H45 680 772 2

D1612886

Spitfire Dive-bombers Versus the V2

Spitfire Dive-bombers Versus the V2

Fighter Command's Battle with Hitler's Mobile Missiles

Bill Simpson

Pen & Sword
AVIATION

First published in Great Britain in 2007 by
Pen & Sword Aviation
an imprint of
Pen & Sword Books Ltd
47 Church Street, Barnsley, South Yorkshire S70 2AS

ISBN 9781844155712

Typeset in Palatino by
Phoenix Typesetting, Auldgirth, Dumfriesshire

Printed and bound in England by
CPI UK

Pen & Sword Books Ltd incorporates the Imprints of Pen & Sword Aviation, Pen
& Sword Maritime, Pen & Sword Military, Wharncliffe Local History,
Pen & Sword Select, Pen & Sword Military Classics and Leo Cooper.

Contents

Acknowledgements

This work could not have been completed without the encouragement and support of a large number of individuals, many of whom were actively involved in the campaign against the V2s or were under the rockets in the south of England or the Spitfires' bombs in the Netherlands. Much of the factual base of the account comes from the squadron records but the human side draws on written and spoken recollections which have been made freely available to me. Those whose exploits are recounted are getting on in years and some are unwell – sadly a few have passed away during the four years it has taken to complete the work – but all have given their help, advice and encouragement unstintingly and I am grateful to them all. The research has been made more difficult because so many of the pilots live in Australia, but the internet and the ability to e-mail has made it easier than I would have believed to resolve issues, answer queries and keep in touch.

It is almost inevitable that a work of this nature will contain errors and, as always, they are mine and mine alone. If I have omitted to thank any particular person or organization then I apologize – it has not been done deliberately.

Of course, the most important contributors are those who took part in the campaign, either in the aeroplanes or on the ground, and some who had no involvement in the campaign but could comment from personal experience during the war. In particular I have to thank Flight Lieutenant Russell Leith, who has been my main contact in Australia, along with Flying Officer (now Sir) Brian Inglis, the late Flying Officer Norman Marsh, Flying Officer Tom Hall and Russell Baxter. In Europe my thanks go to the late Warrant Officer Eric Mee (for permission to quote freely from his memoir), the late Flight Lieutenant Bob Sergeant, Warrant Officer Max Baerlein, the late Flight Lieutenant Raymond Baxter, Flying Officer John Moss, Warrant Officer Tom O'Reilly, Pilot Officer Freddy van Dyck, Flying Officer Michael Francis, Warrant Officer Roy Karasek, Sergeant Arthur Inch, Flying Officer George Pyle, Warrant Officer Stan Sollitt, the late Sergeant Bill Vine, Flight Lieutenant Jack Batchelor and Flying Officer Nick Machon.

I also thank the late Jan van't Hoff and his wife Betty in the Netherlands for their hospitality and interest in the project, and for sharing with me their experiences during the war, and Jos Borsboom for his interest and help and for spending a weekend in 2003 guiding me round V2 sites in The Hague and western Holland as well as recounting to me his family's experiences in Bezuidenhout and allowing me to write about them. Bart Tent gave help in researching the attacks on the BIM building, and Rita Gathercole provided recollections of the V2s hitting the south-east of England. Geoff and Richard Zuber gave me information about their father, Cec Zuber of 602 Squadron, and I am grateful to them.

Paul Baillie and Geoff Dewing carried out sterling research for me at the UK National Archives, and the help and encouragement given to me by fellow authors Squadron Leader Bruce Blanche and David Ross is greatly appreciated. Professor Dugald Cameron, who has an abiding interest in 602 Squadron, also provided encouragement, and I am very grateful to him for allowing me to use his profile of the 602 Squadron Spitfire XVI in the book. Lieutenant-Colonel David Bashow also helped and gave me permission to quote from his excellent history of the RCAF in the war, *All the Fine Young Eagles*. Michael Francis kindly allowed me to use his poem which appears as a postscript and I am grateful to him.

The source of most of the photographs is acknowledged beside them but I have to thank all who have helped me find appropriate illustrations. These include the late Eric Mee, the late Jan van't Hoff, Tom O'Reilly, George Pyle, Tom Hall (who also allowed me to quote from his book *Typhoon Warfare*), John Moss, Russell Leith, the late Bob Sergeant, Freddy van Dyck, Sir Brian Inglis, the late Raymond Baxter and his family – particularly Mrs Jenny Douglas – Geoff and Richard Zuber, Rob Lawa, Senior Archivist with Shell International BV in The Hague, Yvonne Oliver at the Imperial War Museum, staff at the Australian War Memorial, Hugh Alexander at the UK National Archives at Kew for permission to reproduce the aerial photograph of The Hague illustrating the tragic bombing of Bezuidenhout, Mr Norbert Ludwig at Bildarchiv Prussischer Kulturbesitz in Berlin, Margrit Prussat of the Photographic Archive of the Deutsches Museum in Munich, Mr G.I. Smit and KLM for permission to use one of their aerial images of Bezuidenhout, John Coulter of the Lewisham Local History and Archives Centre at Lewisham Library for permission to use the image of the V2 damage at New Cross. Others who helped with images and/or approvals to copy were Judy Nokes at the Office of Public Sector Information in Norwich, Harco Gisbers of the Netherlands Institute for War Documentation, Mel Knight at Mirrorpix, Jane Cramb at Macmillan Publishers Ltd., Venetia Bridges of Osprey Publishing Ltd, Heather Thomas of ITV, Rebecca Barnard at Solo

Syndication on behalf of Associated Newspapers for permission to quote from the *News Chronicle* and to reproduce an article from the *Daily Sketch* of December 1944, Joanna Sinclair of BBC Information for permission to quote from the BBC Scotland radio broadcast *Beware the Crossed Lion*, Michael Neufeld of the Smithsonian Institution in Washington for his help with photographs of forced labour at Nordhausen and information about Hans Kammler, and Harry Griffiths, the Executive Chairman of The Spitfire Society, for his agreement to my use of quotations from the society's journal. In particular, I would like to thank miss Sjoukje Atema of the Haags Gemeentearchief in The Hague who was very patient with my queries and requests for photographs.

Phil Makanna of Ghosts in San Francisco (www.ghosts.com) has been very generous in allowing me to use his beautiful picture of a refurbished Spitfire flying over the mountains of New Zealand, and I am grateful to him.

In a few cases, it has not been possible to identify the photograph owner. In such instances, I would be pleased to be made aware of the ownership to make appropriate corrections in any future issue of the book. In the meantime, I apologize for any omissions and/or errors.

In a more general way, I need to thank Bob Ogley of Froglets Publications, who helped me and gave me permission to use various parts of his book *Doodlebugs and Rockets*; my old school friends Andrew 'Danny' Kay, an airline pilot who has suffered uncomplainingly my interest in flying over the years, and Bill Campbell an ex-RAF Vulcan pilot who has been helpful and encouraging, and who gave me an introduction to Air Marshal Cliff Spink, to whom I am particularly grateful for writing the foreword. Group Captain Dan Needham helped me contact Ray Hart, Secretary of the Australian Spitfire Association, who in turn helped me contact some of the Australians, and I am grateful to both of them for their help. Jim Porteous, who was a ground crew member of 453 Squadron before it re-formed in Britain has been keenly interested and I thank him for that. Members of the 603 Squadron Association in Edinburgh have always taken an interest and one of them, Andy Wanstall, gave his time in cleaning up some of the poorer-quality photos for me. Modern-day Auxiliaries Group Captain Bob Kemp, Wing Commander Alasdair Beaton, the previous commanding officer of 603 Squadron, Squadron Leader Graeme Lyall and Squadron Leader Derek Morrison – the current commanding officers of 602 and 603 Squadrons respectively – have taken an interest and I appreciate this. Stan Murray-Zmijewski gave me helpful insights into the lives and philosophies of former Polish servicemen who remained in Britain rather than return to a Communist Poland. I would like to mention the late James Sanders a Kiwi pilot in Coastal Command who wrote an excellent book called *Of Wind and Water* and inspired me to plod on in the more tedious moments.

    Finally, I must thank my wife Marion for putting up with my evenings spent hunched over the computer, trips to the Netherlands and elsewhere and for those (few) occasions when instead of listening to her, I was miles away thinking about V2s and Spitfires.

Foreword

by Air Marshal Clifford R. Spink CB CBE FCMI

Bill Simpson has produced a very readable work of great detail and historical importance that covers a key chapter in the operations of the Royal Air Force during World War Two. The V2 rockets were a last desperate attempt by Hitler to strike back at the Allies and they caused huge and indiscriminate damage and loss of life. It was the indiscriminate nature of the rocket that brought such terror – it was inaccurate and therefore used for area targets where no warning was possible against this entirely new class of weapon.

The use of assigned Spitfire Squadrons to target the launch sites of these weapons was vital in the fight to limit the use of the V2 until the advancing ground forces could reach these areas. Operating in sometimes appalling weather, and faced with a long transit over the North Sea, these Squadrons did not let up in their search and destroy missions against a clever and evasive adversary who frequently and cynically used urban areas for the launch platforms.

The aircraft that these Squadrons operated was, in the main, the Mark XVI Spitfire which was very simiar to the ubiquitous Mark IX but with a Packard built Merlin 266 engine. Much has been written about these aircraft and folklore developed about the American-built Rolls

(Richard Paver Photography)

Royce engine. Today I am privileged to fly a Mark XVI Spitfire on a regular basis and it is a thoroughbred – a pure delight. The engine, an original Packard Rolls 266, is as sweet a Merlin as you could wish – indeed, the engineering build standard is exceptionally high.

However, I usually fly this wonderful aircraft in clear blue skies and cannot begin to imagine the hardships that the pilots of these aircraft faced in the final bitter months of World War Two. It is a unique story of their bravery and in the telling Bill Simpson keeps their memory, and history, alive.

Cliff Spink
Keyston
January 2007

Introduction

When the Germans started firing V2 rockets at London in September 1944, the outcome of the war was pretty much decided and the rockets were never going to change that, but they represented a new aspect to warfare and also a tragedy to those who got caught up in the campaign – the slave labourers who made them, the German troops who were firing them, the British, French, Belgian, Polish and Commonwealth airmen who tried to counter them, the British civilians underneath them, and not least the Dutch civilians hoping for an end to their oppression and the privations of a vicious winter without food and heat. Many died, and the tragedy was that they had survived the violence since 1939 only to become its final victims – indeed the last British civilian casualty of the war was a housewife killed by a V2. The tragic but accidental bombing of a residential area of The Hague on 3 March 1945 by medium bombers of the 2nd Tactical Air Force as part of the campaign which killed 500 Dutch civilians is still remembered each year in the Netherlands in a ceremony, although with remarkably little antipathy towards the RAF and the British.

The sight of the RAF aircraft gave these Dutch civilians hope that their trials would soon be over – as indeed they were, but only days before Germany finally surrendered.

The V2s and the campaign against them was a sideshow to the world-shaking events taking place to the east as Germany crumbled, and they have been rather overlooked by history. But the campaign was significant and those who gave their lives should be given their due place in the history of the Second World War, as should those who fought and endured.

If nothing else I hope that this account will record for posterity just what happened in the skies and towns of western Holland in these final days of the second European catastrophe of the twentieth century.

Readers may notice that the account concentrates on the activities and experiences of 602, 229/603 and 453 Squadrons and that 303, 451 and 124

Squadrons are not covered in the same detail. This was not a deliberate strategy, but has come about purely because I was unable to make contact with any members of these three Squadrons. Nos 451 and 124 only came into the campaign a few weeks before it ended, so the lack of detail about them is not as important as it might otherwise be, but I would have liked to include more about them and 303 Squadron and its men, not least because of what they represented – both in the contribution of the Polish until September 1944 and also because of their shameful treatment once the war finished. If any reader served with any of the six squadrons involved in the campaign, I would be more than happy to hear from them.

I hope that the more we document past wars and their consequences, the more we will understand them so that my grandchildren and their generation will not have to suffer its horrors again; I think it may be a forlorn hope.

CHAPTER ONE

The Rockets Uncovered

I t wasn't a particularly impressive explosion; just another to add to the thousands – tens of thousands – that had rocked London since the start of the war. Hardly worth commenting on in fact. Something else to deal with on the long road to a peace that looked as if it might just, at last, be in sight.

But this explosion was different somehow.

The weather in London in the early evening of Friday, 8 September 1944 might well have been described by a Scotsman as 'dreich' – damp and miserable. The morning had been bright, but as the day progressed, cloud thickened to threaten rain and in the early evening cast a moisture laden gloom over the city. It may not have seemed out of place then, when at just after half past six, what sounded like two gigantic peals of thunder boomed across the city – hot on the heels of each other – although it may have struck some who heard them that the conditions were not what they would have called 'thundery'. Five years and five days after Britain had declared war on Germany, Londoners were well used to bombs and blasts, but these latest explosions felt odd, and some of those who heard them puzzled as to just what the cause had been – not necessarily thinking that they could be enemy action. But Professor R.V. Jones, the Prime Minister's scientific adviser, knew all about them. He looked at his assistant when the double boom arrived and said, 'That's the first one.'

Staveley Road is in the London Borough of Brentford and Chiswick, about 5 miles west-south-west of Westminster. Then, and at the beginning of the twenty-first century, it was a middle-class street with mainly tra-ditional brick semi-detached two-storey houses and a few detached as well. A quiet, pleasant dormitory district, lined with cherry trees, which Queen Mary, the King's mother, used to visit every year in the spring to view the blossom.

Few ventured out on this dank evening. On the wireless, the BBC Home Service Six o'Clock News had just finished and the war news was good. Allied armies moved steadily across Europe towards the German

Damage at Staveley Road. *(Syndication International.)*

homeland. On 25 August, Paris surrendered. On 2 September, the Red Army reached the border with Bulgaria. On the 3rd, the British Second Army liberated Brussels and on the 4th Antwerp. Only on that day, the 8th, the US First Army took Liège, when an end seemed to be in sight.

The residents of Staveley Road washed the dinner dishes, read the papers and looked forward to an half hour of Jack Payne and his band on the wireless, due to start at a quarter to seven, but at 6.34 their peace was rudely shattered when, with absolutely no warning, there was an explosion and a crater appeared in the road outside number 5. By some quirk of atmospherics, many in the area were spared the double thunderclap and heard only a 'plop' followed by a rumble. But the damage was extensive and three people were killed, including a three-year-old girl asleep in her bed at number 1. She was suffocated by the blast, which left not a mark on her body. Her six-year-old brother at the rear of the house survived, but with some injuries to his hand. Robert Stubbs was the caretaker in the nearby school. 'I was blown 20 yards across the playing fields by the blast. I picked myself up and staggered to the nearest wrecked house. A woman – I later learned that it was Mrs Harrison – crawled out of the wreckage and died in my arms.[1]'

Ten people were seriously hurt and another ten sustained 'slight injuries'. Some of the houses in the immediate vicinity of the hole collapsed, and the blast damaged others to a greater or lesser extent – blowing tiles off roofs and shattering windows as well as cracking walls and collapsing floors. Eleven dwellings were demolished, fifteen needed extensive repairs and their owners temporarily rehoused, twelve also needed significant repair work, although those living there could stay on during the work, and over 500 sustained light damage of one kind or another. By 8.15, all the casualties were removed.

The crater was reported as being 40 feet in diameter and 10 feet deep. Brian Rogers was a schoolboy who lived at number 58 and he ventured down the street to have a look at it. When he returned home, his parents told him that people were saying it had been a gas-main explosion, but even the young boy could see that it must have been a pretty big gas main. Of course, the authorities knew differently but it suited them to leave the speculation uncorrected, although some journalists already suspected that it was a new weapon.

A few seconds after the explosion in Staveley Road, there was another similar one in Epping, 20 or so miles from Chiswick. It caused little damage and no injury so it attracted much less attention.

In reality, the two explosions marked the opening of a new chapter in

Despite the poor quality, the typical launch trail of a V2 is clearly captured by this photograph taken by a PRU Spitfire.
(Australian War Memorial Negative no. SUK14314.)

the history of both the Second World War and warfare generally.

Five days later, on the 13th, six Typhoon 1Bs of the Royal Air Force's 247 (China-British) Squadron lifted off from the cryptically named B58 Melsbroeck airfield in Belgium on yet another armed recce, this time in the Tilburg-Venlo area. Into the flight, they noticed a thin smoke trail climbing vertically into the cloudy sky some distance from them. This was new and whilst they did not know what it was, the pilots realized that the phenomenon should be reported. They returned to B58 at midday and the incident found its way into the Intelligence Officer's report.

The two incidents were part of the same thing – the use by the Germans of a new weapon that had the potential to change the course of the Second World War even at this late stage. It would be two months before the truth of the situation came out – two months during which the long-suffering people living in the south-east corner of England became used to the strange double boom accompanied by a rushing noise that announced yet another 'gas main incident'.

The cause, of course, was not faulty gas pipes, but Germany's rockets – the V2s.

On Saturday, 3 February 1945, five months after the Staveley Road incident and with the RAF's campaign against the V2s running in high gear, newly operational Spitfire pilot Warrant Officer Eric Mee found himself about to take off on a dive-bombing mission against German V2 mobile launchers hidden in the wooded Haagsche Bosch area of The Hague, the capital of the Netherlands. He was apprehensive. This would be his second operation – the first had been aborted without encountering the enemy – so the whole thing would be a new experience for him. He would be one of a section of four Spitfire XVIs, each armed with two 250-pound bombs, taking off from an airfield in Norfolk to face a return flight across the wintry cold and grey North Sea to the Netherlands.

At five past one the green-and-grey camouflaged Spitfires took off, racing over the ground in a close group as their elliptical wings gradually developed the lift they needed – flexing and smoothing out the bumpy path until they parted company with the ground. Mee was number 4 – tail-end Charlie – the last in the group. Those watching saw them make a sharp turn to port as the undercarriage legs folded up outwards and awkwardly into the mainplanes, then they disappeared into the thin cloud that covered the sky. They were on their way.

Climbing hard, they soon reached 12,000 feet and levelled out, easing into a looser formation, roughly four wingspans part, to cross the sea. Later, as they neared the Dutch coast, the section leader ordered them to 'change gear' – the instruction to get rid of their belly tanks after changing over to internal fuel. The main tank was just in front of the instrument panel – potentially lethal if it should catch fire. Eric Mee was small and this procedure always caused some fun. The tank release lever was low down in the cockpit and he had to lower his seat as far as it would go, then bend down to give the lever a good tug. To do this, his head disappeared below the cockpit canopy rails and the exertions of pulling at the lever with one hand and trying to fly the aeroplane with the other meant that those flying with him suddenly saw his Spitfire bouncing about the sky, apparently with no pilot controlling it – always good for a few digs at him when they got back to base. Crossing the enemy coast, the section attracted some flak, which Mee recalled as looking like fluffy black balls, but despite the innocuous appearance, the natural instinct for survival pulled the small formation together as they changed course and height in case the flak was radar predicted.

Soon they arrived over The Hague, just in from the coast, and the section leader ordered the four Spitfires into echelon – line abreast – and they started to reduce height and speed gently. The target was a wooded area, and looking out for it Mee at first saw many houses and buildings. Then the woods came into sight over the port wing. As he reached 8,000 feet and just under 200 knots, the target area slowly came into view under the trailing edge of the section leader's wing. The leader rolled the Spitfire into a steep dive and the others followed, with Eric Mee last. By the time he tipped into his dive, the enemy had opened up and he could see what he described as a 'thick carpet' of flak through which he would have to pass. Then he saw little balls of fire speeding past him, seemingly languid as they approached but fast and urgent as they came near, and he knew that for every one he could see there were ten that he could not. But he had no time to dwell on them; there was a job to be done. He found the target and got it into the centre of the gunsight. The task now was to dive accurately without sliding or slipping, as this would mean the bombs missing their target. He saw the others release their bombs then pull away as he continued his seemingly vertical dive, hurtling down but holding it for just a little longer than the others because, as number 4, he had the additional task of taking photographs. He let the bombs go and pulled out, by now at about 3,000 feet.

The pullout G-forces were huge and he blacked out for a moment. Then, yelling madly, he made his escape, pushing the plane all over the sky to spoil the flak gunners' aim and heading out for the nearby coast. In its dive the Spitfire had gained kinetic energy, and he now reversed it by pulling the Spit into a steep zooming climb to reach the sea. The others had disappeared, but they had agreed a rendezvous point and he headed over towards it and found the other Spitfires joining up. His first real operation was more or less over and the flight back across the sea should be without incident.

It was a matter of pride to put on a bit of a show on returning to the airfield. Back into tight formation to fly low across it into wind. Then on the command 'Break port. Go!' the leader would peel off into a steep turn to the left, the rest of us following at about two second intervals. The object was to do a very tight circuit followed by a stream landing. The drill was for number 1 to touch down on the left of the runway with his number 2 landing slightly behind on the right. Then 3 and 4 would come in behind them.

Climbing out, the mechanics took over, first looking for any damage and asking how the trip went. Then came 'Spy' our Intelligence Officer. His priority was to get back the escape kits and the money in them for which he was responsible and then debriefing.

They landed at 14.35. The section told 'Spy' that the bombing had been accurate, with black smoke and debris seen afterwards. They also reported damaging a long white vehicle crossing a bridge on the south side of the target area. A successful operation as far as they were concerned, and another couple of hours in the log book.

Eric Mee was one of over a 100 pilots from six squadrons, all flying Spitfires, charged with the heavy responsibility of defending London and the south-east of England from the now constant bombardment of German V2 rockets, which could number up to sixteen a day. The origins of the six squadrons represented, unintentionally, a fair mix of the nations and peoples fighting for the Allies, with the exception of the United States which was not represented. Two were Scottish Auxiliary squadrons, two Royal Australian Air Force (RAAF), one regular RAF, and the last the *Polskie Sily Powietrzne* or Polish Air Force. And the pilots came from all corners of the British Commonwealth and Occupied Europe – Englishmen, Scots, a Guernseyman, Australians, New Zealanders, South Africans, Canadians, Poles, Belgians, French, even some from the Royal Indian Air Force – and all had reached the squadrons in different ways. Some, like the Poles, had literally fought their way to the shores of Great Britain for the privilege of continuing the struggle against the Germans. The Guernseyman first had to escape from one of the few parts of Britain to be occupied by the Third *Reich*.

Among the native British men, some did their entire training in the UK at places such as Carlisle or Hawarden, Tealing or Eshott, or other airfields suddenly constructed for the emergency, while some in the Empire Training Scheme went to Southern Africa for theirs. Some went under the Arnold Scheme to the USA, enduring dangerous voyages across an Atlantic Ocean full of U-boats to find the bright lights of Florida, Georgia, Alabama or Carolina and the granting of USAAF silver wings to mark their success as trainee pilots. For the Aussies and Kiwis there was the hard decision to join their countries' air forces to fight a battle thousands of miles from their homes and families and then make the journey to Britain. After basic flying training in their home countries, they often made the voyage to Canada for advanced training and then to

Britain for final operational training and posting to a squadron. Many of them were only teenagers, and most had not had the chance to start a career, although some were apprentices. For many the next logical step was college or university, but that would have to wait until they had fought their war. Some celebrated their twenty-first birthdays with their new squadron mates in the nearest pub to the airfield. They did not know how many years it might be until they returned home to pick up the threads of their lives and their families – and of course, many of them would not return because they had been killed in action. Some came on their own, some had brothers in other squadrons – or sometimes the same squadron – or other branches of the service. Some had distant relatives in Britain to whom they could turn if they felt the need or wanted to get away from the fighting and noise for some peace. Some had nobody that they could call on and the squadron became their family, with the loss of another pilot feeling like the death of a brother or a father. But of course, in this family there could be no time for grieving, or brooding over someone who did not come back. Perhaps there would be a funeral, but often there was no body and the epitaph was a toast to the departed the next time operations allowed a trip to the pub or a night in the mess bar.

When it came, death could be sudden and terrible. A burning Spitfire became a deathtrap. With the petrol tank directly in front of the pilot's instrument panel fire spread literally in seconds and if the cockpit hood had been damaged and would not open, and the pilot had not switched off his radio, then his fellows and those back at base could hear the screams, which eventually became silence. Or they could see a mate's Spitfire suddenly explode in mid air if caught by flak. Or they sometimes saw a pilot they had been drinking with at the pub the previous night bale out over the sea or enemy territory and the parachute not open. Death and injury came in many forms – and it usually came suddenly.

Eric Mee may have been new to operational flying in 1945, but many of the others on the squadrons attacking the V2s were not. Some were battle-hardened warriors who had been flying since just after the Battle of Britain in 1940, raids across the Channel to France in 1941 and 1942, Malta in 1942 and 1943, North Africa and Sicily. Many had flown cover over the D-Day landings on 6 June 1944, and the sight of that great armada steaming towards Normandy would stay with them for ever. Some flew at Arnhem. Some had fought in the air with the *Luftwaffe*'s Heinkels, Junkers, Messerschmitts and Focke Wulfs and beaten them. Some had been shot down, evaded capture and returned to the fight. Some bore the scars of old wounds received in these battles. But wherever they came from and however they had got there, they all brought their skills and experiences, at whatever level, to this last battle. For some the campaign against the V2s would be their only one and for a few it would be also the one which would kill them.

Jan van't Hoff. *(Jan van't Hoff.)*

Those who survived it and the war returned to their countries and families, although for the Poles the Allied victory in Europe became a bitter pill with their beloved Poland falling under the influence of Stalin and the Soviet Union – one tyrant replacing another. Many of them could not return home and settled eventually in the West, in the countries which they believed had betrayed them. Some of them married and had children, some did not. Their lives varied hugely. They became captains of industry, artists, accountants, a newspaper editor, a journalist and TV presenter, a joiner and undertaker, salesmen, teachers. . . And many continued as pilots, either remaining in their air force or moving into civil flying.

The Germans fired the V2s from the woods and street corners of The Hague and its suburbs. The Dutch civilians who lived there in 1944 and 1945 found themselves caught between the devil and the deep blue sea –

rockets on the ground, bombs from the air. Fifteen-year-old Jan van't Hoff lived in the area of The Hague called Bezuidenhout with his elder sister Riet and his parents Pieter and Truus. The young Jan saw the Spitfires coming over day after day, and they gave him hope that one day the family would be released from the dreadful occupation they had endured since 1940. Pieter van't Hoff worked for the post office. The Germans issued him a permit or *ausweis* which allowed

Pieter van't Hoff, Jan's father, in his Post Office uniform. *(Jan van't Hoff.)*

him to move about the city – and the country – on his bicycle rather more freely than he might otherwise have been able to do as an ordinary citizen, with an undertaking that his bicycle would not be confiscated if he wore his postman's uniform. According to Jan, from that day he never left home in anything other than his uniform.

In the middle of September Operation Market Garden started. Designed to create a corridor into Germany by dropping paratroops to capture key bridges at Arnhem, Nijmegen and Eindhoven whilst a ground force thrust through the opposition to relieve the airborne troops at each bridge, it failed when, many days later, the British at Arnhem, the bridge furthest away from the relieving column, had to withdraw before the ground troops could reach them. On the orders of the Government of the Netherlands in exile and in an effort to support Market Garden, the Dutch railways started a strike intended to disrupt the German supply lines, but the response of the Germans was to use their own people to run the railways exclusively for their own purposes. Because of the bitter winter, the Dutch could not use the canal system to move food and other vital supplies around the country, although there was plenty in the north of the country. When the Allies swung away to the east to drive into the German homeland, the western part of the Netherlands remained occupied for months whilst the strike continued and the people ran out of food. They starved and froze over the winter of 1944/45, a bad one by any standards, and it became known as the *Hungerwinter*. Being able to travel meant that

Bezuidenhout in 1930. 1e Van den Boschstraat.
(Courtesy Haags Gemeentearchief. Photo no. 0.71809.)

Bezuidenhout in 1935. Juliana van Stolbergplein.
(Courtesy Haags Gemeentearchief. Photo no. 0.35598.)

Pieter was more able than others to forage for food for his family – either scavenging or buying it on the black market – although only two months into the railway strike, the final awful effects of hunger had yet to become apparent. Jan said, 'My parents did everything they could to keep us alive, like many others, roaming the farmland to try to get anything to eat.' From time to time Pieter carried documents for the Resistance, hidden deep in the piles of mail.

Bezuidenhout was a pleasant suburb of The Hague, dating back to the mid-1800s, hard on the south side of the Haagsche Bosch. With wide tree-lined cobbled streets along which trams rattled on their rails, parks and open spaces, three- or four-storey town-houses and tenements, it was a pleasant, middle-class district, home to artisans, artists and intellectuals. And the people who lived there did so in grand company for not far away, immediately to the north, was the royal palace – the *Paleis Huis ten Bosch* or 'House in the Woods'. It was a safe place for children to play on their bicycles and home-made carts, and for the adults to stroll on a summer evening.

At first the German troops tried to make friends with the families but their advances were rejected and, although attempts to fraternize reduced, to their credit the ordinary German soldiers mainly kept a distant formality. Jan recalled one occasion when a drunken German soldier forced himself into their house and terrified the family, although he did not actually cause them any harm. Pieter went to see the local commander to complain and as far as he knew the soldier was disciplined. But it was not always so, and on occasion, the German troops forcibly entered the Dutch houses seeking evidence of the Resistance or booty that they could take back home. Anything that might be of use was taken with no thought of what the effect might be on the Dutch. The trams which rattled through the streets of The Hague disappeared to Germany, as did machinery from factories, tools, equipment, vehicles. The Dutch reverted back to using bicycles, but with tyres in short supply, they soon ran on the canvas of the inner tyre, then the metal rims – a fact noticed later by some of the more enterprising Spitfire pilots. But even then, the Germans confiscated or stole the bicycles so the only option for many of the Dutch was to walk.

With the Germans operating a policy of firing V2s from street corners, the young Jan experienced several launches from nearby. He recalled that the Germans would shoot people for being near the launch sites or attempting to watch them. But apart from night-time curfews, the Dutch civilians were not stopped going about their business in the streets, even although the rockets might be fired from nearby at any time without any warning and without any apparent concern for the safety of the civilians. Jan lived near the Haagsche Bosch and they always knew if one was about to be fired. The first indication would be a humming noise about half an hour before the launch and eventually the roar of the rocket engine as the missile appeared above the tree tops accelerating into the sky, turning and rolling towards the west, heading for Antwerp or London. Sometimes, though, the humming stopped suddenly and then would come a tremendous explosion as the missile failed on the launch pad.

For the civilians living nearby, the launch of a V2 brought the immediate worry that it might be a rogue and explode, and if it did so, where would it land? Would they become casualties? The whole thing could be extremely unsettling. But for Jan and his family and the others, the constant sight and sound of the Spitfires flying overhead gave their morale a much needed boost. With the Allied armies swinging east into Germany leaving western Holland in the hands of the hated enemy, and with the combined effects of the *Hungerwinter* and the brutal occupation, the courageous and long-suffering Dutch civilians needed something to believe in – and the Spitfires gave them a little of what they needed.

Han Borsboom was born on 3 March 1936 and also lived with his family in Bezuidenhout. His ninth birthday was memorable for all the wrong reasons. His father, Jules, was a coal merchant and the family house was beside a well-known white swimming pool building called *Bosbad*.

But the RAF, the Dutch and the German rockets had come a long way before that February day in 1945 when Eric Mee got his first experience of real combat. The reasons why he found himself tipping his Spitfire into a 70 degree dive to attack a German rocket site in the Netherlands go back as far the First World War. The way that war ended sowed the seeds of the whirlwind which engulfed Europe and then the world twenty years later. The war finally ended in 1919 with the signing of the Treaty of Versailles on 28 June, which humiliated the defeated Germany by demanding reparations for the damage and destruction its aggression had caused and attempting to make it impossible for Germany to rearm. Many of its citizens, and many of the soldiers who had endured the fighting, were outraged that their leaders should have agreed to the Armistice and the subsequent capitulation, believing that their sacrifices had been for nothing. Adolf Hitler was one. The treaty placed fierce restrictions on German rearmament but crucially did not prohibit certain activities which the new *Luftwaffe* and *Wehrmacht* could exploit and develop. One was the development of military rockets.

Curiously, though, in the Weimar Republic which followed the upheavals of the war, rocketry and space flight became a civilian, not military, fad. In 1927 some enthusiasts started the Society for Space Travel, allowing rocketry to become available to a much wider audience and whetting interest. In 1929, one of the enthusiasts, Hermann Oberth, published a book discussing the use of long-range strategic missiles which could be used to attack cities – although he regarded this as impractical because of the lack of accurate guidance systems, and he was right, guidance would be a problem for many years.

The army appreciated the significance of rocketry as well; if the development of artillery was curbed by the Treaty of Versailles, rockets had the potential to provide a weapon that would be more fearsome and better than any long-range gun. But looking at rockets in this way, the soldiers saw them only as extensions or improvements to artillery. They did not see their full strategic value, thinking of them mainly in terms of tactical weapons. Much of their effort concentrated on solid-fuelled rockets which could be used as battlefield weapons, although they also hoped to develop a long-range weapon that would operate as a ballistic gun. A long-range gun which could hit major cities far behind the front lines might, it was thought, destroy civilian morale. The rocket dispensed with the paraphernalia of the gun – transport, weight, bulk – and they wanted it to be more accurate than conventional artillery and expected it to bring 'shock and awe' when first used. After that, however, it would be just another 'big gun' and indeed, it would be some years before Hitler became enthusiastic about it – and only once the war was beginning to go badly for Germany. For all his faults, Hitler had a good grasp of weaponry and what technology could achieve. He seems to have understood the limitations of the rockets and finally felt that they could be of use only when it was really too late and the war was more or less lost.

Amongst those helping in the development was the young Baron Wernher von Braun. His father, a banker and government minister, found it difficult to accept Wernher's love of engineering and spaceflight – unusual for someone of his background. His interest in rockets started with the civilians but in 1932, twenty years old and only part-way through his university course – reading mechanical engineering at the Technical University of Berlin and also a doctoral candidate at the University of Berlin in applied physics – von Braun moved over to the army in a leading role.

The *Luftwaffe* left the development of rockets to the army, but in 1935, the Development Division of its Technical Office, headed by Wolfram Freiherr von Richthofen – a cousin of the famous 'Red Baron' – could see the potential of rocket and jet engines and was keen to research them. The *Luftwaffe* followed its own programme of work to develop rocket engines fuelled by liquid oxygen, but during 1935, the army and the air force came to an agreement that they would co-operate at a new experimental centre at Peenemünde on the Baltic coast in northern Germany not far from the Polish border. The first of the rocket men moved there in May 1937 and von Braun, now twenty-five, was given charge of the east side, with control of about 350 workers.

Development of the rockets continued slowly and painfully. In September 1939 the onset of war brought pressure to set out programmes of production and likely dates for the delivery of weapons, and this continuing pressure would become a feature of Peenemünde. In order to avoid the closure of the programme, von Braun and his colleagues found themselves agreeing to timescales they did not meet, which in turn brought more criticism and pressure with changes in the priorities for labour and materials as the success of Germany's war effort flowed and ebbed. At the end of 1939, they were assuming that the development phase would be completed by May 1941 with production starting in a plant which was also being built at Peenemünde. But reductions in the priority given to them between then and the middle of 1941, as well as difficulties with the development, resulted in this deadline not being met.

Test firings of the rocket version intended to be used as a weapon, the A-4, only started in 1942, and did not go well. The first attempt to test fire one in March 1942 failed on the launch pad without damaging the pad itself, although the missile was beyond repair. Three months later, on 13 June 1942, the first successful launch took place but celebrations were short-lived because shortly afterwards it was seen tumbling out of the clouds and crashing about ½ mile from the shore. The engineers discovered that the problem had been a failure of a roll-rate gyro, possibly compounded by the wind, which may have made the rocket roll faster than the guidance system could cope with. The next launch took place on Monday, 16 August, but the rocket still did not perform as intended, although it was an improvement on the last attempt. For forty-five seconds all appeared to be going as planned, but then the engine cut out and the rocket turned out of control to fall in pieces to the sea almost 5½ miles from the launch point. This time the engine failed. On 3 October, the fourth A-4 was ready for firing. In the late afternoon, in excellent weather, it rose impressively, leaving a white condensation trail behind it. Then, just before the full minute, the engine cut and the missile continued on its trajectory to fall into the sea 125 miles away about four minutes after

A-4 launch from Peenemünde.
(Courtesy Deutsches Museum, München. Image no. BN_09674.)

Director of the Rocket Development programme Walter Dornberger and
Wernher von Braun savour the first successful A-4 launch at a
celebratory dinner.
(Courtesy Deutsches Museum, München. Image no. BN_30959.)

engine cut-off, having reached a height of almost 50 miles. It was a nearly
perfect shot and they celebrated it that night.

By the spring of 1943, the rockets were far from being ready for mass
production. Technical problems still had to be resolved, certain drawings
were not available and contractors were not in place. Of eleven test rockets
fired between October 1942 and March 1943 not one was a success – most
failed utterly. The army group was paying the price for its earlier promises
that they had a war winning weapon; they now had to provide it.
Ominously, the SS *Reichsführer* Heinrich Himmler was becoming interested in the possibilities that rocketry provided. This interest was whetted
by the news of the successful launch in October 1942 and he travelled to
Peenemünde two months later in December to witness one of the launches
for himself. It was an abject failure, but Himmler was not put off.

By now, von Braun was a member of the SS, having been 'invited' to
join in 1940, but after the end of the war and once he had moved to the
United States, his membership was played down and in fact, it seems that
in joining, his main motive was probably to ensure the priority of the
rocket research and his own ability to contribute to it. He was only seen
in his SS uniform on a handful of occasions – some reports say only once,
when Himmler visited Peenemünde for a second time in June 1943 (when

the launch he witnessed was a success). However, his membership is significant, particularly in conjunction with the use of concentration camp and slave labour in the production of the V2s. To say the least, such workers were not treated humanely and it seems that this may have been with von Braun's knowledge and tacit approval.

During the first half of 1943, the rocket work at Peenemünde carried on against a backdrop of the political machinations of various groups trying to increase their control and influence on the project. But also during this period the rockets became a top priority for the *Reich*. With the war generally beginning to turn for the worse Hitler needed a decisive weapon to win it. Over the years, whilst Peenemünde East and the *Wehrmacht* concentrated on rockets, a few miles away in Peenemünde West, working independently, the *Luftwaffe* was developing its own new weapon – the flying bomb. Wednesday, 26 May 1943 was a critical test for both systems when they were to be compared in a competitive 'shoot' of two each. The demonstration attracted some high-level military and civilian attention. The two A-4s flew perfectly, but the two flying bombs failed. Nonetheless, it was decided that both projects should proceed. In reality, the two missiles were complementary to each other, the flying bomb being relatively cheap and easy to deploy while the A-4 was more complex and expensive to produce but with a greater payload and (hopefully) greater accuracy. At the beginning of June 1943, the A-4 programme was given a high priority. Now the *Führer* could see a potential war winner and became fired with enthusiasm to such an extent that von Braun and his colleagues seem to have become unsettled by it and the expectations being generated. The demands on the development team increased as production and deployment expectations spiralled.

For the technicians and scientists working at Peenemünde that summer of 1943, life was almost idyllic. With cutting-edge technology to stimulate them, the possibility that the rockets could be the means of winning the war, the beautiful wooded surroundings, beaches, walking, and the absence of any direct connection with the brutality of war, it was a protected and comfortable life. True, northern Germany lay on the routes of the British bombers flogging their way to targets further east, but when the air-raid sirens started their eerie wailing in the dark, the residents tended not to tumble into shelters and over the months became complacent. Peenemünde escaped attention – for the moment.

During the 1930s, the British Government adopted a somewhat ambivalent attitude towards Germany and its rearming. To dismiss British policy merely as 'appeasement' is probably too simplistic. Britain and its empire, whilst perhaps reluctant to deal with the German problem head-on, also regarded it as a threat which could be contained; German ambitions seemed to be limited to Europe and its immediate borders. When Germany allied itself with Italy and the Axis was a fact, the threat became more direct and in the end, albeit with a measure of external pressure, Britain (and France) had little choice but to confront the Axis. In the early thirties the British knew that the provisions of the Treaty of Versailles were being 'overlooked' but chose to do nothing. Even as German aims for expansion were becoming overt, Britain still tried to control them without confrontation. As late as June 1935, two years after the creation of the *Luftwaffe* was out in the open and Germany had withdrawn from the League of Nations and the Disarmament Conference, the two countries signed an accord that limited the size of the German navy to about a third of the size of the Royal Navy. However only two months after a tripartite conference at Stresa following which Britain, France and Italy announced that they would oppose German rearmament, Germany started a major build-up of its navy.

In September 1938, Germany's threats against Czechoslovakia resulted in the Munich Crisis and what is seen as Britain's low point when the Prime Minister, Neville Chamberlain came back from his meeting with Hitler declaring 'peace in our time'. In fact, although the agreement allowed Germany to annex the Sudetenland and effectively dismember Czechoslovakia, it prevented Hitler taking control of the whole country, although he did so in March of the following year. If any doubts that war with Germany was inevitable remained, it was not long before they were dispelled. In Chamberlain's defence, it would have been difficult to gain popular approval for a huge increase in military spending in the mid-thirties because of the state of Britain's economy as it tried to recover from the effects of the Depression. Further, there was no obvious threat – no 'clear and present danger' in the parlance of the twenty-first century – to warrant such expenditure. And whilst Britain was humiliated by the Munich Crisis, it did give the country and its empire some much-needed breathing space to continue a desperate rearming, even if the time was insufficient. In September 1939, when war was finally declared, Britain's forces remained woefully inadequate to meet the numerically and technologically superior armed forces of the *Reich*.

In September 1939, the same month that Britain declared war on Germany, information about German plans to develop rockets dropped into the lap of the British in the form of a seven-page document which was left at the British Legation in Oslo apparently by a German sympathetic to the British and Allied cause. It was timely, because on 19 September, during a speech at Danzig, Hitler made reference to weapons which were as yet unknown and Dr R.V. Jones was asked to try to uncover what might be meant by the reference at much the same time as he received the Oslo Report, as it was to become known, for assessment. The Oslo Report was the first to mention a research facility at Peenemünde, and of the *Wehrmacht*'s investigation of the use of rockets, although from the information given it was not possible to be absolutely precise about what the

Germans intentions were. Dr Jones seems to have taken the Oslo Report seriously although clearly, the veracity and reliability of the document needed to be assessed – it might be a clever fiction planted by German intelligence and designed to mislead the British.

Despite the mention of Peenemünde in the Oslo Report, nothing was done to try to confirm whether or not it was what it was purported to be. It was not until 15 May 1942 that a Photo Reconnaisance Unit (PRU) Spitfire overflew the site during a routine sortie. The pilot noticed the airfield at the north end of the peninsula and took some photographs of it.

But these did not trigger a significant reactiom. PRU photographs were sent to RAF Medmenham for detailed interpretation, where one of the interpreters was WAAF Flight Officer Constance Babington Smith. Not a conventional airfield, RAF Medmenham was built around and in the grounds of a large country house called Danesfield, overlooking the River Thames between Henley and Marlow near the village of Medmenham. PRU photographs sent there were subjected to three levels of scrutiny: the first phase for any immediate and high-priority intelligence, to be reported within three hours; the second phase for a more considered view as to changes and progress, to be reported within 24 hours; and the third phase for long-term, detailed developmental trends. The second phase interpretation of the Peenemünde photographs noted the presence of circular earthworks under construction but this was not passed on for any action. After carrying out the third-phase interpretation, Babington Smith duly filed the pictures. However, whilst she noted the presence of the earthworks, she did not know what they were so took no further action, but she made a mental note of the name of the site.

For the next eleven months – until April 1943 – information about the rockets continued to trickle on to the desks of the various British intelligence agencies, allowing them gradually to piece together a picture of what was going on at Peenemünde. Between December 1942 and March 1943, a number of reports and dispatches came in from various sources; in a conversation Professor Fauner of the Technical University of Berlin was reported to have been heard discussing a rocket that could carry 5 tons of explosive 125 miles; another source reported a rocket 50 – 60 feet long carrying 550 pounds of explosive and successfully tested at Peenemünde; another that a rocket with a range of 70 miles was being deployed on the English Channel coast. In January 1943, a report from Sweden announced that there was a new German factory at Peenemünde where rockets were being fired from a testing ground. One crucial piece of intelligence came from a recorded conversation on 22 March 1943 between two captured German senior officers, Generals von Thoma and Cruwell. Captured in North Africa and brought to the UK, their conversations were recorded, transcribed then reviewed by Dr Jones and one of his team members, Dr Charles Frank. Dr Jones considered von Thoma to be a reliable technical source and when he heard him discussing rockets that he had seen it seemed to be confirmation that they existed.

Jones' reaction was quite low-key however and before setting off any hares, he decided to gather more information. But Military Intelligence in the War Office also saw the same transcript and raised the alarm. On 12 April, the War Office issued a paper *German Long Range Rocket Development* and three days later, 15 April 1943, the Prime Minister received a note intimating that the suspected rockets apparently did exist. The need for a single individual to be responsible for gathering and assessing the intelligence was clear, and Duncan Sandys was appointed, not for his technical knowledge but because of his political position. Educated at Eton, he went up to Oxford, becoming MP for Norwood in 1935. He served in the army, reaching the rank of Lieutenant-Colonel, but following a car crash was invalided out and became a Joint Parliamentary Secretary in the Ministry of Supply. He was close to Churchill, being married to his daughter Diana.

PRU photograph of Peenemünde showing the rockets and the distinctive elliptical earthworks.
(Courtesy Imperial War Museum. Negative no. C4782A.)

The strains within the scientific and intelligence communities continued after Sandys' appointment, but from now on, the pace of action increased. Soon after his appointment, the Air Ministry asked Medmenham's Station Commander, Group Captain Peter Stewart, to investigate the German secret weapons programmes. On Thursday, 22 April 1943, a Mosquito from RAF Benson in Oxfordshire took photographs of Peenemünde. They yielded some interesting results. The circular/elliptical earthworks were confirmed, as well as what appeared to be two large factories at the south-east of the site. One photograph showed a large object pointing to the north-west from a building, and in another, taken a few seconds later, the object had gone and a small cloud of steam or smoke was observed coming from the structure. On 14 May, another Mosquito came back with a photograph of what appeared to be a lorry, on which was a large cylindrical object 38 feet long near to the earthworks.

Quite what all of this meant was unclear.

On the 17th, Duncan Sandys submitted his first interim report which concluded (provisionally) that the Germans were attempting to develop a rocket which was potentially able to reach London. It was roughly 20 feet long with the capability of carrying an explosive warhead of 10 tons up to 150 miles. Two weeks later, on 4 June, a report was received from a scientist who had been conscripted by the Germans to work at Peenemünde giving much more accurate details of the rocket being developed – saying that it was 33 feet in length with a range of between 95 and 150 miles. But clearer evidence was to come shortly after. On 12 June, a PRU sortie to Peenemünde produced a photograph that arrived on Dr Jones' desk six days later. The quality of the definition was poor, but Jones was convinced that he could make out the slim pencil shape of a rocket and shortly after, on the 23rd, another PRU Mosquito took some good quality photographs and the interpreters were able to discern quite clearly the shapes of rockets on vehicles within one of the elliptical earthworks.

The Prime Minister, clearly concerned at the developments, instigated a meeting of the War Cabinet Defence Committee on Tuesday, 29 June at the Cabinet War Rooms in Great George Street. 'We cannot delay much longer in taking stock of this serious matter.'[2] He specifically wanted Sir Stafford Cripps and Lord Cherwell to be present.

On the 27th, Duncan Sandys submitted a paper for discussion at the meeting. Running to seventeen pages, it made interesting, if somewhat disturbing reading. There were four sections: the first for reports from secret agents, the second covering statements made by prisoners of war, the third evidence from refugees and neutrals, and the fourth interpretation of PRU photographs of Peenemünde and the Baltic coast. Clearly, it was difficult to establish the reliability of the contents of some of the reports, and this made drawing conclusions difficult. There appear to be references to three different weapons: a gun which would fire rocket-propelled projectiles, an 'air mine' with wings, and finally rockets. With hindsight, some of the reports are remarkable in the information they provide, although within the report it would have been difficult to recognize which items were fact and which were not. The meeting duly convened and included the Prime Minister, Clement Attlee, Anthony Eden, the Chiefs of Staff and General Ismay, Herbert Morrison, Stafford Cripps, Sir Robert Watson-Watt, Lord Cherwell, Dr R.V. Jones, Duncan Sandys and others. It would be a turning point because it debated the issue of whether or not the rockets existed and what should be done. By the end of the discussion, it was generally accepted that a rocket-type weapon did exist, and that it presented a real threat to the United Kingdom. As for what was to be done, Peenemünde should be bombed but not until there was confidence that a raid would be entirely successful – it was noted that a half hearted attempt might only warn the Germans that their activities were known to the Allies and they might move them elsewhere.

But in principle the action was clear: Peenemünde should be attacked.

The night of Tuesday, 17 August 1943 at Peenemünde was clear and moonlit, with a breeze blowing from the land. Some of the young men and women stayed up late to enjoy the setting of the sun and the lingering scent of the pine forests. They strolled and talked as the shadows lengthened. Some swam and then walked slowly back to their accommodation. By 11 p.m. the installation was pretty much deserted and the residents in their beds. At about 11.30, the sirens sounded. Some went to the shelters, others stayed in bed but nothing happened and it seemed that it must be a false alarm. Many of those who had sought the protection of the shelters eventually returned to their beds, despite the fact that the 'all clear' had not sounded. An hour and a half later, most were asleep. Those still awake heard aircraft in the distance but because of the lack of flak thought that they must be German. In fact, they were British bombers that had arrived early. At 1.10 a.m. cascades of 'fireworks' began to descend on Peenemünde – Pathfinder target markers – and five minutes later, the first bombs exploded.

Peenemünde's idyllic days were over for good.

But did the raid delay the rocket programme? The answer has to be 'Yes'. Some estimate that it delayed deployment of the rockets by six months, but others, possibly nearer the mark, say that it caused a delay of only two months. Target-marking problems meant that more damage than intended was inflicted on the labour camp, and in other areas an element of bad luck allowed some buildings and facilities to escape the total destruction desired by the Allies. Perhaps one of the most significant results came from the increasing involvement of the SS as the question of Peenemünde's vulnerability as a production facility became an issue.

Forced labour, Nordhausen.
(© *Bildarchiv Preussischer Kulturbesitz, Berlin. Image 30023140. 1 April*)

The Germans now realized that the Allies knew what was going on and the moment for dispersal had arrived. For Heinrich Himmler it presented an opportunity to convince Hitler that the SS should be more involved. By coincidence, he was with the *Führer* at the *Wolfsschanze,* his headquarters at Rastenburg in East Prussia, on 18 and 19 August, and he proposed to him that now was the time to move underground. The SS could supply labour from the concentration camps and the nature of underground production facilities meant that they would be secure from both escaping workers and the prying eyes of outsiders. Further, because the activities at Peenemünde had been compromised, development work could be moved further east to a *Waffen-SS* camp in Poland at Blizna, where there was a former Polish army artillery range. The camp was called Heidelager or the 'Heather Camp', the same name as was given to the small concentration camp sited there originally. Hitler agreed. On 25 August Nordhausen in Thuringia

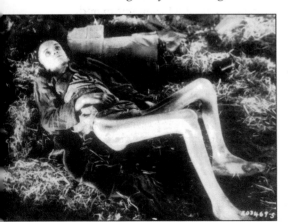

was selected as the site for the main rocket production plant. It would become known as the *Mittelwerk,* a term meaning 'central works' and suitably non-specific as to its real purpose.

The facility was in huge tunnels built into the mountainside. Prior to being handed over for rocket

Forced labour, Nordhausen.
(*US National Archives via Michael Neufeld.*)

production, it was a partly completed dump for fuel, oil and poison gas and responsibility for turning it into an operational production facility was given to SS *Brigadeführer* Dr Hans Kammler. Tunnels still had to be driven and a huge task faced him. It seems that he had no thought for the human cost and the concentration camp labourers used in 'Work Camp Dora' were treated as badly as those in the concentration camps themselves, if not worse. The workforce ultimately comprised many thousands housed in the damp, dank tunnels in bunks four levels high, although before the bunks were built they lived and slept on the bare rock of the tunnel floors. Once available, the beds were used on a 'hot bunking' system and soon became filthy. The sleeping tunnels were anything but peaceful – noisy with the rock blasting from nearby and full of dust. There was not enough water, and washing and sanitary facilities were inadequate. The whole place stank and the cruelty of the guards and *kapos* brutal in the extreme.

Once the complex was completed, the numbers of labourers reduced as attention turned to the need for a more technically skilled labour force, but even then, the living conditions were still poor and the quality of the manufacturing left much to be desired. On 10 December 1943 Albert Speer visited Nordhausen. He seems to have thought the conditions he saw quite barbarous, and made various improvements which, as well as providing more space, saw the construction of a camp outside, in the open air. But even then, it was still a concentration camp, *Konzentrationslager* Mittelbau, whose primary *raison d'être* was extermination. It is interesting that with their preoccupation with violence and brutality, the Germans did not seem to appreciate that their workers might have responded more positively if they had been treated more sympathetically. As it was, the quality of the manufacturing was at best mediocre and at worst suffered from deliberate sabotage from some particularly courageous individuals. More lives lost were in the production of the V2s than they killed, and many of those died from the brutal treatment meted out to them. The history of Dora and the monstrosities perpetrated in the name of the rockets is well covered in many other historical works and whilst they do not directly affect the air campaign in the Netherlands, any student of the air war needs to be aware of the conditions under which the rockets were manufactured and to which their defeat would bring an end.

New problems arose. Test missiles from both Blizna and Peenemünde (once it had recovered from the bombing) exploded prematurely because of friction overheating the nose cone. The engines continued to cut out just after launch, and the long-standing difficulties of guidance continued to dog the development. And at the same time, the general quality of missiles coming out of the new production facilities was poor. These factors all combined to create yet another crisis for the rocketeers. Information

A-4s at Blizna.
(© Bildarchiv Preussischer Kulturbesitz, Berlin. Image 30015476. 1944.)

continued to come over to the Allies from various sources operating at great danger under the noses of the Germans. In March 1944, it was learned that the missiles at Blizna used liquid oxygen, that they had a range of at least 6¼ miles and that there seemed to have been an explosion near Siedlice (about 160 miles from Blizna). With such a range, it seemed clear that these reports could only be referring to the suspected rocket. PRU sorties continued, but the next breakthrough came on 13 June 1944, the day that the first V1 landed on British soil a week after the D-Day landings in Normandy. A 'special' A-4 was launched to test a guidance system known as *Wasserfall*, but for whatever reason, control of the missile was lost and it headed north to crash eventually on Swedish soil about 100 miles away near Malmo. Two RAF officers were despatched to Sweden to inspect the wreckage but the amount of electronic equipment they found led to conclusions which were not quite accurate. They decided that the rocket must be carrying a very large warhead; larger than the 1 ton anticipated.

The Swedes allowed pieces of the A-4 to be taken to Britain by sea, and during the latter half of July attempts were made to reassemble it at Farnborough or at least glean as much information as possible from the wreckage. Dr R.V. Jones was once again in the limelight, trying to come to a definitive conclusion about the rockets by assessing the various conflicting reports in his possession. In August he reported that the rockets weighed about 12 tons and carried a warhead of about 1 ton. At last, their true dimensions were more or less known. Whether or not there was any guidance remained to be discovered, with the *Wasserfall* electronics continuing to cloud matters. But with defensive preparations in anticipation of a rocket campaign already in place – and, although they did not know it, about to start – those responsible in Britain for conducting the defence now knew what they were up against.

The *Reich* Propaganda Minister, Josef Goebbels renamed the two weapons systems V1 (the *Luftwaffe* flying bombs) and V2 (the rockets) the 'V' standing for *vergeltungswaffe* or 'revenge weapon'. The rockets were never going to bring Britain to its knees, however, and whilst larger ones to attack America were on the drawing board, they could never have brought the USA down unless their destructive power could be hugely increased. Fortunately, Germany's atom bomb never reached operational stage, and even the Allied bomb was too big to be fitted into the warhead of one of the rockets. But given time and a different set of circumstances, Germany might have been able, eventually, to attack American cities with atomic weapons.

Despite all the developmental problems, operational deployment of the V2 was not forgotten. As early as 1942, instructions were issued for the establishment of a unit to be responsible for A-4 operational training and experiment and *Lehr und Versuchs Batterie 444* came into existence – *lehr und versuchs* meaning 'training and experimental'. Its task was to train other units in the maintenance and operation of the rockets, but of course, before this could be done, procedures had to be defined, set down and practised. Whilst development of the rockets moved painfully slowly, progress and the deployment of operational A-4s seemed a forlorn hope, the operational processes could not be left until a fully tried and tested weapon was ready. Time would not allow it and so the preparations for deployment started.

The personnel establishment of a rocket firing battery was 210 men, and that of a fuel battery 156.

To begin with the German commanders expected the rockets to become available before an Allied invasion of the continent took place and assumed that the launch sites would be along the northern French coast within good range of London. At the same time, V1 launches would be taking place from these areas and launching facilties were built in readiness. These were concrete ramps up which the pilotless missiles were fired and looked rather like small ski-jumps. For the V2s, underground bunkers seemed the most appropriate launch sites and construction started, but the delays in turning the A-4 into a reliable weapon meant that the Allies overran the French launch sites in 1944 before they could be used to fire V2s. However, as well as fixed underground sites, the mobility of the rockets was also recognized, and an alternative method of firing was devised using only small concrete hardstandings; in fact, any suitable hardstanding including street corners – literally. For some time, it was assumed that the two weapons systems would be deployed operationally simultaneously and in December 1943, *XVI Armee Korps* of the *Wehrmacht* came into being commanded by Lieutenant-General Heinrich Heinemann. It had two arms: *Flakregiment 155(W)* commanded by Colonel Wachtel, responsible for V1s and *HARKO 191* commanded by Major-General Richard Metz, which would fire the V2s. Metz's command comprised a single *abteilung*[3] for the launching of missiles from the bunkers, three *abteilungen* for firing from mobile launchers and an independent unit.

But things changed in the late summer of 1944. In July, a number of senior officers of the *Wehrmacht* attempted to kill Hitler by leaving a bomb in a briefcase under a conference table at the *Wolfsschanze*. Although it exploded and caused significant damage, the *Führer* escaped with his life, although not without suffering psychological effects and losing trust in his army commanders. The failure proved to be to the advantage of the SS, whom Hitler felt he could still trust. Control of the V2 project passed to them, and reporting directly to Himmler SS *Brigadeführer* Kammler took the title 'General Commissioner for the A-4 Programme' and became responsible for the operational troops, now in two *gruppen*, *Nord* and *Süd*. Key units in *Gruppe Nord* were *Artillerie Abteilung 485* and *Lehr und Versuchs Batterie 444*, which would carry out most of the firings from The Hague. The main unit in *Gruppe Süd* was *Artillerie Abteilung 836*. As the campaign went on, changes would be made, with various technical and other units being activated.

Kammler took command on 30 August, by which time the Allies were sweeping through France, having liberated Paris a few days before. On the same day, American troops liberated Nice in the south. The following day, the 31st, British troops took Amiens. If the V2s were to be used against the Allies, then no time could be spared to build more bunkers. Mobile launches from constantly changing locations would have to do – as had always been envisaged. Not surprisingly, the rockets could not be fired without preparation – installation of the warhead, fuelling etc. – but those fired from transportable bases required preparation to be reduced to a minimum to avoid being caught in the open by aircraft.

The factories sent the completed V2s to the launching regions by train on flatcars where a technical troop took them over for initial checking and the installation of the warhead. Although the V2s could be launched quickly, they needed an infrastructure of storage areas with technical facilities, and of course the road and railway infrastructure to get them there. The Hague provided just such an infrastructure and the wooded areas proved to be ideal launch sites, with the trees giving good camouflage and protection of the newly launched rocket from surface winds. Because the coast of the Netherlands formed part of the Germans' defence line against an Allied invasion of Europe – the Atlantic Wall – much of The Hague had been cleared of civilians so that it lay empty and provided accommodation and some of the facilities needed for the V2s without the added problem of potentially hostile residents. This area was called the *Sperrgebeit*. V2s came in on flatbed railcars from Germany to Leiden station, where they were unloaded then taken to assembly areas where warheads were installed and they were generally checked and readied. The gyroscope used for guidance proved to be particularly problematic and needed careful attention. Storage of more than a few days meant a greater chance of the rocket failing and so the aim was to get them to the firing troops and launch them without undue delay. A *meillerwagen* – a skeletal cradle with arms to hold the rocket secure – carried the V2s horizontally, towed by lorries, but served also to raise the missile to a vertical alignment and act as a pre-launch gantry. It was ingeniously engineered. Fuel – liquid oxygen – arrived by rail. With its low temperatures (-183°C) it needed careful handling. Metal containers became covered in frost that

A V2 on its *meillerwagen* – possibly a development model. The 'lemon squeezer' blast deflector is clearly seen.
(Courtesy Deutsches Museum, München. Image no. BN–10639.)

would take the skin off an unprotected hand. The liquid oxygen was pumped into a special road tanker and transported to the launch site as part of the convoy. Other bowsers brought the alcohol and other chemicals needed. On arrival at the chosen launch site, the firing platform or *abschussplattform,* moved on a towing dolly to the spot selected, was made stable by screwing 'spud' legs down to the firm ground base. The dolly was then removed. The firing platform included a cone-shaped metal plate, known by some as 'the lemon squeezer' because of its shape, to deflect the hot exhaust gases of the launch away from the hardstanding towards the side. The *meillerwagen* and missile (tail first) would be winched to the firing platform and then, controlled by one man, hydraulic rams raised the cradle of the *meillerwagen* to the vertical, setting the rocket gently on to the firing table apparently standing on its fins. Fuel and chemicals were loaded, carbon graphite exhaust rudders were fitted to the fins and the final preparations completed. The arm of the *meillerwagen* returned to the horizontal and the support vehicles then moved away to a safe distance.

Each rocket had to be oriented to the right direction for its trajectory to take it to target, and this was done using a dial sight on the firing platform immediately before the cradle of the *meillerwagen* was removed. Ready to launch, the operation passed to the firing troop, who controlled the final moments from the protection of a *feuerleitpanzer*; a vehicle looking not unlike an armoured car with small horizontal slits for viewing. These firing control cars were usually about 150 yards from the rockets. Within a minute the missile was launched and on its way. Once launched, there was very little left to move from the site. It took an hour or so from arriving to seeing the rocket launched, and then about twenty minutes to clear the site. Clearly, the rocket troops were vulnerable to attack – particularly from the air – whilst setting the rocket up. The liquid oxygen and alcohol were highly explosive, not to mention the 1 ton warhead. Being caught in the open would be fatal and so the launching sites chosen were often in wooded areas where the prying eyes of Allied pilots could not see them through the branches – which nonetheless would not affect a launch. But in selecting launch sites, the Germans seemed to deliberately use locations near to civilians which meant that the Allied aircraft could only bomb them when they were confident that civilian casualties would be minimal, or if higher would have to be accepted. Street corners were often used – they had the advantage of strong, level hardstandings, and nearby civilians to act as 'human shields'. A significant number of V2s exploded immediately before or after launching; some went out of control plunging to earth and exploding in the immediate launch areas, killing both German soldiers and nearby civilians. But the casualties did not deter those in command. The launches went on. With the invading Allied armies pushing through Belgium, heading towards northern Germany,

The deceptively tranquil site of the launch of the first V2 fired at London
in September 1944 in Wassenaar, The Hague taken in 2003 but much as
it was in 1944.
(Author)

one of Kammler's first orders was to send *Abteilung 485* into the
Netherlands, to The Hague whilst *Batterie 444* moved to St Vith, near
Malmedy in Belgium.

The V2 campaign was about to begin.

The first attempt to fire a V2 in anger took place at about 9 a.m. on
Wednesday, 6 September 1944. The unit concerned was *Batterie 444* at St
Vith; the target Paris. The engine shut down just as it was launching but
with no explosion, and the rocket remained standing on the firing platform. About three-quarters of an hour later, a second attempt to fire failed
in the same way. The next day, *Batterie 444* moved to Houffalize in
Belgium and on the morning of Friday, 8 September, attempted to fire two
V2s, once again at Paris. This time, both rockets launched successfully, but
the first seems to have exploded at altitude because no impact was
recorded. The second, however, did as it was intended and exploded at
Alfort to the south-east of Paris, killing several people and injuring about
three dozen more.

In the meantime, *Batterie 2 Abteilung 485*, prepared to launch two
missiles against London from a peaceful residential, leafy suburb on the
northern side of The Hague. Wassenaar is still where the well-heeled
professional and middle classes live – university professors, lawyers,

surgeons, successful merchants. In Britain it would be called 'stockbroker belt'. The houses are large and imposing – two or three floors – and standing in their own grounds, or at least large gardens surrounded by walls and high hedges. Wildlife lives here in peace – blackbirds, thrushes, foxes and other innocuous creatures. Once off the main arterial roads, many of the smaller access roads to the houses are more like quiet lanes and walkers might be surprised to find a motor vehicle coming up behind them – even at the beginning of the twenty-first century. The lanes have names that add to the sense of tranquillity, and three of them – Lijsterlaan (Thrush Lane), Konijnenlaan (Rabbit Lane) and Koekoekslaan (Cuckoo Lane) – meet at a small intersection not far from one of the houses. Perhaps 150 yards along Lijsterlaan, there is another junction, this one with another lane called Schouwweg.

Civilians were summarily cleared out of this area so that in the early

evening of Friday, 8 September, there were no witnesses as the tranquillity of Wassenaar was rudely destroyed by the sounds of motor vehicles, pumps and men, and then the dreadful roar of a rocket engine, which peaked, then reduced as the V2 lifted off accelerating into the sky, leaving its corkscrew vapour trail behind it. Then, almost simultaneously, came a second, after which there were only the sounds of the men of *Abteilung 485* packing up their equipment, slamming doors, starting engines and finally the grinding of gears as the vehicles left and peace returned once more as night fell. The leafy lanes were not quite the same though. A Dutch civilian noticed later that each launch left a large circular burnt patch on the ground and that nearby trees had been burnt as well, up to a height of about 3 feet.

A V2 rises from the protection of woods.
(Courtesy Deutsches Museum, München. Image no. BN_38439.)

Christina Nieuwenhuits then twelve years old lived in The Hague with her family, and saw the first V2 being launched. 'I heard this great noise and saw a big flame and then this "torpedo" rising. I asked my mother what it was but she did not know.'

The first V2 launched from the junction of Lijsterlaan, Konijnenlaan and Koekoekslaan beside a house called Klein Wildhoeve, the second just along at the junction of Lijsterlaan and Schouwweg. It is perhaps ironic that the first V2 to land in London, the first of yet another weapon of indiscriminate mass destruction, should start its fateful journey from a leafy, suburban lane in one city and end it a few minutes later causing death and destruction in another suburban street in a different city in a different country. The innocent citizens of Wassenaar in The Hague and Staveley Road in Chiswick were surely the first victims of the latest outrage of human barbarism.

Notes

1. *News Chronicle* 7 September 1946. Reproduced by kind permission of Associated Newspapers.
2. Memo from the Prime Minister dated 25 June 1943. National Archives Premier 3/110.
3. Usually three batteries.

CHAPTER TWO

A Shaky Start

The RAF's Fighter Command was divided into groups based on geographic boundaries. No. 10 Group covered the south-west of England, with 11 Group responsible for the east of southern England and London as far north as Bury St Edmunds. The Midlands was covered by 12 Group with the north of England and Scotland the baillie-wick of 13 Group, although by the beginning of 1941, the very far north of Scotland was designated another Group, No. 14.

Prior to the Second World War, the organization responsible for defending Britain's air space was called Air Defence of Great Britain (ADGB), but in time it became Fighter Command. In 1943 ADGB was back. Fighter Command turned to the offensive in 1941 when the half-expected resumption of the attacks on southern England by the *Luftwaffe* failed to materialize and by 1943 the expectation was of an Allied invasion of Europe, not a German invasion of Britain. The threat to the UK main-land was much reduced, as was the need for numbers of defending fighters. Allied planning for the invasion got under way. The air arm of the invasion force became known as the Allied Expeditionary Air Force (AEAF), commanded by Air Chief Marshal Trafford Leigh-Mallory, who had commanded 12 Group during the Battle of Britain. This would be a joint British and American formation which included a resurrected ADGB (Fighter Command having been disbanded) to be responsible once again for the defence of Britain's shores. Although the threat of German invasion was much reduced, ADGB's role before the invasion was vitally impor-tant in preventing enemy reconnaissance aircraft seeing the enormous build-up of troops and ships in the south of England and ensuring that they were not attacked. Command of this critical formation passed to the current Air Officer Commanding (AOC), of 12 Group in 1943, Air Marshal Roderic Hill, who assumed command of ADGB on the day that it came into being – 15 November 1943.

In both experience and temperament, Roderic Hill came from a different mould from many of his colleagues and peers. Born on 1 March

1894 at Parliament Hill Fields in London, the eldest of three children – two boys and a girl – his parents were Micaiah and Minna Hill. At the time of Roderic's birth, Micaiah Hill was Professor of Mathematics at University College, London, and Roderic and his brother Geoffrey soon showed an interest in matters technical – Roderic having an early and long-standing fascination for trains and flying. But he also developed an interest in art. After prep school, he attended Bradfield College and in 1912 went up to University College with the intention of becoming an architect, but like many young men at that time, the outbreak of the First World War changed his life dramatically, and two days after the declaration of war, he enlisted as a private in the 18th Royal Fusiliers. Little thought went into the decision and yet it would change the whole course of his life. By this time he had met Helen Morton, the woman who would eventually become his wife and the mother of his children.

Towards the end of 1914, he was given a commission in the 12th Northumberland Fusiliers and after nine months' training, found himself a subaltern on the Western Front and taking part in the Battle of Loos, which started on Saturday, 25 September 1915. But he was wounded, hit in the side and evacuated from the front to be Mentioned in Despatches, the first of his many awards and decorations. Whilst recovering from his wounds, he applied for a transfer to the Royal Flying Corps, and so found himself arriving at the fledgling School of Instruction at Reading on St Valentine's Day 1916. Much of the work was what would now be called 'ground school'. Successfully passing out of the school, but not yet a qualified pilot – as was the way – his first posting was to No. 9 Reserve Squadron based at Norwich, where he soloed. Later he joined No. 13 Reserve Squadron at Dover and gained his wings on 19 June 1916. Then after training on Morane Bullets at Gosport, he left by train for the front on 25 July 1916, posted to 60 Squadron taking part in the Battle of the Somme, which by then had been under way for almost a month. The squadron flew Nieuports and Moranes on offensive patrols over the battle area tasked with keeping the skies clear for British bombers and reconnaissance aircraft, as well as acting as close escorts for the bombers. By the end of September, 60 Squadron was equipped entirely with Nieuports and Hill was playing his part in the fighting which at times was intense and bloody. He had his share of adventures and was awarded the Military Cross for an action on 26 September.

Later in November Hill was made 'A' Flight Commander and he rose to the challenge superbly. On 30 January 1917, he travelled once more to 'Blighty' on leave, but before he could return to the front was posted with immediate effect to replace Major Frank Goodden (who had been killed) as the Officer Commanding the Experimental Squadron at the Royal Aircraft Factory at Farnborough. By this time Hill had been Mentioned in Despatches again. He seems to have enjoyed the flying at

Farnborough – glibly described as test flying, but in reality distinctly hazardous in that it involved the testing of experimental and prototype aeroplanes to ensure that they were sufficiently robust to withstand the rigours of flying operationally at the front. Hill's flying was anything but routine but he enjoyed the combination of the physical act of flying with the technical issues arising from the aircraft he flew. On 26 September 1917, the second anniversary of the Battle of Loos and the anniversary of his gaining the MC, he married Helen Morton. The date was at his specific request; its significance not lost to him.

Hill did not lack physical courage. In 1918, he flew an FE2B fitted with a device on the wings to deflect balloon cables in an experiment at Martlesham Heath. It was not entirely successful and the young pilot needed all his skills to nurse the aeroplane back to earth. This exploit earned him an Air Force Cross (AFC). On a later occasion he made a parachute drop and was subsequently awarded a second AFC. When the Royal Air Force formed in April 1918, Major Hill became Squadron Leader Hill but continued his work at Farnborough (now known as the Royal Aircraft Establishment), being awarded the R.M. Groves Aeronautical Research Prize for 1921 and elected Fellow of University College, University of London in 1924 – making an unusual combination of awards for bravery in the air and aeronautical technical research. Despite some of his own misgivings, those who controlled Hill's destiny seem to have had him earmarked for great things in the fledgling service and in May 1923, he attended the second course to be run at the RAF's Staff College at Andover, but only with great reluctance on his part. He considered his work at Farnborough to be far more important and although selected for the first course to be run at Andover – surely an indication of his high reputation – he delayed his entry until the second course by digging in his heels and simply refusing to go!

After Andover, Hill's next appointment was to Iraq as Officer Commanding 45 (Bomber) Squadron, where he relieved Squadron Leader Arthur Harris. The squadron base was Hinaidi, south-east of Baghdad. Hill had concerns about his ability to follow such a charismatic and dynamic leader, but he did so, bringing his own attributes to the position. One important task of the squadron (along with 70 Squadron) was to fly the mail between Baghdad and Cairo operating Vickers Vernons along a route that for its day was quite hazardous and testing; over mountains where forced landings were simply not possible, and then desert where a successful forced landing meant immediate danger from a hostile local population. Hill found the desert scenery beautiful and exhilarating – it touched the artist in him – and the pioneering nature of the work, the mail flights in particular, caught his imagination. He made a success of his tenure as the squadron commander, bringing to the position a rather unusual – for that time – concern for the welfare of the ordinary airmen who were his responsibility. After Iraq, Hill was posted to the technical staff of Middle East HQ in Cairo until 1927, when he returned home to be one of the teaching staff at the Staff College at Andover – having been a student there himself only a few years before. Two years followed as the Commanding Officer (CO) of the Oxford University Air Squadron – a post with the title of 'Chief Instructor' rather than 'Commanding Officer' – and during this period he made such an impact on the university that he was given an MA.

Then followed a series of high-level appointments utilizing his technical and administrative abilities and in 1938 promotion to Air Vice-Marshal. But to his chagrin and disappointment, within days of war being declared in September 1939, instead of an operational command, he was sent across the Atlantic to Canada to mobilize Canadian and (where possible) American industry to the production of aircraft for the British war effort. Back to the UK in 1940, as an acting Air Marshal, Hill became Director-General of Research and Development before being returned to the USA as the Controller of Technical Services, British Air Commission, again to his great disappointment. The lack of any operational appointments weighed heavily with Hill, who interpreted this as an indication of

his standing with his superiors. It seemed somehow wrong to him that he should be in the comfort and luxury of the United States when there was so much hardship at home. Back in Britain in 1942, there was further disappointment for him when he was given the position of Commandant of the RAF Staff College, which meant a reversion to his substantive rank of Air Vice-Marshal. When this tour ended, it seemed that he might be retired, but he became AOC 12 Group with the rank of Air Marshal and shortly afterwards the AOC of ADGB.

Hill's daughter Prudence wrote a biography of her father[1] and it reveals a sensitive man with an

Roderic Hill.
(Courtesy Imperial War Museum. Negative no. CH10275.)

artistic bent – it will be recalled that he originally wanted to become an architect – but also a man racked with self-doubt, particularly on taking up a new appointment when, on each occasion, he seems to have endured agonies wondering if he would be able to cope with the demands made of him – to find invariably that he was more than capable and well able to rise to the challenges.

His daughter wrote of him:

> *Although deeply inclined to the private and unassuming way of life, he constantly found himself weighed upon by public commitments, and a sense of the strangeness of this was always with him. There on the one hand were his pencils and his drawing board representing to him what he really felt himself to be, and there on the other hand were his gold braid, his medals and his academic gown representing what life was making of him. He would laugh about it gently, with a kind of resignation, and a kind of quiet pride.[2]*

And he was charmed by both the technical act of flying and the qualitative aspects too.

> *Climbed up through clouds from three thousand to four thousand and found them in waves like great Atlantic rollers rolling from the east. In the western distance, a great shadow barred the cloud surface and beyond it the sun made a pathway of light exactly like the distant sea. I have never seen such perfect waves before, about six hundred yards from crest to crest. In the north, clouds stood up like distant mountains, blue and faintly gold where touched by the sun.[3]*

He painted pictures of the desert and his great fascination and love for the Cairo to Baghdad mail run drove him to write a memoir of it, called *The Baghdad Air Mail*, which at the beginning of the twenty-first century, seventy years later, is still recognized as a classic and the few originals on the market were changing hands for £200 a copy. He and Helen had three children: Peter, Prudence and Phoebe-Ann. Peter followed his father's footsteps into the RAF but was killed flying a Baltimore bomber on night operations in Italy in 1944. His father was devastated – he was a great family man and never happier than when pottering about at the family home on Hayling Island, which Hill designed himself.

There can be little doubt that there would be some who thought Hill unsuitable for operational command because of his general lack of operational experience, despite the fact that he had taken part in the air battles above the Western Front in the First World War and had fought as an infantry subaltern too. He was nonetheless a formidable pilot, and with his intellect, commitment and interest in things technical, was well suited for his responsibility for defending British skies against their latest attackers.

Two days after the re-creation of ADGB, Hill received a directive from Leigh-Mallory setting out his duties. The first was to be responsible for the air defence of Great Britain and Northern Ireland and the second to command Nos 9, 10, 11, 12, 13, 60 and 70 Groups. Another was to conduct 'defensive and offensive operations which involve the use of squadrons of both ADGB *and TAF* (Tactical Air Force)[4] as heretofore under instructions issued to both headquarters until fresh instructions are issued'. In reality, the communications and command problems were complex and difficult. Hill wrote later that although control of his (Hill's) handling of operations was exercised by Leigh-Mallory, it was 'little more than nominal'.[5] This meant that Leigh-Mallory was effectively by-passed, with Hill going directly – but with Leigh-Mallory's knowledge – to the Air Ministry and the British Chiefs of Staff. But on the other hand, it was 11 Group Headquarters, under Hill, that issued orders and requests to the TAF which was not under his command. Despite these anomalies, Hill's prime responsibility was to defend British air space and this he set out to do.

When Hill assumed command of ADGB in November 1943, it was unclear just what he was up against. He was aware that the Germans had been experimenting with a long-range rocket with the potential to devastate large urban areas and kill many people and he inherited some initial measures to give warning of them. Five radar stations on the south coast between Dover and Ventnor were able to detect rockets launched from across the Channel and the operators were trained to recognize the returns on their screens. Also, artillery units based nearby were instructed to report visual signs of a launch – 'flash-spotting' – and others, including the Royal Artillery's 11th Survey Regiment, were told to report noise indicators – 'sound ranging' – in the hope they might allow warning maroons to be sounded in London and also to pinpoint the launch sites so that they might be attacked.

Early in 1944, Hill received instructions to reduce these anti–V2 measures and to concentrate on the V1s, the flying bombs, but he wisely decided to make sure that the operators skilled in detecting the Big Ben (the code for V2s) targets remained in place allowing the precautions to be reinstated quickly should it prove necessary. When the V1s started to come over in force in June 1944, he ordered that they should be re-activated, by then a further two radar stations were operational. In the meantime, his knowledge of the rockets gradually clarified as 1944 wore on. By the end of August he knew that they were roughly 45 feet long with an all-up weight of about 14 tons, including a warhead of about 1 ton. He also knew that the rocket did not need a massive bunker for launching, but that it could be fired from a simple platform and that the time needed to prepare it for launching was no more than two hours. Finally, intelligence information led him to believe that the rockets might very well be ready for use in September. The Allied armies moving through France captured concrete slabs which they took to be prepared positions for V2 launches and Hill commented that similar positions must exist in areas that the Germans still occupied but that their locations were not known to the Allies and 'there was not the slightest chance of our detecting them on air reconnaissance photographs'.

The use of fighters flying 'armed reconnaissance' ('armed recce') sorties against the launch sites constituted a key element in the preparations for the anticipated onslaught of the V2s. Because of the expectation that they would be used first in early September, such sorties started on 30 August (the same day that SS *Brigadeführer* Kammler took command of the V2 troops) but they could only be haphazard and depend on luck to succeed because of the difficulty of spotting the launch sites. This problem would never really be solved, even although the general areas used by the V2 troops might be known. But the expected rocket attack did not materialize and on Monday, 4 September, with the invading Allied armies in the Pas de Calais and Flanders putting the rockets out of range, the sorties ceased. However, whilst some thought the threat had gone, Hill's intelligence staff were less sanguine, having noted that the Germans still occupied the Netherlands, from where rockets able to land on British soil could still be fired. Their advice was that this might happen within ten days.

Ironically, having stopped the armed recces over France on the Monday, the first two rockets fell on Staveley Road and Epping at the end of that week. The onslaught had begun. To their credit, the authorities were not panicked by the rockets. Over the next week or so, V2s continued to arrive, but in small numbers and not the deluge that might have been expected. According to Roderic Hill, between 8 and 18 September, twenty-six landed, thirteen of them in the London Civil Defence Region.[6] Rockets continued to fall on Woolwich, Southgate, Wembley and East Ham. Other records suggest that the troops fired fewer than twenty rockets during this period. What was significant for the British were the lessons learned. According to Hill the radar stations set up to pick up V2s fired from France – the expected launching area – found it difficult to track rockets coming from the Netherlands and so the number of stations along the coast from Lowestoft to Dover was doubled from three to six and extra flash spotting and sound ranging units were deployed to liberated areas of the continent. No. 105 Mobile Air Reporting Unit was formed under Hill's command in the middle of the month and was sent to near Brussels to 'correlate and transmit the information from technical sources across the Channel'. The other significant factor was that the radar and sound-ranging information about individual rockets' trajectories did not allow, as had been hoped, the launching points of the rockets to be calculated with a sufficient degree of accuracy, only to within a mile or so. This was not enough to give the pilots an accurate target to look for – by the time the aircraft were over the launching site, the launcher convoy would have moved on.

However, they did know roughly where the first two V2s were fired from, and Hill quickly despatched aircraft to seek out the launchers.

Squadrons flying Tempests and Typhoons were soon attacking the launch site areas which had been identified in some of the wooded areas in and around The Hague. No. 80 Squadron used Tempest Vs operating from their base at Manston. Just previously they were one of the squadrons trying to bring down the V1s, and as confirmation that the perceived threat from them had receded is a comment to the effect that on the 7 September 'with the Diver[7] menace quickly declining, a relaxed state of readiness was brought into effect'. But on Monday, 11 September, whilst escorting some Invader bombers attacking Leeuwarden airfield in the Netherlands, 80 Squadron's CO, Squadron Leader R.L. Spurdle, noticed what he thought might be a V2 site south east of Den Helder – clearly the squadron knew about the new threat. Two days later it was official – they were to attack the V2 in the Netherlands. At 6.50 a.m. eight Tempests led by the CO took off to attack what was believed to be a V2 storage site north of The Hague. Because of the woods, no specific target could be identified but the Tempests gave the general area a good 'going over' with cannon. Whilst in the air, they saw other British fighters to the south, one of which exploded. This turned out to be Squadron Leader Wigglesworth of 3 Squadron, whose aircraft was apparently caught in the explosion of a V2 he had hit. Whether or not it was about to be fired is unclear. One sortie resulted in a massive explosion which left a huge crater and might very well have been a V2 being caught just on the point of launching. For the next few days, 80 Squadron continued the armed recces of the The Hague area. On the 15th, they reported a V2 launch during an early afternoon sortie[8], and then on the 17th, attention turned to support for Operation Market Garden, although interest in the V2s continued.

At this time, 229 Squadron, based in England and commanded by Major N.F. Harrison, a South African, and flying Spitfire IXs, was carrying out several different types of sorties in the general area of the Netherlands – Jim Crows (reconnaissance operations looking for enemy shipping and usually carried out by two aeroplanes), bomber escort missions, and on the 13th there were two consecutive escort operation by two Spitfires piloted by Flight Lieutenant McAndrew in 9R●B and Flight Lieutenant Burrett in 9R●D, who took off at 16.45 returning at 19.15, and by Flight Lieutenant Lillywhite in 9R●T and Pilot Officer Clarke in 9R●N, leaving at 18.30 to return at 20.40. The squadron Operations Record Book (ORB)[9] says:

> *McAndrew and ... Burrett were airborne on an escort project of which little was really known and much speculated. A Wellington and/or a Halifax*

*patrolling over the North Sea, and said to be either on air/sea rescue work,
or some radar operation plotting 'Big Ben' was reported to have been
attacked earlier in the day and in need of protection.*

The two Spitfires climbed to 17,000 feet and twenty minutes after taking
off, found a Wellington at 15,000 patrolling 15 minute legs on a course of
210 degrees and the reciprocal. A Halifax was also seen in the vicinity. The
second pair reported similar activities although 'knowing even less of
their purpose of duties'. The weather was good with a haze over the sea
and thin stratus at 40,000 feet.

For the pilots of 229 it was their first inkling of the V2s.

Already based in Norfolk, having been operating frequently over the
Netherlands and with the topography familiar to the pilots, 229 was well
placed to take on the V2 campaign and they would be heavily involved in
the campaign. Formed briefly at the end of the First World War, it re-
formed at RAF Digby in October 1939 flying Bristol Blenheim IFs, but
these were replaced in March 1940 with Hawker Hurricanes. It fought in
France and in the Battle of Britain before going to the Mediterranean
theatre until 1944 when it returned to the UK to fly protection for the
Normandy landings on 6 June 1944 from RAF Detling. This was a sight
that created a great impression on at least one of its pilots; Flight Sergeant
'Paddy' O'Reilly recalled seeing a myriad of tiny black specks on the water
in the moonlight all going south, making for France.

From Detling, in short order 229 operated from Tangmere, Merston and
Gatwick before arriving at Coltishall at the beginning of July. From then

until September there came a round
of sweeps and bomber escort operations across the sea to the
enemy-occupied continent. At this
time, the squadron's identification
code was 9R. Besides strikes
against ground targets, many of
their operations were directed
against shipping. Even then there
were losses. On Friday, 15
September Flight Sergeant John
Manley (in 9R●D) ditched in the
North Sea whilst on a Jim Crow
with his great chum, Flight
Sergeant O'Reilly.

John Manley of 229 Squadron.
(Tom O'Reilly)

The weather today was better, although still not good flying weather. But in spite of this, F/Sgt. Manley and F/Sgt. O'Reilly were airborne at 09.10 hours on a Jim Crow to patrol Ijmuiden [sic] to Terschelling. The weather on crossing became worse and a heavy sea fog was below them. At 10.05 hours approx. they suddenly saw through the mist that they had made landfall and F/Sgt. O'Reilly thought it was 6 miles South of Den Helder but most probably they were somewhat North of Ijmuiden [sic]. They immediately turned north and crossed out again at 200 feet to be met by intense light flak from the coastal area. F/Sgt. Manley (Black 1) was hit and they set course of 280° for base climbing to 3,000 feet as Black 1 knew he would probably have to bale out. Black 2 formated on him and saw that Black 1's rudder ailerons were shot away. When about 30 miles West of Den Helder (according to Black 2, but probably Ijmuiden) Manley was seen to prepare to bale out, at about 10.15. Flames and white smoke came from its exhaust and he went into a spiral. His chute was seen to open at about 500 feet and it remained upon the water for 5 mins. About 200 yards from the position where the aircraft crashed. An oil patch appeared on the surface. The pilot was seen at no time.

O'Reilly climbed to 3,500 feet and reported the loss of his friend waiting until two other 229 Spitfires arrived to take over the watch, having been

'Paddy' O'Reilly of 229/603 Squadron. His Spitfire was called 'Lightning Strike'. Note 229 Squadron identification code '9R'.
(Tom O'Reilly)

scrambled at 10.20 and getting airborne in 'the record time of one minute and 35 seconds'. They stayed in the area looking for Manley but found nothing. At 11.40 another two pairs of Spitfires left to continue the search but all they reported was a Hudson on a similar duty. Finally, at 17.00 a further four Spitfires took off in a final effort to find the missing pilot but to no avail. They returned at 19.20, at which time it was decided that Manley was indeed lost. This came as a huge blow to his fellow pilot and friend Paddy O'Reilly, who despite having witnessed the loss, was airborne again at 12.45 with Flight Lieutenant Patterson to resume the original ill-fated Jim Crow, knowing that his friend might very well be somewhere below them waiting for rescue.

O'Reilly was born in 1923 in Birkenhead and despite his nickname and his part-Irish ancestry, his accent was more the Mersey rather than the Liffey – he preferred 'Tom' to 'Paddy' but it was the latter which stuck. He left school when he was sixteen and volunteered for the RAF a few months later. He was an impressive boxer and although he did not make the professional ranks, he counted Pat and Les McAteer amongst his friends. He joined 229 in Malta and fought with it for two years. He was a pleasant and easy-going man with a lively sense of humour and a mop of dark hair that fell across the right side of his forehead. Manley and he shared a room in the sergeants' mess and also an interest in motor bikes – O'Reilly owned a red Panther and Manley a Norton – which allowed them a certain independence in getting off the camp and into nearby villages and Norwich on their frequent escapades. Paddy O'Reilly recalled that in some ways, they possessed different characters despite being good mates. Returning to Britain from the Mediterranean, O'Reilly was flat broke because he had lost his money playing cards. John Manley was well off – he had not drawn on his air force salary because there was so little for him to spend his money on, and he found that he had the best part of half a year's salary to spend! They were young men and they carried on like all young men but with perhaps more intensity given the risks that they ran almost every day.

That evening, Paddy O'Reilly had the difficult and unenviable job of sorting through his friend's belongings and sending them to Manley's wife Norma. His feelings can only be imagined, but he must have spent a miserable night wondering if Manley was still alive and might even then be tossing about in a dinghy on the North Sea, cold and possibly hurt. And of course, even at this stage of the war there was no compassionate leave when friends were lost. O'Reilly would know that his duties would continue to take him over the same area of sea day after day. Eventually, Manley's body washed ashore on the Dutch coast. He was twenty-one years old when he died and is buried in Plot 2, Row A, Grave 20 in Bergen General Cemetery. His parents were Denis and Cathrine Manley, who lived in Cardiff, and he had a sister, who was living in the USA at the turn of the twentieth century. Although not strictly a casualty of the V2 campaign, nonetheless Flight Sergeant John Manley RAFVR (1338749) was 229 Squadron's first casualty of the period.

On the 17th, most of the pilots were involved in patrolling activity as protection for the Market Garden landings but saw no action. However, in the early afternoon, just after 13.00 they reported seeing what they took to be a V2 launch: 'It was a vapour trail beginning at 28,000 feet and ending at 55,000 feet going up vertically at terrific speed originating somewhere to the south of the Zuider Zee.' A V2 was reported as exploding at Coulsdon on the south side of London at 13.11 – possibly the same one.

Roderic Hill was now responsible for all the air operations against the V2s, and he had the authority to request attacks from Bomber Command and the 2nd TAF – although these were only requests and would only be squeezed in when other operational needs allowed. Nonetheless he became convinced that three properties in Wassenaar were being used by the rocket troops and asked that they be attacked by Bomber Command, which they were on 14 and 17 September. The attacks were thought to have been successful.

During the next week or so there was a lull. Operation Market Garden meant that Allied troops were getting a little too close for comfort and *Abteilung 485* moved to Burgsteinfurt in Germany and *Batterie 444* to Rijs. Intelligence from the Netherlands told Hill that the rocket units were being ordered away but not exactly when, and *Abteilung 485*'s farewell launching of a V2 on the evening of the 18th made him and his advisers doubt what they were being told. Accordingly, Hill decided to play safe and to continue the operations over the suspected firing areas until he was sure that the danger had gone.

On Monday 18 September, 12 Group issued Operation Instruction no 19/44 titled *Counter Measures to 'Big Ben'*. It makes interesting reading. Orders such as these followed a predefined format – Information, Intention, Execution, Administration and Communications – and within each section, the subsections were equally well defined. The instruction is couched succinctly to give as much information as possible as briefly as possible. Key paragraphs are reproduced below:

INFORMATION

1. The enemy is launching long-range radio controlled rockets against this country from sites in Holland, this operation being known as "Big Ben". The sites from which the rockets are fired are not large permanent structures as was originally thought, but consist simply of numerous well concealed concrete platforms. The firing equipment, radio control apparatus and operating

personnel are transportable and may therefore afford, if spotted, only a fleeting target.

2.   In addition, No. 12 Group is being reinforced and has been made responsible for

  (i)   The provision of fighter aircraft to special aircraft of 100 Group employed for observing "Big Ben" activity and taking radio-counter measures.

  (ii)   Armed Anti-rocket reconnaissance patrols.

  (iii) The immediate despatch of fighters to attack "Big Ben" sites and radio installations when located.

4.   No.100 Group aircraft employed on "Big Ben" counter-measures will be operating as follows:-

  (i)   Pairs of Halifax or Wellington aircraft operating together will patrol continuously throughout the 24 hours on patrol line 'A' (51.50'N 03. 00'E – 52.20'N 03. 30'E) at 15,000 feet.

  (ii)   A patrol of one Fortress aircraft will be operating throughout the 24 hours on patrol line 'B' (52.22'N 04.15'E – 51.45'N 03.45'E) at 20,00 feet.

[This explains the mysterious operations carried out by 229 Squadron on 13 September!]

5.   The rocket launching area, known as the "Big Ben" area, consists of that part of Holland bounded on the South by Latitude 51.20'N; on the East by Longitude 05.10'E on the West by the coast and on the North by Latitude 53.00'N.

INTENTION

6.   In conjunction with 100 Group to locate and destroy:

  (i)   Erections, personnel, vehicles either road or rail, and water-borne traffic, which appear to be connected with the rocket firing.

  (ii)   The Radio Control stations connected therewith either static or mobile.

EXECUTION

Forces Available

7.   The following fighter forces will be available in the Coltishall Sector to meet the commitment:-

(i)	COLTISHALL.	Nos, 80 and 274 Tempest V Squadrons
		No. 229 Spitfire IX Squadron.
(ii)	MATLASK.	Nos. 3, 56 and 486 Tempest V Squadrons.

Armed Reconnaisance

9. Should the 100 Group aircraft be unable to operate for any reason, a continuous patrol consisting of one Section in the Northern part of the "Big Ben" area and one Section in the Southern part of the "Big Ben" area, will be maintained in an endeavour to locate the launching points of any rockets. If seen, they are to be reported immediately, after which the section concerned is to take immediate offensive action against any enemy activity on the site.

10. In addition to the escort to the 100 Group force or to the armed reconnaissance patrol in their absence referred to above, Squadrons will be employed on armed reconnaissance over the "Big Ben" area, operating either as a Squadron, Sections of eight, or Sections of four. It is most likely, however, that standing patrols of four aircraft will be required throughout the hours of daylight.

Strike Force

11. One squadron will be held at readiness to attack sites reported to be operating.

Tactics

14. Sites will not be attacked by the Section Leader until his R/T report has been acknowledged.

15. Fighters attacking vehicles which appear to be connected with the rocket firing, should not go below 1,000 feet, in view of the possibility of very large explosions resulting from the attack taking place on the ground.

16. Since the sites will be extremely well camouflaged, armed reconnaissance patrols are to be carried out above light flak height.

19. It is considered that flak may be considerable on the sites, but is unlikely to open fire until aircraft commence to attack.

20.   All pilots are to be instructed to be particularly observant when passing over or operating in the "Big Ben" area and are to make note of any installations or activities that might connect with the long range rockets, especially if there is any indication of rocket firing.

Reports on Rocket Firing

21.   All reports on rocket firing received by R/T or from pilots on landing will be passed immediately to No.12 Group Controller, in order that the Readiness Squadron may be despatched to attack the firing site it if (sic) is located.

ADMINISTRATION

24.   Nos. 80 and 274 Tempest V Squadrons will move to Coltishall on 19th September, 1944.

25.   Nos. 3, 56 and 486 Tempest V Squadrons (150 Wing) will move to Matlask on 20th September, 1944 and will be administered by R.A.F. Coltishall.

    The players appeared to be gathering but with the exception of 229 Squadron, they flew Tempests.
According to Roderic Hill, there was a lull in the rocket activity between 19 and 25 September, and although the Germans did continue to launch them, none landed on British soil. Hill also reported that 'On the 19th three whole squadrons from No.12 Group . . . were sent to attack objectives in an area south-east of the race-course at the Hague. . .', although according to the 12 Group ORB, there was, in fact, little activity. Four Spitfires of 229 Squadron carried out a shipping recce off the Dutch coast in the morning with a second similar recce in the afternoon at Den Helder and IJmuiden. Other than that, eight Mustangs of 316 Squadron flew a coastal Roadstead (An operation to find and attack enemy shipping) to the Norwegian coast. Similarly, the 12 Group ORB notes that 3, 56 and 486 Squadrons moved from Newchurch Advanced Landing Ground (ALG) in 11 Group to Matlaske, but according to the squadron records, 3 Squadron did not move until 21 September and 56 not until two days after that, having been forced to divert to Manston because of bad weather on the 20th and then being stuck there. No. 80 Squadron, however, managed the transfer to Coltishall despite the weather.
    In the event, the Tempest Squadrons did not spend much time in 12 Group, despite being earmarked specifically for Big Ben work in

Operation Instruction 19/44. Within a week they were ordered to the Continent, to B60 at Grimbergen in 122 Wing of the 2nd TAF. By the 30th, the squadrons were replaced by three others, which all flew Spitfire IXs. Why, having been selected for the rocket campaign, the Tempest squadrons were quickly ordered away again is not clear. Typhoons and Tempests were legendary in their ground-attack support of the Allied armies in Europe, but much of this would be 'skip-bombing' and strafing with rockets and cannon rather than dive bombing. It might be that the Spitfires performed better as dive bombers, and this more accurate method of attack was necessary to keep civilian casualties down. However at the same time as the Tempests left, so did the Spitfires of 229, which was posted to Manston – although they returned a few weeks later. There seems to have been some doubt about how the V2 threat should be tackled in the first few weeks of the attack and it would be the beginning of October before a properly structured response was in place and operating. The Readiness Squadrons mentioned in Paragraph 21 did not last long either – timescales did not allow warnings to come through from the Netherlands and the aircraft to scramble and reach the launch sites in time.

On that fateful Friday when the first V2s landed in London, the Spitfire IXEs of 602 (City of Glasgow) Squadron Auxiliary Air Force (the Auxiliary Air Force being a reserve arm of the RAF) flew sixteen sorties between 14.00 and 18.45 from the rough ALG – cryptically numbered B52[10] – near Douai in France to which it had moved on the 5th. They were all patrols in the vicinity of Arnhem, and all proved uneventful. There had been no flying the previous day because of the bad weather – poor visibility and rain – but even so, the pilots were getting fed up with the lack of action and thought that they had been relegated to a backwater. The CO was Flight Lieutenant A.R. Stewart, who held the post in a temporary capacity because of the loss of the incumbent, the South African Squadron Leader Johannes J. 'Chris' le Roux DFC and two bars, in an accident on 29 August. Due for a spell of leave, le Roux took off in atrocious weather during the afternoon to fly across the Channel to England, but had to return as the conditions worsened. He tried a second time in the evening but seems to have lost his bearings. In his last transmission he requested a position, but nothing was heard of him again.

No. 453 Squadron of the RAAF, like 602 currently part of 125 Wing and based at the same ALG, having moved there on the 4th, was in much the same position. They carried out twelve uneventful sorties in their Spitfire IXEs between 07.00 and 10.30, patrolling Brussels and Antwerp. The pilots considered these operations to be 'milk runs' because of the regularity of the trips and their monotony. They too had not been flying the day before. On 8 September, the CO was Squadron Leader D. H. 'Don' Smith, who had been in post since 2 May but was a long-standing member of the unit credited with a single Bf109 kill and two probables, as well as a Focke Wulf

190 kill and three damaged. He was no mean fighter pilot. For 453 Squadron, on the Continent, life continued to be frustratingly quiet because of the poor weather and their distance from the front line, but on the 17th, they moved to ALG B70 at Deurne, near Antwerp. They subsequently flew a number of sorties to the Nijmegen area. At the same time, 602 also moved to Deurne, within striking distance of Brussels which was visited on several occasions by the pilots, who enjoyed the festivities and hospitality of the newly liberated Belgians. During the next ten days, 602 continued its patrols of the Flushing and Arnhem areas, which seemed to be relatively uneventful. No. 453 flew four patrols each of eight aircraft on the afternoon of the 17th – the day that Operation Market Garden began. The second patrol reported clouds of smoke at Nijmegen and the third 100 gliders and a building at Arnhem on fire as well as a large explosion (possibly an arms dump) and an oil fire.

No. 175 Squadron, an RAF squadron and part of 2nd TAF's 121 Wing, operated Typhoons, and it also moved to Deurne on 17 September. Operating in the close support role, usually using rockets, one of its pilots was another Aussie, Tom Hall. He remembered that they received a warm welcome from the enemy when they arrived at their new base on the 17th:

602 Squadron group.
Back Row l to r. ?, 'Spy', Flying Officer Raymond Baxter, Squadron Leader 'Max' Sutherland, ?, Adj, Cec Zuber
Front Row l to r. Warrant Officer Max Baerlein, ?, ?, Flying Officer W.J.H. Roberts, Flight Sergeant S. Gomme, Pilot Officer Michael V. Francis. *(Max Baerlein)*

We had just completed taxiing to the designated squadron area when German artillery opened up from about 4 miles away on the other side of the Albert Canal. We had personal belongings stuffed in the gun bays and did not have a chance to take anything out of the aircraft before we ran to the slit trenches. But the barrage did not last very long . . .[11]

The Spitfire needs little introduction. The early Mark I and IIs – victors of the Battle of Britain in 1940 – soon became outclassed by the improved variants of the *Luftwaffe*'s Bf109 and in particular the Bf109F. The RAF introduced the Spitfire Mark V which in turn became the prey of the brand new Focke Wulf 190 'Butcher Bird' towards the end of 1941. The performance superiority of the 190 over the Spitfire V threatened a mortal blow to the RAF's aspirations to take the air war across the Channel, and the Mark IX was the solution. There were three versions: the L, the HF and the LF. The HF was a high-flying variant and the LF was designed for use at low altitude; it incorporated the new Merlin 66 engine. Once introduced, the new Spitfires proved a match for the 190. To check just how they did compare in detail, trials conducted with a captured FW190 showed that the performance was similar, with each possessing slight superiorities and different attributes at different heights. As a generalization, the Spitfire IX proved a match for the 190, although as time went on the different variants of each introduced by the opposing air forces meant that they took turns in having the edge.

Visually, the IX was very similar to the V. It had a wing span of 36 feet 10 inches and a length of just over 31 feet. The maximum permissible take-off weight was 7,500 pounds and for the LF IX the Merlin 66 produced 1,580 horsepower to turn the 10 foot 9 inch diameter Rotol four-bladed propeller. The 66 was not without its problems, however. George Pyle flew Spitfire LF IXs with 129 Squadron from Hornchurch in 1943. He recalled that in new aeroplanes just delivered, the Merlin 66 had a tendency to cut out at about 20,000 feet. This was resolved without too much trouble, but it meant that each new Spitfire had to be checked. On 18 August 1943 he found himself detailed to carry out an air test on a Spitfire LF IX which had needed to have the adjustments made to the engine, having failed the previous day.

My Flight Commander told me to 'take it up as high as it would go'. It was a nice afternoon with occasional broken cloud, and being an obedient and inquisitive character I just kept climbing, past the 21,000 level and then steadily upwards. At 40,500 I was obviously losing power, staggering a bit, and getting cold and having felt that I had proved something I rolled over on to my back for a quick descent. In so doing, of course I toppled my instrument gyroscopes and as I dived through the first layer of cloud I pushed forward on the stick to counter the natural tendency of a Spitfire in a dive to go tail heavy. I overdid it because as the speed built up I was suddenly thrown forward in the cockpit as the violent shaking of hitting compressibility commenced. The controls were solid as the speed seemed to wind up and I imagined either disintegration or a very deep hole in the ground somewhere. Unable to move the stick I then did something desperate and potentially destructive – I rolled the elevator trimming tab marginally back. The result was instantaneous and once again I had to hold the stick slightly forward to control the resultant zoom. Later calculations allowing for height, pressure and humidity showed that I had reached in excess of 600 mph in diving from a corrected altitude of 43,000 feet. And all of this from a low-level version. When the fitter had done a check for wrinkles, popped rivets and the like without finding a fault, I asked for and was given 'ownership' of DV●B which saw me through most of my subsequent operations.

At this time, few journeymen service pilots had come across the phenomenons associated with Mach numbers and the so-called 'sound barrier'. George Pyle regarded the Spitfire IX as a beautiful and responsive plane to fly without any vices, although like any high-powered aeroplane it had to be respected. But it could also take substantial punishment should the need arise, and this was not lost on the pilots flying them.

It carried 85 gallons of fuel in two tanks just in front of the pilot imme-

George Pyle.
(From 'Broken Mustang' by kind permission of George Pyle.)

diately behind the instrument panel – the upper with 48 gallons and the lower with 37. Fuel load could be increased by the addition of drop tanks, up to 170 gallons. The LF IX had the 'B' wing and the LF IXE the 'C' wing but both carried a total of two 20mm cannon and four .303 Browning machine guns fired with a reflector gunsight in earlier versions and the Mk IID gyroscopic gunsight later.

But, significantly, and importantly for the attacks on the V2s, as Roderic Hill later wrote: ' The Spitfire IX could carry at most one 500-lb bomb and that only by refuelling in Belgium.' Operating from bases in Norfolk and not able to use airfields on the continent, the main weapons available were the Spitfire's guns.

As far as rated performance went, the Spitfire had a maximum speed of about 408 miles per hour at 25,000 feet, with a cruising speed of about 324. Rate of climb was 3,950 feet per minute and it could get to 20,000 in just under six minutes. Most versions could get to a maximum altitude of 43,000 feet, as George Pyle found. These performance figures are typical. Different aeroplanes had slightly different performance affected by factors such as their age and the amount of surface damage to the skin – a highly polished skin could add several miles per hour to a top speed so the inevitable host of scratches and blemishes on the metal surface would add to the skin friction to increase the total drag.

Like all the Spitfire variants, its pilots adored it – with its graceful ellipses for wings and the ease of handling, each successive mark that came merely made it an even more beautiful aeroplane to fly! But it did have some drawbacks. The main undercarriage legs were close together and retracted outwards into the mainplanes, unlike the Typhoon and the Focke Wulf 190 for example, which retracted inwards, giving the under-carriage a much wider track and making it more suitable for rough landing fields. The long nose also created difficulties in landing and moving on the ground. Pilots usually adopted what became known as 'the Spit approach' – the straight-in approach used for most other aeroplanes was not recommended to land a Spitfire. The technique was to turn in early on the downwind leg and then approach the airfield in a descending curve which ended at the beginning of the landing run. By looking down the side of the nose the pilot could see the touch-down spot and straighten up at the last moment. Once on the ground, being unable to see directly ahead, the pilot had to 'fishtail' the aircraft to have any chance of avoiding a collision.

At the beginning of the war, as a generalization, Fighter Command camouflaged its aircraft dark green and brown on the upper surfaces and sky blue on the underside (different variations did exist – e.g. black port and white starboard underside). The green and brown was fine when the aeroplanes might very well be parked on a grassy airfield, but in 1941, when flying operations across the Channel, the brown in particular did

602 Squadron Spitfire IX.
(From 'Glasgow's Own' by kind permission of Prof Dugald Cameron)

not suit the new situation, and in August 1941, the Air Ministry instructed a new scheme: dark green and dark grey on the upper surfaces and light grey on the underside. To be strictly accurate, the greys were 'ocean grey' above and 'medium sea grey' below. The spinner colour became 'sky' and to help identify friendly fighters in the midst of the confusion of a dogfight, the outboard leading edges of the wings received a yellow strip. Just forward of the tail unit, there was an 18 inch band in 'sky' colour. Finally, the various markings also changed over the years. The original fuselage roundels of 1939 and 1940 with equal widths of red white and blue surrounded by a yellow ring changed to make them less visible by increasing the thickness of the red and blue circles, and decreasing the widths of the yellow and white ones (and the white strip on the red, white and blue tail flash). Aircraft flying with the 2nd TAF on the Continent had their spinners painted black and they did away with the 'sky' coloured band around the rear fuselage.

A typical aircraft was NH150 a Spitfire IXB issued to 602 Squadron, identification code LO●N. Ordered from Supermarine Aviation (Vickers) Ltd under Contract B19913/39, it arrived at 9 Maintenance Unit (MU) on 29 April 1944 for final testing and gun adjustment before being issued to 66 Squadron on 8 June. No. 602 received it on 5 October 1944 and it flew on operations regularly but failed to return from a sortie to The Hague on 2 December 1944 when piloted by Warrant Officer Roy Karasek.

On 18 September 229 Squadron were engaged in practice dive bombing, perhaps because of their new role. But whatever the reason, it was significant, if only because there had been no time for practice flying in recent weeks. On the 20th, Operation Instruction No 19/44 reached them and the squadron clearly realized its significance for them. Things were going to change, although they took it to mean that they would primarily be working with 100 Group on escort duties. There was no chance that night to get into Norwich, or out to the pub, because of briefings and reorganization to allow them to start their new tasks the next day – realizing that with their familiarity with the Netherlands, they were best placed to begin the operations. The first was allocated to Flying Officers Walker and Andrews with a wake-up call at 04.00 and take-off at 05.52!

But it was not to be. Dawn found the airfield covered in thick fog and it took until lunchtime for it to clear, but then patrols came thick and fast: four sorties over Leeuwarden airfield, two for a Jim Crow and six on 'Boffin Cover' – escorting the 100 Group aircraft on their patrols. On the 24th they received the order to move to Manston, which they did the following day – although, to be accurate, although the aircraft made the quick hop south during the afternoon of the 25th, the ground party did not leave Coltishall until about 17.30 and their train took just under twelve hours to get to Margate, the disembarking station. So they arrived at 04.15 on the 26th. Inexplicably, the change took them away from the immediate attacks on the V2 sites in Holland and they spent the rest of September and much of October engaged mainly in operations escorting bombers (Bostons, Mitchells, Halifaxes) to various targets in Germany and on the Continent (including Duisburg, Deventer and Bonn). They would, however, return to 12 Group three weeks later later in October to resume action against the V2s in the Netherlands.

Roderic Hill believed that 25 September saw the beginning of a second phase of V2 attacks which lasted until 3 October, but with the main target area Norwich and East Anglia – for *Batterie 444* in Rijs only this part of England was within range. It seems that *Abteilung 485* was still in The Hague but not firing missiles at London. Whatever the reason, the southeast of England experienced a lull – bearing in mind that the explosions were still being attributed officially to gas main problems. On the same day that 229 moved out and possibly as a direct replacement for them, 303 Squadron moved to Coltishall from RAF Westhampnett in Sussex and 11 Group. It flew Spitfire IXs too. A few days later, 602 and 453 Squadrons moved back to the UK to 12 Group, on 29 and 30 September respectively. These three squadrons, together with 229 when it returned to 12 Group, would be the four main Spitfire squadrons involved in the campaign to bomb the V2s – one a regular squadron, one an Auxiliary, one Australian and one Polish.

Polish squadrons in the RAF became almost legendary for their courage and fanatical determination to kill Germans, and 303[12] is one of the best known. The second Polish fighter squadron, it formed at Northolt on 2 August 1940 (shortly after 302) commanded by Squadron Leader

Ronald Kellett and took the title 'Warszawki im. Tadeusza Kościuszko' or sometimes simply 'The Kościuszko Squadron'.

The Polish Air Force acquitted themselves well against the *Luftwaffe* in 1939 – their aircraft were not destroyed on the ground as many believe, but in truth were overwhelmed by the numbers and technical superiority of their enemy. When Poland surrendered, the pilots fell back to Romania, as had been planned, but found that the support they expected did not materialize, so they made their way to France via Hungary and Budapest. Many of them fought with the *Armée de l' Air*, although the French seemed distinctly ambivalent about using these refugee airmen. After France fell, yet again, the Poles found themselves facing hardship, and struggled to make their way to Britain which despite its moral support for Poland in the autumn of 1939, was seen by some Poles as having let them down when it did not add practical and military support when the attack came.

Once in Britain, it seemed to the Polish that the RAF was reluctant to make use of them, although they received a warmer welcome than they had in France. In the eyes of the Poles, they gifted the RAF a cadre of ex-

Pilots of 303 Squadron gather round the inscribed tail-fin of their 178th victim, a Junkers Ju 88, at RAF Kirton-in-Lindsey, Lincolnshire prior to the campaign against the V2s. In the background is Flight Lieutenant J.E.L. Zumbach's Spitfire VB, BM144 RF●D, displaying a personal score of eleven destroyed and two probables.
(Courtesy Imperial War Museum. Negative no. MH 13763.)

perienced fighter pilots who, unlike many British pilots, had fought the enemy twice, albeit being on the losing side both times, but the RAF wanted to use them as bomber crews! From the RAF's perspective, they were unsure of the ability of their new recruits and in particular the language problem. Many of the Poles had little English and as Britain faced the might of the *Luftwaffe* and the threat of invasion in the summer of 1940, Fighter Command's defences depended on strong verbal communications with controllers. The potential for disaster through misunderstanding had to be addressed. Eventually two Polish fighter squadrons formed, and as is now well known 303 entered the fray flying Hurricanes from Northolt at the height of the Battle of Britain when the RAF's need for fighter pilots was most urgent, and they acquitted themselves as they promised they would.

Such is the stuff of legend. On 30 August 1940, the squadron was on a training exercise when Ludwik Paskiewicz spotted a formation of German bombers being attacked by Hurricanes. He later claimed that he tried unsuccessfully to raise Squadron Leader Kellett, although some accounts suggest that Kellett did not bother to reply. Whatever the truth, Paskiewicz, followed by his No. 2 Miroslaw Wojciechowski, peeled off on their own to join in and Paskiewicz subsequently became the first of the Poles to shoot down a German. The incident was portrayed in a somewhat stereotypical way in the classic film *The Battle of Britain* and although Paskiewicz received a reprimand for his indiscipline, he was also congratulated on his success. One other consequence was that the Poles were now considered as able to be fully operational and became a welcome addition to the hard pressed ranks of 11 Group.

On 11 October 1940, 303 moved north to Leconfield for resting and remained in the United Kingdom for the rest of the war. The squadron's identification code was 'RF'. On 28 September 1944 Squadron Leader B.H. Drobinski DFC took over command.

No. 602 Squadron's pedigree was impeccable. It had the distinction of being the first squadron in the Auxiliary Air Force to form in September 1925, so was not far off its twentieth Anniversary. Originally a bomber squadron, by 1939 it had turned to the day-fighter role and equipped with Spitfire Is – the first auxiliary squadron to get them, and this before some regular units of the RAF. The decision to give Spitfires to 602 was vindicated only a month into the war when, on 16 October 1939, it shared in the action of shooting down the first German aircraft (a Ju88) over the UK land mass with its sister squadron and rival, 603, the City of Edinburgh Auxiliary Squadron, also equipped with Spitfires. Two weeks later, on 28 October 1939, 602 and 603 were again jointly involved in what proved to be the first occasion that a German aircraft was shot down onto British soil. This time it was a Heinkel 111 which crashed near Haddington in East Lothian. No. 602 fought magnificently during the Battle of Britain and then, like 303, remained on British shores until after D-Day, when it moved to France to support the advancing armies. On 29 June, its Spitfires spotted an enemy staff car near St Fey de Montgomerie, strafed it and reported seeing it overturn. The occupant was none other than Erwin Rommel, and he suffered a fractured skull. He survived but committed suicide only a few weeks later. This attacking role continued into September, accompanied by many changes of base and personnel. They became one of the few squadrons with its own pub, the Get Stuk Inn, put together from bits and pieces salvaged and scrounged!

By this time, none of the original Glasgow Auxiliary pilots remained – all having been either killed, injured, captured or posted to other squadrons. Whilst all units have their own *esprit de corps* and camaraderie, the Auxiliary squadrons had an edge because of their links to their various home towns and regions, Glasgow especially. Although the original pre-war 602 pilots were no longer there the current cosmopolitan group still retained the interest and enthusiasm of the people of the city, who were anxious to know about their successes and rightly treated 602 as 'Glasgow's own'. Even the ground crew had few of the original Auxiliaries left despite the intention that they should only be asked to serve within 5 miles of home. The identification letters on 602's Spitfires were 'LO'.

On 27 September, Squadron Leader R.A. Sutherland DFC took over command of 602. German artillery shelled the airfield and made life

A Spitfire IX of 453 Squadron taken before D-Day, probably undergoing an engine test. Note the ground crew holding down the tail and the lack of flying kit worn by the 'pilot'.
(Australian War Memorial Negative no. UK0090.)

uncomfortable for the men. The Spitfire IXEs were swapped with IXBs of 126 Wing at Brussels – a precursor to a change. On the 28th rumour was that 602 would be moving back to the UK and it was finally confirmed that this would happen on Friday the 29th. At 14.00 on that day, the ground crews and some of the pilots flew to Coltishall by Dakota, with the Spitfires following three hours later. The move was uneventful.

The history of 453 Squadron and its path to 125 Wing and then Coltishall could not have been more different. For a start it was Australian. It formed at Sydney on 29 July 1941 to fight the Japanese in Malaya. Shortly afterwards, on 15 August, it moved to Sembawang to be issued with eighteen Brewster Buffalo Mark II aeroplanes. Declared operational on 19 November, its initial role was the defence of Singapore, but after the loss of the Royal Navy ships *Repulse* and *Prince of Wales*, it moved to Ipoh in December to be thrust immediately into furious action. But the Buffalo was no match for the Japanese Zeros. Decimated in the intense fighting, 453 eventually arrived back in Australia at Adelaide, where it disbanded on 15 March 1942. The squadron motto 'Ready to Strike' lived on though when it re-formed three months later on 18 June in Scotland at RAF Drem on the south bank of the Firth of Forth near Edinburgh (and one of the airfields from which 602 and 603 Squadrons flew in October 1939 to shoot down the first German aircraft to be lost over the United Kingdom). In terms of an order of battle, it replaced 452 which moved back to Australia. The new 453 flew Spitfire Vs. Like 602, it remained in the UK until 1944 when it too moved to France operating alongside the Glasgow squadron with IXs. Their Spitfires bore the identification code letters 'FU'.

During this final week of September 1944, the pilots of 453 Squadron could not complain about a lack of excitement. The 27th saw them involved in dogfights, and on both the 27th and 28th the heavy shelling by the Germans caused damage to the airfield and disrupted the daily activity, as described by Typhoon pilot Tom Hall. It was late that evening that the orders to move back to Coltishall arrived and it was to be a straightforward exchange with 80 Squadron (previously operating against the V2s as per Operation Order 19/44), which would take over the 453 dispersals, equipment, and the 6453 Service Echelon on a 'walk-in walk-out' basis. Flight Lieutenant Ernie Esau also assumed command of the squadron that day.

On the 28th, like 602, it exchanged its Spitfire IXEs for IXBs from 126 Wing. They were concerned at the poor state of serviceability of their new mounts. After the usual party to celebrate the move, at 17.00 on the 29th 11 Spitfires took off from ALG B70 to fly to Britain. Warrant Officer Carmichael was left behind – he was to collect another IXB the next day and fly it across. Unfortunately, and illustrating the risks of flying at this time, what should have been a simple transit resulted in a loss when Flying Officer Jim Ferguson was hit by flak over Ostend[13]. His Spitfire was

'Fergie'.
(Australian War Memorial Negative no. UK1946.)

seen to receive a direct hit and he turned back inland, presumably to make
an emergency landing, but shortly after this an explosion in the air was
seen by the other pilots and it was assumed that 'Fergie' perished. Esau
decided that it would be prudent to set down as quickly as possible to
check for flak damage to the remaining aircraft so they touched down at
Bradwell Bay at 18.20. There was another problem when the undercarriage of Flight Lieutenant Baker's aeroplane would not come down and
he had to make a belly-landing. The squadron overnighted at Bradwell
Bay and the nine remaining Spitfires flew on to Coltishall on the 30th.
Warrant Officer Carmichael duly picked up the Spitfire from 126 Wing but
suffered an engine failure over Dungeness and had to make a forced
landing near Old Romney in Kent. He was unhurt. 'Fergie' survived too,
managing to bring his crippled Spitfire down to a crash landing. He was
captured, but at the end of the war returned to 453 at the beginning of May
the following year.

    After a somewhat uncertain start, the squadrons that would carry out
the campaign were in place, but just as they arrived the command structure changed again. On the evening of Monday, 25 September, a V2 had
landed at Hoxne in Suffolk to the east of Diss and the following day
another had landed near Norwich. Roderic Hill now tried to understand
the implications of the apparent change of target away from London. His

information was sketchy. The flashspotters and soundrangers saw and heard nothing – the firing locations could not be identified – but by chance and quite independently, on the Tuesday, the crew of an aeroplane flying 14 miles to the west of Arnhem reported seeing a rocket trail rising from a wood near the small town of Garderen and timed five minutes before the V2 exploded near Norwich. Garderen lies to the east of Amsterdam between Amersfoort and Apeldoorn. They also reported seeing the wood catch fire. Other observers saw the same trail but located the firing point either on Ameland or Schiermonnikoog, two of the necklace of seven islands which curve around the north of the Netherlands from Den Helder in the south to Borkum in the north and east.

Hill had further evidence that the rocket might have been launched near Garderen. Intelligence reports indicated that a train carrying rockets and fuel had arrived at Apeldoorn the previous week and he believed that at least some of the V2 troops previously in The Hague had moved to this general area. Finally, further careful examination of films of the radar data taken before the Monday rocket landed concluded that perhaps there were faint indications that the rocket had been launched from a site much further away and Hill was advised that on balance, the missiles had probably come from the general area of Garderen. Hill acknowledged himself that 'the case for Garderen as the new firing area now looked stronger than, perhaps, it really was'[14] but he had to act on the information and advice available to him. On the 27th, 12 Group sent 274 Squadron on two armed recces of the area, the first at lunchtime and the second in the late afternoon/early evening. Each operation was carried out by four Tempests, which attacked railway targets and various buildings in the woods that seemed to be being used by the German military. But they reported nothing that would confirm that the activity observed had anything to do with the V2s.

Hill was in a quandary. Whether or not the rockets were now being launched from Garderen or some other undiscovered location, they were beyond the range of the single-engined aircraft operating from the British mainland, and the airfields on the Continent now in the hands of the Allies were too congested to operate more aircraft under Hill's command. Hill concluded that in these circumstances, the attacks on the V2s would have to be carried out by aircraft of the 2nd TAF over which he had no direct command – an invidious arrangement in that Hill could only supply daily intelligence summaries of the rocket situation, known as 'Benreps', to 2nd TAF and advise which targets might usefully be attacked. There were no 2nd TAF squadrons earmarked specifically for V2 operations, and they could only be fitted in with the myriad other demands on their pilots. This arrangement came into being on 1 October.

Two days later, on 3 October, intelligence suggested that the V2 troops were returning to The Hague and that evening a V2 exploded in

Leytonstone. Two weeks later on 15 October, the command structure changed again with the disbandment of the AEAF. The significance for Roderic Hill was that he became the AOC of the newly reconstituted Fighter Command, with his own aircraft once again able to reach the rocket targets which had returned once more to the west of the Netherlands and particularly The Hague. For Hill, October marked the end of the phase of attacks on East Anglia and the commencement of a new phase of attacks on London and the south-east. But even so, until the 15th, the responsibility for the attacks on The Hague still remained with 2nd TAF and not 12 Group.

Even after the 15th, with Hill in command of his own aircraft operating against targets once again primarily within their range, there was still a wrinkle to be smoothed. Although the main target of the rockets was London, some still operated from sites in the east of the Netherlands or over the border in Germany, and these were still outside the range of the Norfolk-based squadrons. Accordingly, Hill proposed that Fighter Command would deal with the rocket operations in the Netherlands west of a north-south line approximately 45 miles east of The Hague with those to the east (nominally being fired at Continental targets) being dealt with by the aircraft based on the Continent, and this is what happened.

With the clarity of hindsight, the operational command and control does seem muddled and unsatisfactory. Considering the situation on the ground at the time – the lack of reliable intelligence information, the changes in the targets of the V2s, the conflicting demands being made on the operational squadrons of the 2nd TAF and the consequences of the Arnhem problem, the decisions taken are understandable. Further confusion arose from the change to the original decision to use Tempest squadrons, as promulgated in Operation Instruction 19/44, to using Spitfire squadrons instead. The reasons for this change are not clear. It did however, result in 229 Squadron being moved away to Manston a few days later to be employed on bomber escort work and a further delay in getting the other three squadrons positioned in 12 Group and ready to start the campaign and then to move 229 back a few weeks later. No. 12 Group did not really get its act together until the start of October, almost a month after the first V2 arrived at Staveley Road. Despite this, Hill must be given credit for remaining steadfast in carrying out his instructions to defend the British landmass against the backdrop of the critical fighting going on across the North Sea at the time. Balancing the conflicting circumstances was not a simple task.

Notes
1. *To Know The Sky* published by William Kimber 1962.
2. *To Know the Sky*, page 12.
3. *To Know the Sky*, page 74.

4. Author's italics.
5. Supplement to the *London Gazette* of Tuesday, 19 October 1948, 'Air Operations by Air Defence of Great Britain and Fighter Command in Connection with the German Flying Bomb and Rocket Offensives, 1944–1945.'
6. Supplement to the *London Gazette* October 1948, 'Air Operations by Air Defence of Great Britain and Fighter Command in Connection with German Flying Bomb and Rocket Offensives 1944–1945'.
7. Code name of the V1s.
8. A V2 is reported as landing in the Thames north of All Hallows at 2.20 p.m.
9. The Operations Record Book (Form 540 and 541) is a 'diary' which each unit in the RAF (squadrons, groups, stations etc.) had to complete and submit. It recorded day-to-day activities; operations, movement of personnel etc. and is a base of information for the historical researcher. Usually compiled by the Intelligence Officer and signed by the CO, the content varies depending on the individuals. Some have only the briefest of facts, others include anecdotes about life on the unit – some highly amusing!
10. With the Allied armies moving swiftly across the continent, the supporting aircraft of the 2nd TAF needed to move with them. With no time to build new airfields, they used anything they could – from open fields with hastily laid tracking for runways to newly captured airfields just vacated by the *Luftwaffe*. These temporary bases – ALGs – were referred to by number rather than name.
11. *Typhoon Warfare*, by Tom Hall published 2000.
12. To avoid confusion when the same squadron number was being used by the air arms of the different countries fighting under operational control of the RAF, separate number sequences were allocated to squadrons from different air arm groups. The 300 series were squadrons drawn from the occupied European countries, e.g. France, Poland and Czechoslovakia, and the 400 series from Commonwealth countries, notably New Zealand, Canada and Australia.
13. Recorded as Dunkirk in the squadron history *Defeat to Victory*.
14. Supplement to the *London Gazette*, October 1948, 'Air Operations by Air Defence of Great Britain and Fighter Command in Connection with German Flying Bomb and Rocket Offensives 1944–1945'.

Chapter Three

Into the Groove

There is no doubt that the Dutch Resistance made a huge contribution to the campaign but its full extent is unclear. Some of the pilots think that whilst in the air they were directed to specific areas because the Resistance had spotted the Germans preparing a V2 launch and managed to radio the information to England, but no evidence has been found of this happening on any specific occasion. Since it took an hour or so to set the launches up, it seems unlikely that there would have been time for the Resistance to get to a radio, pass the information to Britain, then for it to get to 12 Group and ultimately to the Spitfires in the air. But perhaps it did, nothing was found to indicate that it did not happen this way. What is clear, is that information about the storage sites, the areas being used for firing and other installations like motor parks, office buildings and troop billets was being passed to Britain by the Resistance and was a vital component of the intelligence-gathering process, along with PRU photos and the observations of the pilots. Any account of the campaign against the V2s needs to include the contribution of the Resistance because it would have been less effective without it. Another aspect is that several of the pilots who came down in the Netherlands on one of the attacks were soon picked up by the Resistance and held safe until the Allies ended the German occupation. The full extent of the work of the Resistance and the intelligence services may be unclear, but it was considerable and valuable.

The Dutch people were generally sympathetic to the British cause, and the Germans underestimated the strength of the resentment that their invasion and occupation engendered amongst the ordinary Dutch folk. There were many who were sufficiently roused to carry out acts of defiance. Over the years, a number of organizations sprang up, and the Dutch became expert at different kinds of resistance – including those of passive nature. The silence that fell in bars or cafés when the occupiers entered could be quite intimidating. Underground newspapers and newssheets soon appeared – the first one the day after the Netherlands surrendered –

and whilst many only circulated for short periods, it is thought that more than a thousand different clandestine publications were produced during the occupation. Of course, resistance could not be carried out in isolation; it had to be directed and supplied with intelligence, weapons, explosives, money and people, and it was from the British that such support was sought. On 19 July 1940, the British Special Operations Executive (SOE) was granted its charter, in the words of the Prime Minister, 'to set Europe ablaze'. On 19 July, the Dutch Government in exile also established an intelligence service, the *Centrale Inlichtingdienst* (CID), and over the years, other agencies which encouraged resistance and intelligence gathering were also set up in exile with varying degrees of success.

Hitler always intended that resistance in any of the occupied countries should be dealt with harshly, but the Nazis believed that the Dutch, with their blond hair and blue eyes, were near relatives of the Aryans and over the years would be assimilated into the 'Master Race'. The first Governor-General of the Netherlands, responsible for civil affairs was an Austrian, *Reichskommisar* Artur von Seyss-Inquart . The military side was initially the responsibility of General F.C. Christiansen and the SS commander, *Obergruppenführer* Hanns Albin Rauter, another Austrian. Under him, he had a police commander of security, *Befelhshaber der Sicherheitspolizei,* and there were four incumbents during the period of German occupation. The armed forces had their own secret service and counter-espionage group called the *Abwehr,* which included Hermann Giskes who over the years would be a dangerous opponent for the SOE and Secret Intelligence Service [SIS].

Helping the Dutch Resistance proved to be unexpectedly awkward for the British agencies, for several reasons. In such a small country, the Dutch agents who made their way there could not be sure that their anonymity would be maintained – chance meetings with old friends, relatives and colleagues were more likely than in, say, France, with its larger population and size. The flat and low-lying nature of the land also made it difficult for RAF aircraft to search for landing grounds and dropping zones without attracting the attention of the *Luftwaffe*. Particularly once the British bombing offensive began to gather momentum, the *Luftwaffe* stationed radar-controlled night fighters in an arc from Denmark to France (including the Netherlands) because they were across the route of many Allied raids. This Kammhuber Line (named after its designer Colonel Josef Kammhuber) and the closeness of night-fighter airfields provided a strong disincentive for British aircraft to linger. Finally, the coast, which might have been a means of clandestine access, was too risky.

Also, the SOE created problems for itself. Most agents inserted into the Netherlands were of Dutch origin. Some were ex-military, some came from Dutch possessions in the Far East and some from South Africa. They received training in Britain at various country houses in the skills they would need – explosives, weapons, clandestine operations – and were dropped in by parachute (having received jump training usually at Ringway). On the ground would be a reception committee, supposedly from local Resistance fighters. For a period of perhaps fifteen months at the start, SOE's operations were known to the Germans in the Netherlands. Agents parachuted in were almost literally falling into the arms of the occupiers, who used Dutch traitors to meet them. The normal 'drill' called for the reception committee to meet the newly arrived agent on the dropping zone and for an hour or so let him or her think that they had made a successful entry. With the adrenalin flowing after the tensions of the parachute drop and the fear of capture – supposedly overcome – the new arrival was likely to be garrulous and susceptible to giving away information. After an hour or so, they would be arrested and handcuffed. Many finished up in the jail at Haaren and ultimately lost their lives in the concentration camp at Mauthausen.

Agents brought money, weapons, explosives, radios, codes and intelligence. Reports which filtered back to SOE should have given them clues that all was not well with the agents they were sending in, but because those captured were accompanied by wireless sets and codes, the Germans could 'work' them and did so in such a way that the SOE in Britain saw nothing amiss and assumed that their agents were working as instructed, even ignoring more deliberate attempts to warn them that this was not the case. Later in the war, after the reality of the situation was discovered, Dutch agents were treated with some suspicion and the result was that the co-ordination and direction that should have been implemented when the invasion happened was not fully in place, with the Resistance less effective than it might have been. At the beginning of December 1944, the SOE estimated that there were about 11,700 Dutch armed members of the various Resistance organizations and planned to arm another 10,000 during the following three months – unrealistically as it turned out

Major Dr J.M. Somer of the *Bureau Inlichtingen der Nederlandse Regering* (BI) in London was keen to gather information about both of the 'vengeance weapons' – details of the location and nature of the launch sites and the units carrying out the firings, supply routes, logistical information, storage sites etc. One very successful Resistance group in the Netherlands established under Somer's leadership was code-named 'Packard'. Originally set up to transmit meteorological information back to the United Kingdom, because of its success its remit broadened to include the V-weapons and it is reported that they were contacted the same day that the first V2s landed in Britain. One of its members was A.J. Houck, who already knew another Dutchman with comprehensive knowledge of the rockets gained clandestinely and at enormous personal risk – Johannes (Jan) Wilhelmus Huybert Uytenbogaart. Uytenbogaart's knowledge would be critical for the Allies, both in supplying technical detail about the

V2s during the offensive and then subsequently re-engineering, or piecing together the make-up of the missiles after the war ended.

Uytenbogaart was born in Utrecht in 1897. He was a slim, austere-looking man with high cheekbones whose father was an electrical and chemical engineer and whose forebears in the eighteenth century included two painters. He graduated in 1921 with a degree in chemical engineering from the Delft University of Technology. Between then and 1938 he worked in the chemical industry, developing man-made fabrics, particularly rayon. After a spell with the First Netherlands Rayon Industry ENKA in 1930 he moved to *Vereingte Glanzstoff Fabriken* in Berlin as Scientific Director, staying there until 1938 when the increasing belligerence of the Third *Reich* convinced him that he should return home to the Netherlands. He worked for *Bataafsche Import Maatschappij* (later Shell Nederland) in The Hague. However, in Germany his interest in rockets was triggered by the various groups pursuing their development, and this would bring a serious element of risk to his life in the years to come. In 1941 in a Netherlands now occupied by the Germans, he became part-time Professor of Synthetic Fibre Technology and Mechanical Technology at his old university in Delft, with other appointments in the faculties of chemistry and mechanical engineering.

Uytenbogaart received appointments in two ministries and as a director of the Central Institute for Industrialization was well placed to work for the Allies. His interest in rockets continued to develop, and at the beginning of 1944 he felt that he possessed information which would be of use to the Allied powers in Britain. Accordingly, he managed to send information to the BI in London. Thus, in September 1944, when the authorities in Britain suddenly had to find someone to help pass information over from the Netherlands, Uytenbogaart found himself with excellent contacts, an appropriate technical knowledge and background and, perhaps most

Johannes W.H. Uytenbogaart.
(Reproduced by kind permission of Shell International B.V., The Hague.)

crucially, the moral courage to accept the responsibility which duty now placed on him. If he decided to accept the task it would mean risk and danger. He lived comfortably in a large house in the wealthy district of Wassenaar, not far from where the first two V2s were fired at London, but this would all be lost if the Germans should ever discover his work against them. And some of his neighbours in the street were German sympathizers – some highly placed German officers even lived nearby.

Uytenbogaart gathered together some trusted colleagues and started collecting the intelligence requested. They set about finding the locations of the storage and production areas, the routes used to transport the rockets in the area of The Hague and launch sites. As the intensity of the launches increased, so did the number of failures. The destruction of the rockets which exploded on take-off or shortly afterwards when they plummeted to earth – often on the homes of innocent Dutch families living nearby – left wreckage and debris, and although the Germans discouraged any interest in the V2s by summary execution, Uytenbogaart and his teams would rush to the spots where the missile debris fell and try to examine it or spirit it away for further examination before the Germans arrived. And Uytenbogaart led from the front. In his house in Wassenaar, he had a secret room in the attic where pieces of the rockets were taken. Even his wife knew nothing of the room, such was his secrecy, and it survived at least one thorough search by the occupiers. As well as their observations and the debris from failed launches, the group also gathered photographs, manuals and launch diaries by bartering with the enemy soldiers. With his technical knowledge, Uytenbogaart was able to analyse what he was seeing, and he produced remarkably accurate drawings of various components found and seen. After the war, it transpired that he had managed to construct a more or less complete V2 from bits of wreckage scavenged from the launching areas. Information reached London via the Packard group transmitters and one in his villa. Microfilm and debris from exploded rockets passed down the Resistance chain via Eindhoven and Brussels.

But in addition, and of more importance for the Spitfire squadrons, his group watched the launches, divining the locations of storage and assembly areas, launch preparations, activity near stations and on roads. This information was passed to London to provide targets for the dive bombing attacks. Then the results of attacks would be assessed and passed back. Watching the launches was enormously risky – not least because of the possibility of a V2 becoming a rogue and exploding at lift-off. The Germans dealt with spies ruthlessly, and if caught summary execution was probably the best to be hoped for. At least twelve of Uytenbogaart's group died at the hands of the enemy for their espionage work. There is one anecdote about an occasion when Uytenbogaart himself almost came to grief. In November 1944, during heavy rain, he managed to find a V2 being launched, but it was one that went wrong. He noticed a German truck stopping and the troops baling out to take cover from the uncontrollable rocket. Logic told him that he would be safer underneath the truck than in the open so he dived underneath it. When the missile had crashed and the Germans troops approached, they congratulated him on his survival – the lorry was full of grenades! After the war, Major Dr J.M. Somer wrote an eloquent tribute to Jan Uytenbogaart: 'Through his daring and professional work his name inspired great gratitude amongst the British Intelligence . . . These quiet workers . . . operated in silence, so much so that they became virtually untouchable for the enemy.' Uytenbogaart survived the war, dying in 1964.

There can be little doubt that the information which the men and women of Uytenbogaart's group and others passed to London via the Resistance influenced the conduct of the aerial attacks on the V2 sites and the targets chosen. Although it was in the background, the history of the air campaign against the rockets needs to be viewed with the activities of the Dutch Resistance in mind.

Sunday, 1 October found 453, 602 and 303 Squadrons all at Coltishall – 453 and 602 settling into their new quarters, which they clearly found more acceptable than the series of ALGs which had been home to them in the previous weeks and months. 'Certainly one cannot complain of the living conditions and the food here, both are excellent,' wrote the compiler of the 453 Squadron Form 540. No. 602 also enjoyed being back in Britain: 'Although they all [the pilots] have mixed feelings about our return to the Old Country – happy to be back again, but unhappy at being so far away from the War Front, on one thing they all agree – that there's no beer in all the world as good as a pint of English bitter . . .'

Coltishall is just north of Norwich. Built in the expansion period of the 1930s the airfield buildings were of brick and solid, with good facilities unlike some of the more primitive conditions prevailing on those airfields hastily constructed during the war – its satellites Ludham and Matlaske,[1] for example.

Both 602 and 453 were released until 13.00 on Monday, 2 October, and many of the pilots took advantage of a 48-hour leave which allowed them to go up to London for Saturday and Sunday night. All arrived back safely – some no doubt the worse for wear – in time to resume the war. For 303, having been at Coltishall for a week by now, there was no respite and on the Sunday from 08.20 until 17.50, they had six sections of Spitfires airborne carrying out uneventful Big Ben patrols protecting 100 Group Liberators – probably from 223 Squadron. In the late afternoon, another section searched successfully for damaged motor torpedo boats (MTBs) and radioed a 'fix' back to control. Monday was similar – six sections of two on Big Ben patrol with a Liberator.

On their return from leave on the Monday, the 453 pilots completed 'Sector reccos' to familiarize themselves with the lie of their new territory in Norfolk, whilst 602 operated the Big Ben patrols to protect Liberators.

Tuesday started what would become a pattern – mixtures of Big Ben patrols, sometimes escorting Flying Fortresses and Rangers [Operations to find and engage suitable targets within a defined area] over the Continent – particularly the Netherlands, but not specifically targeting the V2s. The events are neatly summarized in the Coltishall ORB entries for the day:

> *Escort to Patrol B was provided from 0700–1855 hours by 602, 303 and 453 Squadrons; all were uneventful except for about 15/20 bursts of in-accurate heavy flak at 1115 hours directed against the Liberator and coming from the Hague.*
>
> *Day Rangers 42, 43 and 44 were laid on 453, 303 and 316[2] Squadrons.*
>
> *The first squadron [453] with 8 Spitfires up at 1234 hours covered the Groningen area, but owing to cloud conditions, nothing of interest was seen except 5 Mine Sweepers and two vessels of about 250 tons in the Zuider Zee – all aircraft returned by 1447 hours.*
>
> *303 Squadron with 10 Spitfires IX airborne from 1545–1845 planned to cover the Wittmunehafen area, but weather conditions North of Spiekeroog were responsible for an early return with nothing of interest to report.*

Patrol B was the line specified in Operation Instruction No 19/44 stretching more or less along the coast of the Netherlands from Haamstede in the south on the island of Schouwen to Zandvoort in the north with The Hague about halfway along. The aircraft flew at 20,000 feet. No. 602 took the morning watch with sections taking off at 07.00, 08.10, 09.20, 10.15 and 11.20. No. 303's sections were off at 13.05 and 14.05, and 453's at 15.05, 16.05 and 17.20. The 602 Squadron ORB comments. 'Each section returned having had an uneventful trip – but – by the colour of their faces and the quick dive made in the direction of the stove – a damned cold one! Stooging up and down for two hours or so at 20,000 ft is apt to raise the gooseflesh somewhat.'

It was only now that the RAF's campaign seems to have taken on a structured and organized aspect. Although the Tempest squadrons and 229 had been operating patrols, it was only now, the beginning of October, that the squadrons finally started to carry out the campaign with clear-cut objectives and operations – Big Ben patrols, armed recces and Rangers.

The Spitfires had no heaters, which meant the pilots had to rely on their clothing to keep them warm, and they might be flying for long periods in sub-zero temperatures. Although bomber crews could get electrically heated suits, the Spitfire pilots could not. Of course many – but not all – had the ubiquitous Irvin jacket but the RAF recognized that despite this,

Flying Officer John Moss of 603
Squadron.
(John Moss.)

there was a need for more warm
clothing, and in 1941, introduced
the 'Suit, Blue Grey, Aircrews
(Blouse and Trousers)' which was a
more or less identical copy of the
khaki battledress issued as standard to the Army except that the
'Hairy Mary' serge was RAF blue/
grey. To start with it was issued to
flying personnel and only worn
whilst flying, but later it became
standard issue to all personnel with
the official nomenclature 'War, Service Dress, Blouse' but called 'battledress'. Additional warmth came from a white crew-neck sweater given
the official, if somewhat quaint and inappropriate, name of 'Frock, White,
Aircrew'. Not surprisingly, the name became a source of amusement for
the flyers. But other clothing was needed. Flight Lieutenant Bob Sergeant,
who flew with 229 Squadron, recalled that he had woollen leg warmers
knitted by his mother – long socks that he rolled up to the top of his thighs
when flying, but rolled down to the top of his boots when on the ground.
Others used similar home-made unofficial items to keep warm. Gloves
helped to keep hands warm but were not always as effective as they might
be and their thickness dulled the 'feel' necessary to fly the aeroplanes,
requiring the pilot to remove them if he had to make a delicate adjustment
to one of the instruments – say to change the altimeter setting. John Moss,
a flying officer with 603 Squadron at the end of the war recalled that he
solved this problem with a pair of wool-lined leather mitts that he could
'whip-off' when necessary.

Apart from the cold, the design of the dinghy pack between the pilot's
rear end and his parachute did not cater for comfort – one pilot
commented that 'it was like sitting for hours on end on a bag of cricket
balls'. Sometimes the dinghy would inflate in the cockpit for no obvious
reason. If it did, it pushed the control column forward and the Spitfire
went into a fatal dive. Some pilots carried a knife stuck into the top of their
right boot so that if this happened, they could puncture the inflated
dinghy and recover control. Bob Sergeant also recalled another problem
on these long flights: the Spitfire had no facility for the pilot to urinate. If
the need came, they had to relieve themselves in the cockpit, then warn the
next pilot to use the aeroplane that they had done so!

453 Squadron's ebullient and fiery CO, Squadron Leader 'Ernie' Esau. The roll-neck sweater was called a 'frock, white'. Tape loops on the front of the Mae West were used as strong points for boat hooks to pull aircrew out of the water, and tugging the large loop on the left-hand side of the jacket ripped open a panel which released a fluorescene dye into the sea around the airman to make him more visible from above. *(Australian War Memorial Negative no. UK2201.)*

Eight 453 Spitfires led by Squadron Leader Esau took off at 12.35 on the 3rd on the first Ranger, but they were back at 14.45, having had an uneventful trip along the route that saw them cross the Dutch coast at Egmond, then fly to Groningen and Leeuwarden, and although they spotted some minesweeper-type vessels in the Zuider Zee, 'the Hun was definitely not playing'. At 16.10, ten of 303's Spitfires led by Flight Lieutenant S. Ocha lifted off to cover much the same ground. They too found little excitement but did see a V2 being launched: 'Landfall on way in was made at DEN HELDER for which point a Big Ben was reported by the Leader. It was at 20/30,000 ft and still using [sic] leaving a white corkscrew contrail appeared to come from the LEEUWARDEN area.' This was probably the V2 which landed at Great Wichingham, a few miles west of Coltishall at 16.55. The German rocket troops were returning to The Hague. For the pilots, seeing V2s being launched in the distance was not unusual. One of 602's pilots, Flight Sergeant Michael Francis recalled: 'On one occasion approaching the Dutch coast at dawn, a V2 launched right in front of us, but alas! a little too far away to waste ammo on! It was a lovely yet sinister sight; like a golden comet hurtling vertically skywards. They got it off with about three minutes to spare because we were approaching at 400 mph.'

The diet of patrols and Rangers was broken on 7 October when ten Spitfires from 303 and eight from 602 flew escort for an operation by 351 Halifaxes and ninety Lancasters to bomb Kleve (Operation Ramrod 1319) and the neighbouring town of Emmerich in Germany. By this time, Operation Market Garden had failed, exposing the Allied right flank at Nijmegen and the aim of this raid was to make it difficult for German units to approach and attack; it was judged a success. The 303 ORB recorded it thus:

> *Difficult to see the bombing results owing to ground mist, but thick smoke was seen to rise 4,000 ft from target area. Spitfires remaind [sic] for 18 minutes over target area at 14,000 ft. No. e/a were seen. There was intense, heavy accurate flak from the target area. Saw a direct hit on Halifax, which disintegrated, 10 – parachutes seen.*

Ten of 229 Squadron's Spitfires from Manston also flew escort on this raid. None of the three squadrons lost any aircraft. No. 303 however lost one of their pilots on the 13th on a Ranger over the Netherlands led by the CO, Squadron Leader Drobinski. They took off from Coltishall just before 14.00 and crossed in over Texel. The route took them over Leeuwarden, Groningen, Hoogeveen, Meppel and finally Egmond on the way out. Whilst still over the Netherlands, Sergeant Pilot K. Stankiewicz, in BS534, reported that he would have to make a crash landing and glycol was seen coming from the engine of his Spitfire. He made a good landing and reported over the radio transmitter (R/T) that he was unhurt. He was advised to get away from the wreckage of his aircraft and head south to try to link up with Allied troops.

The weather was becoming worse, the previous week a number of operations had been laid on then cancelled, with the pilots becoming frustrated and starting to get bored. The Big Ben patrols seemed to be the only consistent operational activity but the pilots found them uninteresting and, because of the cold, uncomfortable. They also carried out Jim Crows from time to time. Some would have preferred to get back to front-line work whilst

'Crossing into the Netherlands north of The Hague . . . '
(Author)

others appreciated the change to a quieter regime. If the weather allowed, some gunnery practice took place at the Pastow range. No. 602 Squadron's Flight Sergeant Roy Karasek scored particularly highly. No. 602 seems to have enjoyed being back in Britain with the opportunities for evening 'sorties' to the pubs in the area.

The 'Glasgow squadron' suffered its own loss the day after Sgt Stankiewicz went down. The operation was Ramrod 1332, an attack by 519 Lancasters, 474 Halifaxes and twenty Mosquitoes with a heavy fighter escort on Duisburg as part of an operation given the name 'Hurricane'. The objective of the operation was to demonstrate to the German population the overwhelming air superiority of the Allied air forces. Fourteen of the bombers were lost. Both 602 and 303 took part. Ten Spitfires from 602 took off at 07.40. Flying Officer G.L. Robinson flew MK729. Just after taking off, the engine cut and Robinson had to bring the aeroplane down in an emergency landing. Engine failure on take-off is one of the most dangerous. He brought the Spitfire down in a field more or less over the airfield boundary but injured his back severely. He was rushed off to hospital. Flight Sergeant Michael Francis (in MJ528 LO●V) recorded the operation as lasting two hours forty minutes and 'uneventful'. A second Ramrod later in the day proved to be uneventful as well.

Although the 15th marked the disbandment of the AEAF and the reintroduction of Fighter Command with all its implications for Roderic Hill, life continued without change for the three Spitfire squadrons until the 18th when the 'Benreps' previously sent to 2nd TAF were now directed primarily to 12 Group. Nos 453 and 602 Squadrons with Service Echelons 6274 and 6080 respectively, moved to Matlaske. Built in 1940 under the wartime emergency as a dispersed satellite airfield, it lay about 12 miles to the north-west of Coltishall but lacked the latter's comforts. It was also plagued with drainage problems – Roy Karasek recalled: 'It was just flat fields which became sodden and unusable in the winter months.'

However, both squadrons seem to have been relatively content with their new home. The 453 ORB comments: 'Frightening reports had been circulated about Matlask, but on our arrival, we were relieved to find it would soon become a habitable spot. Matlask Hall will soon become a very comfortable Officers' Mess. At the moment, food is served in the Sergeants' Mess.' 602 identified a clear improvement: 'For the first time for months, we now have Two Flight Rooms and "A" and "B" Flights are in separate rooms.'

Immediately prior to the arrival of the Spitfire squadrons, the airfield had been on 'care and maintenance', becoming operational again on 14 October under the command of Acting Squadron Leader P.G. Ottewill GM, who arrived on the 16th.

Being the latter half of October, the weather continued to deteriorate and hamper operations. On the 23rd the 453 ORB notes cryptically, 'Bad

Outside the airmen's mess at Matlaske. LAC W.R. Mullin, Corporal A.
W Stanton and LAC R. Hopkinson with some WAAFs.
(Australian War Memorial Negative no.UK2751.)

weather and Matlask seem to be inseparably linked.' But already a subtle
change in the operations regime had happened. The previous day, the
22nd, 303 and 453 both flew armed recces over the Netherlands – a different
type of operation which would become the hallmark of the campaign to hit
the V2s. No. 453 provided four Spitfires for the first of these. They took off
at 09.45 led by Squadron Leader Esau, the pilots being Flying Officer
Russell Leith, Flight Lieutenant M.K. Baker and Warrant Officer R. 'Frog'
Lyall. Unfortunately, the 10/10ths cloud cover only a few thousand feet
above the sea restricted visibility so that the operation was aborted 30 miles
out. Leith's log-book records ,'Abortive – weather u/s.' At 12.50, a further
four Spitfires of 303 Squadron took off on a similar armed recce and
reached the coast of the Netherlands, but again, the 10/10ths cloud forced
an early return to base. The pilots and aircraft involved were Flight
Lieutenant S. Szpakowicz (MB910 RF●S), Flight Lieutenant A. Malarowski
(MA416 RF●A), Sergeant J. Kukuc (MB694 RF●J) and Sergeant K. Sztuka
(MA420 RF●K). They all returned safely at 14.55.

For armed recce sorties, the pilots were ordered to seek out specified
target areas and attack them, whether or not they could see that a launch
was being prepared. Bob Sergeant confirmed that armed recces were not
free-ranging operations, but directed towards a specific target, although
after the attack there was the chance to have a go at any other potential
target seen. At this time the main weapons were the guns.

The two operations by 303 and 453 on the 22nd really marked the change in tactics brought about by the continuing bombardment by the V2s and the passing of responsibility and control to Roderic Hill, although for the pilots there seemed little significance in the resurrection of Fighter Command. Russell Leith said that they knew that the change had happened but it did not appear to change things operationally. 'The reason for the change may have been discussed with wing leaders or squadron COs, but the "troops" just did what the higher ups decided. I have no recollection as to whether Squadron Leader Esau discussed the change with us.'

A further change was the return of 229 to 12 Group at Matlaske at 19.00 on the 22nd from Manston[3], They were singularly unimpressed with their new quarters:

The Squadron tumbled out of their Nissen huts where they had shivered all night to look around at their new home and were far from being favourably impressed. Everyone fervently hopes we might in the near future move to the luxury of life at Coltishall. NCOs and Officers eat in the same Kitchens; meals are very crude and frugal and usually develop into a foraging campaign each man just getting whatever he can from odd and sundry places.

And later:

The Officers' Mess promises to be most intriguing from a historical point of view. Know [sic] actually as Barningham Hall, the ancestral home of the De Winters and dating back hundreds of years it is a remarkable Tudor Mansion of innumerable small rooms, sloping floors and odd corners with huge fireplaces and great rafters. But most interesting of all is its Poltergeist (Ghost) about which many stories circulate and its old clock which though unwound for centuries occasionally strikes at a certain hour the chimes of which are only heard by the inmates and once only by them in a lifetime.

Quite why 229 Squadron was ordered to Manston and 11 Group in September, only to return to 12 Group in October is unclear. They were the one unit that had been in position when the V2s started to arrive and they knew the Netherlands well. Of the six squadrons of Spitfires that eventually made up the RAF's response to the rockets, 229 was the only one specifically mentioned in the Operations Order issued by Roderic Hill on 18 September that remained to complete the task.

Weather prevented flying on the 23rd, but on the 24th, all four of the squadrons earmarked for the anti-V2 raids specifically (303 at Coltishall and 453, 602 and 229 at Matlaske) carried out armed recces, however heavy cloud cover and poor visibility curtailed them all. The daily activities changed subtly. By the 28th, the Big Ben patrols escorting the Halifaxes had pretty well disappeared and the offensive was on. The following table sets out the operations the four squadrons completed during the day. The weather in England started off fine but a belt of rain crossed over eastwards followed by thundery showers with hail. Initially the visibility was poor but it improved over the day.

Take-off	Squadron	Airfield	Pilots and aircraft	Operation Type	Comment
07.30	602	Matlaske	F/L H.RP Pertwee MJ441 W/O L.T. Menzies MK230 W/O C.H. Jenkins MK464 F/Sgt E.S. Bannard ML270	Armed recce over the Netherlands – Egmond. Landed back 09.15	Uneventful
09.05	453	Matlaske	S/L E. Esau 'T' W/O D.G. Jones 'Q' F/L W.R. Bennett 'K' F/Sgt J.F. McAuliffe 'A'	Armed recce over much of Netherlands. Landed back 10.30	Attacked motor vehicles.
10.30	453	Matlaske	F/L M.K. Baker 'F' F/O R.G. Clemesha 'H' F/O R.A.J. York 'J' F/Sgt J.K. McCully 'O'		Observed launch of V2 from general area of The Hague at about 11.55. Accurate heavy flak around Rotterdam.
11.15	602	Matlaske	F/O R.H.C. Thomerson ML381 F/L J.R. Sutherland MJ294 W/O W.P. Ryan MJ873 F/Sgt M.V. Francis NH150 'N' P/O J.F. Farrell MJ848 F/L J.P. Banton MK230 F/Sgt E.E. Duke ML205	Armed recce over Netherlands – Texel. Landed back 12.20.	Two targets attacked but intense flak encountered. Red 1 and Red 3 'shot up'

Take-off	Squadron	Airfield	Pilots and aircraft	Operation Type	Comment
07.11.30	229	Matlaske	P/O McConnochie 'E' F/Sgt Haupt 'Y' W/O Cookson 'O' P/O Norton 'R'	Armed recce of Netherlands. Landed back 13.25	Uneventful
14.20	303	Coltishall	F/L S. Socha EN367 Sgt J. Janicki BR140 F/L J. Frankiewicz BS348 F/Sgt M. Michalak MH787	Armed recce – in at Katwijk out at Noordwijk Landed back 16.35	Railway locomotive and trucks attacked. Light flak around Delft.
16.00	229	Matlaske	F/L Patterson 'M W/O Grant 'I' F/L Sergeant 'J' F/Sgt Honeybun 'G'	Armed recce of Netherlands. Landed back 17.40	Uneventful
16.25	453	Matlaske	F/Sgt J.H. Lynch 'F' S/L E. Esau 'T' F/O H.R. Adams 'J' F/Sgt R.G. Peters 'H'	Armed recce over Netherlands. Landed back 17.05	Uneventful

Four V2s landed on Britain during the day, the first at Ashford in Kent at 04.59 and the last at Camberwell at 18.20. At 11.07 what was taken to be a V2 exploded over Deptford, possibly the one reported by the pilots of 453 Squadron. The times quoted on various official documents are not always reliable because of the use of British Summer Time and Double British Summer Time during the war years. Some appear to be 'local' time and others Greenwich Mean Time (GMT). This would explain apparent discrepancies between reports. In November 1944, the local time would be British Summer Time – one hour ahead of GMT.

Flight Sergeant Michael Francis' log-book entry for the 602 operation which set off at 11.15 was 'Bags of flak. Landed Coltishall.' Francis, like Roderic Hill, had interests in both flying and art which stayed with him all of his life. He wrote: 'As a child, an innocent being, I would return home from our local Public Library with books on air fighting in WWI and on art, thus showing already a broad dichotomy between the allure of flying and love of art.' It could have been written by Roderic Hill!

In 1939, Francis started a course in aeronautical engineering which he recalls being 'manoeuvred into' by his mother who realized that war was coming and that it would be a reserved occupation. Having qualified, however he:

. . . arrived at Kemble airfield, a maintenance airfield where Spitfires and Hurricanes were being rebuilt from the Battle of Britain etc. and I soon saw wounded pilots, recovered now and ferrying out the finished machines. One badly burned hero from the Indian sub-continent settled it; I quickly repaired to a recruitment centre at Weston-Super-Mare to volunteer as a pilot. At home I took my mother for a long walk in the country and explained what I had done. She bravely took it as a natural thing.

After initial training on Tiger Moths, under the Arnold Scheme Francis trained in Georgia, Florida and Alabama, in the USA, qualifying in March 1943 with 'top marks' in a course of 100, to be presented with American wings (which he was not allowed to wear on his RAF uniform) – an 'expert' in ground and aerial gunnery. Returning to the UK, Francis found himself at RAF Redhill and 602 Squadron. One of his distinct memories is of the Battle of the Falaise Gap. He writes of the Germans: 'They suffered constant and continuous attacks from the fighters for almost three weeks, before they were routed and fled towards Belgium. What was left of them! On the 31st July 1944, 602 achieved the highest number of enemy transports destroyed in 2nd TAF.' Francis flew with 602 for the whole of the campaign against the V2s.

The next day, the 29th, only one V2 landed on British soil – and that almost at midnight. Winter really started to set in with showers of hail and sleet first thing at Matlaske. The four squadrons had another full day of armed recces which might very well have helped ensure that the German rocket troops kept their heads down and were unable to get missiles away. The first four Spitfires from 453 Squadron took off at 07.10 followed by sections of four from 303 at 08.05, 453 at 09.05, 229 at 11.00 and 12.55, 303 at 14.25, 602 at 15.30 and finally eight from 229 at 15.45. During their afternoon operation, 303's Sergeant J. Kukuc in MH694 RF●J reported problems with his engine and was instructed to proceed to Antwerp, where he was believed to have landed safely. He returned to 303 two days later on the 31st from Brussels. On their morning operation, 303 reported seeing V2 contrails at about 09.30 but these may have been directed at continental targets and not England. On both of their operations, 453 suffered engine problems which required the aircraft in question to return to base. It clearly concerned Squadron Leader Esau because the following day they were held off operations whilst the ground crew subjected each Spitfire to a 'super DI' (daily inspection) so that they would be in tip-top form in future. The other squadrons reported little: enemy trucks, a hospital barge, civilians on bicycles. A tug and some barges were shot up by 303 and on their last operation, 229 found twenty to thirty stationary railway wagons and strafed them, with each Spitfire making three or four runs. After fifteen minutes, eight Typhoons came along, four of them joining in the attack. The Spitfires landed back at Matlaske at 17.45 despite being advised to land at Coltishall because of the falling darkness – whilst Matlaske was a grass airfield, Coltishall's three runways were made of Sommerfield Track.

The weather clamped down after lunch on 30 October and allowed no meaningful flying until Wednesday, 1 November. On both the 30th and the 31st, six V2s landed in the south-east of England; on the 29th, just one. With an improvement in the weather, the armed recces resumed on 1 November and apart from on the first two operations of the day, all reported attacking either ships, barges on the canals or enemy motor transport. During the afternoon, 303 lost one of its pilots, Sergeant J. Wierchowicz. Flying at 6,000 feet, the section spotted two barges stationary on one of the canals and dived down to attack, but on seeing red crosses painted on them, the attack was called off and they climbed back up to altitude to re-form, only to find that Wierchowicz was not with them. Despite reports from the pilots that they had experienced no flak, it seems that he had been shot down and was killed. He had been flying MH910 RF●G.

Operations continued in a similar vein on the 2nd with all the squadrons flying armed recces. At 09.25, four of 453 Squadron's Spitfires – Red Section – took off, making for the southern Netherlands. The pilots were Flying Officer Russell Leith, Flight Sergeant R.J. Pollock, Flying Officer W.H. Carter and Warrant Officer D.C. Johns. When about 15 miles from the enemy coast at an height of 11,000 feet, they saw the contrail of a V2 launch apparently coming from the general area of The Hague, but on flying across the city not many minutes later no activity could be seen. (This may have been the V2 that exploded on Lewisham at 10.04.) They then flew further inland to Leiden and Amsterdam, spotting and attacking two tugs, one of which was left beached on the canal bank and smoking.

Then a barge on the Haarlem–Amsterdam canal received similar treatment, then a lorry on the Haarlem–Leiden road. Recovering after the attack on the lorry, Red 3, Flying Officer Carter in MH449 FU●D, reported a glycol leak and it was decided that he should try to get to Antwerp accompanied by Red 4 while the remaining two headed back to England. They left

453 Squadron's Flight Lieutenant 'Rusty' Leith at Matlaske.
(Russell Leith.)

A pair of 'Rusty' Leith's RAAF
wings.
(Author)

the Netherlands north of Noordwijk, however, Carter did not make it to
safety. Losing height all the while, he eventually had to bring the Spitfire
down to a crash landing near the front lines at Zevenbergen to the west of
Breda. Red 4 landed at Brussels and returned to Norfolk later. Carter was
rescued by American troops and eventually returned to the squadron.

In the evening, four Spitfires of 229 on a practice night cross-country
reported seeing 'a "comet like" object at 6,000 feet on a course of 215°
magnetic at first in a 15° dive later going into a 45° dive when the flames
and sparks disappeared. The aircraft at the time were over Snetterton at
3,000 feet and the "Rocket" was estimated to be 10 miles away and travelling at 5/600 mph.' The time of sighting was 18.48. A V2 was reported as
landing at Long Reach at 20.58 but this may have been a different one, or
again it may have been the difference in the time regimes used that explain
the difference.

The leader of the 453 operation on the day that Flying Officer Carter
came down, Russell Leith, had already experienced the shock of being
brought down himself, although in his case there was no quick rescue.
Compared with many of the British pilots, 'Rusty' Leith's path to Matlaske
seems positively exotic! He was born in May 1922 in Labasa on Vanua
Levu, one of the Fiji islands where his father, Colin, and his mother, Eileen,
made their living from the Colonial Sugar Refining Company Ltd. In the
1920s, life on the estates was very colonial, but there was isolation too.
Because of this, Rusty and his younger brother Ian had to move away to
be educated, ultimately ending up in Armidale, New South Wales. When
he was fifteen, Russell's father became ill and the family returned to
Sydney, but his mother died in 1938 just as he was about to start work for
his father's employer. While there he met the woman he would later
marry, Meg Gwilliam, a stenographer and one of the first women to be
employed by the company.

He joined the RAAF in 1941 reporting to No. 2 Initial Training School
at Bradfield Park for 'square-bashing'. Then it was on to Narrandera in
New South Wales for initial pilot training on No. 15 Course at 8 EFTS
flying Tiger Moths. He soloed on 4 August, then went to Canada for more
training in what would be a hard winter. But he continued his success and
gained his wings on 27 February 1942. By now his flying hours totalled
174 and the next stage of the adventure beckoned – Britain. On 5 May he
turned twenty and celebrated his birthday in a pub near RAF Tern Hill in

Cheshire, where training continued on Miles Master aeroplanes. He then went to Aston Down and Spitfires. From there, the fledgling fighter pilot received his posting to the newly re-formed 453 Squadron based at RAF Drem near Edinburgh.

After D-Day, with the squadron in France, he came down behind German lines on the 25 July, after chasing and shooting down a Bf109. After some days, he was taken in by a French family and, together with two American airmen, settled down on a farm to wait for the Allies to reach them – which they did on 22 August. However, there were brushes with the enemy and danger for Rusty and his hosts; it was no holiday. But once free, he made his way back to 453 and flying again.

Poor weather on 3 November prevented operations, apart from an early-morning weather recce and a Jim Crow, both by 602, but for the next few days, each squadron had a full programme of armed recces over the Netherlands, disrupting the occupying forces. During these operations, a considerable number of V2 launches were seen by the Spitfire pilots, many coming from the general area of The Hague.

At almost 15.00 on the 6th, a V2 exploded at Bexleyheath. Rita Gathercole, a teenager at the time, lived near the impact point and remembered that although there was no clear warning, the V2 seemed to create a 'disturbance' in the air as it came down – not a sound, more of a feeling, but of course it did not allow time to take any precautions. 'You were in the hands of fate.'

The weather that the 602 Jim Crow encountered on the 3rd set them thinking about the conditions they would be flying in during the winter, and in the absence of operations, the pilots had a brainstorming session to try to come up with ways of making their activities more efficient. They decided that if more than one section was operating, on their return over the British coast they would break into their separate flights, with the first flight opening up to high revs and boost, so that they would arrive over the airfield at two-minute intervals, making air traffic control easier. With large numbers of sorties being carried out from the airfields on good-weather days, such measures must have helped maximize the number of sorties completed.

With regard to the weather, the two pilots on the Jim Crow, Flight Lieutenants Stewart and Sutherland, found that on returning to Norfolk, low cloud and mist forced them to divert to Woodbridge in Suffolk where they landed with the help of fog investigation and dispersal operation (FIDO). Stewart reported back on the experience.

It was visible as a thin red line for a distance of three miles and on the circuit marked out the edges of the runway and the emergency strip very clearly. Slight dazzling effect diminished the visibility of the ground although the heat caused the fog to lift and create a clear channel down the runway.

Coming in to land, bumpiness is felt three to four hundred yards short of the end of the runway but this disappears when one crosses the boundary. Landing is rather more difficult than a night landing which is made easier by the angles created by the single lights of the flarepath, and helps the pilot judge his height from the ground.

On the 8th, the COs of the three squadrons at Matlaske got together to discuss tactics and decided that all the suspected rocket target areas around The Hague should be strafed. Each squadron would take a specific area in turn. One proviso was that pinpoint targets in built-up areas would not be attacked because of the need to minimize Dutch civilian casualties; only open and wooded areas should be attacked. Squadron Leader Drobinski, the CO of the Polish 303 Squadron was a notable absentee. As time went on, 303 would become rather marginalized – not fully equipping with the Spitfire XVIs and having a rather secondary role to the others. There is, however, no suggestion that Drobinski's absence was deliberate, it was just that because he was not on hand on the airfield, he was not brought into the debate.

On the 9th, the weather turned even more wintry with heavy cloud, cold winds and later in the day snow and rain. The following days were as bad – if not worse.

Until now, there had been no public acknowledgement of the V2s, but the stories of exploding gas mains could not continue and on Wednesday, 10 November, the Prime Minister made an announcement in the House of Commons.

For the last few weeks the enemy has been using his new weapon, the long-range rocket, and a number have landed at widely scattered points in this country. In all, the casualties and damage have so far not been heavy, though I am sure the House will wish me to express my sympathy with the victims of this as with other attacks.

No official statement about this attack has hitherto been issued. The reason for this silence was that any announcement might have given information useful to the enemy . . .

The Government could no longer pretend that the V2s did not exist and they had to be seen to be doing something about them and to protect London. But with the effectiveness of the RAF's attacks not really known, good publicity would at least reassure those living under the rockets that they had not been forgotten. Eventually, considerable coverage of the Spitfires' activities appeared in the papers and on the radio, both as news broadcasts and interviews with some of the pilots.

By now Roderic Hill knew that V2s were fired from street corners and wooded areas around The Hague, and its particular importance as an

The Church at Bloemendaal in 2003. Splinters from RAF bombs and premature V2 explosions damaged the brickwork and the repairs were still clearly visible in 2003.
(*Author.*)

operational and logistical centre for the rockets. V2s had to be stored and serviced before being issued to the firing troops, and usually the time between their arrival in the launch zones and launch itself was kept to a minimum – a few days if possible – because of the increased failure rate that long storage induced. Hill's interpreters identified two areas at the south-west end of The Hague, giving them the names 'Hague/Bloemendaal' and 'Hague/Ockenburg Kliniek'.

Bloemendaal was a mental hospital in its own grounds with a pleasant wooded park nearby and a church surrounded by grass and trees. The rocket troops commandeered the hospital and its buildings as barracks and used the grassed area around the church to store V2s awaiting issue to the firing units. The park with its trees made an ideal firing site. Ockenburg was another park – perhaps not unlike St James's Park in London – immediately to the north of Bloemendaal, which made it an ideal launching area with its relative closeness to the stored rockets at the hospital. Because of the proximity of the two potential targets areas and their use as a single operating facility, the two were regarded as a single complex, suitable for larger-scale bombing. Hill requested that they should be bombed by Bomber Command, but with its other commitments (and possibly Arthur Harris' fixation with the area bombing of German cities) the attacks never happened. With the benefit of hindsight and the knowledge of what could go wrong if the bombing was inaccurate, it is probably just as well that it did not.

Other potential targets identified included the station and railway yard at Leiden, through which rockets and their various supplies passed, and another suspected storage area near the Hotel Promenade in The Hague. These areas would have been ideal targets for the Mosquitoes of 2 Group and requests were made for attacks to be carried out, but they never happened. Yet another storage area at Raaphorst, previously identified as such but believed to have been abandoned when the rocket troops withdrew to the north and east, was now thought to be back in use. Hill and his staff also believed that V2s were being launched from the shores of the Zuider Zee, wooded areas near Rijs and the islands of Terschelling and Vlieland.

But The Hague seemed to be the centre of activity with rockets being stored on the Duindigt racecourse for firing from the Haagsche Bosch[4]. The Haagsche Bosch is a large, rectangular heavily wooded shaped area with a lake, Grote Vijver, near the Royal Palace which, it was drummed into the pilots, was not to be bombed under any circumstances. Its long axis runs north-east/south-west, with a narrow road, the Leidse Straatweg, running its length. At right angles to the road are smaller roads allowing vehicle access to and from Benoordenhoutseweg which forms the northern boundary of the park as well as a myriad of tracks also giving access to Bezuidenhoutseweg on the south. Bezuidenhoutseweg acted as a boundary between the Haagsche Bosche and Bezuidenhout, where the van't Hoff family lived. And then to the north of the Duindigt racecourse was Wassenaar from where the first V2 had been launched against London on 8 September and other park areas, including Langenhorst and Beukenhorst. The Hague was riddled with potential V2 targets (see photograph in Appendix 2).

Eventually, it became clear to Roderic Hill that help from Bomber Command and 2nd TAF was going to be mixed at best, and if he was going to fulfil his obligations to defend British airspace from the V2s, he really would have to depend on his own resources. But if the Norfolk-based Spitfire IXs were to deliver bombs on the targets in the western Netherlands, they had to refuel on the crowded Continental airfields. This was a serious drawback which needed to be addressed. The answer arrived on the 8th, when an improved variant of Spitfire, the XVI, started to arrive at Matlaske. On the 11th, 453 Squadron took delivery of its first batch of XVIs. Later, 229 and 602 would also get them, although 303 would not. One of the other two squadrons which would become involved later would also fly the XVI, leaving two squadrons, one of them 303, with the IXs for the duration.

By the 17th, Hill concluded that the RAF's activities in trying to stop the V2s were not reducing the numbers arriving on London enough and he wrote to the Air Ministry[5] pointing this out and asking again for Bomber Command to assist in the fight against the rockets. He also asked that the previous policy of not bombing any target where there was a risk to Dutch life or property be relaxed. In the introduction he said: 'The scale of the attack is on the increase and this is attributed to the comparative freedom from interference which is being emjoyed (sic) by the enemy Rocket launching organisation.' His appreciation of the situation is interesting:

> *So far as active intervention by this Command* [Fighter Command] *is concerned, this is limited to armed reconnaissance of areas known or suspected to be used for the launching of rockets and the storage of supplies (including vehicles) and of supply routes. The reconnaissance sorties are flown by Spitfire aircraft throughout the hours of day light whilst* [sic] *weather conditions permit. At this time of year the weather is often unfavourable and at times days may pass without it being possible to fly many armed reconnaissance sorties. Moreover, the enemy has been very cunning in the selection of his launching points, vehicle parks and storage sites. They are mostly situated in fully or partly built-up areas in and near THE HAGUE and are well protected by light flak. They are usually well camouflaged and cannot be seen except from very low level. The reconnaissance aircraft are, however, prevented from flying low by the quantity of light flak and thus rarely succeed in seeing targets (such as vehicles, personnel, or rockets in the firing position) that would be suitable for attack with cannon and machine guns. An alternative would be for the aircraft engaged on armed reconnaissance to bomb the sites associated with launching, the parking of vehicles and storage, but pilots are at present prevented from doing this by the fear of causing casualties among Dutch civilians. As for supply routes, the present ban on attacks on barge traffic and the enemy's ability to move by road and rail at night makes it impossible for fighters to interfere to any appreciable extent with the movement of supplies to the forward area.*
>
> *It is, therefore, clear that armed reconnaissance is not an adequate method of limiting the enemy's rocket offensive unless combined with other forms of offensive action.*

He then pointed out that both Bomber Command and 2nd TAF have had targets of a higher priority to deal with and that '2nd T.A.F. is reluctant to take on the precision targets which require to be attacked by Mosquito aircraft at low level, owing to the risks from exploding rockets'. He goes on: 'The question now arises as to whether bombing attacks against suitable targets should, under the circumstances, be permitted with less discrimination than hitherto insisted upon on account of the risk of injury to Dutch civilians.' And then: 'It is a question of balancing the certain injury to British civilian life and property.'

The balance was between British lives and damage to British property and Dutch lives and Dutch property. There can be no doubt that if Britain had been seriously threatened by the V2s, then the balance would have swung against the limiting of Dutch casualties. As it was, at all levels, from the pilots in their cockpits to the Prime Minister, minimizing Dutch casualties had a high priority and to the credit of the RAF and the pilots, they took great care not to injure needlessly the civilians under their bombs and bullets, although even with the dive bombing techniques used, accidents did happen.

On 21 November, Hill's suggestions received an airing at one of the Deputy Supreme Commander's conferences and his proposals for relaxing the rules were approved. However, it was also decided that the only help he could expect from 2nd TAF was their continuation of attacks on rail targets as part of their general campaign of interdiction: a limited outcome at best. In the meantime, his staff drew up a list of rocket targets which were at least 250 yards from Dutch property or people and the new rules came into effect immediately – more or less on the 21st. Thereafter the target list changed from week to week as the Germans' use of the various sites changed and the RAF became aware of the changes. It was now almost inevitable that the numbers of Dutch civilians who would be killed and injured would increase.

The Spitfire XVI is sometimes described simply as a IX with an American-built Merlin and clipped wings, but there was more to it than that. It could deliver two 250-pound bombs mounted under the wings onto targets in the Netherlands from Norfolk without the need to refuel in Belgium, and if it could be refuelled, the overload tank mounted on the underside of the fuselage could be replaced by a 500-pound bomb, allowing a potential total bomb load of 1,000 pounds. As well as the clipped wings, the fin and rudder looked larger than those of the IX and the rudder had a more pointed, angular top, unlike the rounded top of the IX and other previous variants. Where the IX had the Rolls Royce Merlin 66 engine, the XVI had the Packard Merlin 266. It was effectively the same engine, but built to American standards and using American components but it was not identical, and it gained a reputation in some

The Reply. A Spitfire XVI of 602 Squadron in the 70 degree dive needed to deliver its bombs on to the target.
(Reproduced by kind permission Prof Dugald Cameron.)

quarters for unreliability. And the aeroplane itself attracted some criticism:

> The Mk XVI was, in the words of one distinguished veteran who flew it, a 'dog's breakfast'. This troublesome variant was a marriage of convenience between the Mk IX airframe and the low-altitude Packard-Merlin engine built under licence by the Americans and available in surplus numbers at the time. Producing 1,705 horsepower, it was slightly more powerful than the standard Mk IX, but exhibited treacherous performance characteristics and was prone to catching fire and throwing connecting rods in flight.[6]

It has to be said that this is not the view of the pilots whose exploits are recounted. Without exception they regarded it as a fine aeroplane to fly – one commented that it was the best Spitfire that he had flown and none had any serious qualms about the reliability of the single Packard Merlin even though most of their sorties involved a long return flight across the North Sea in winter, when ditching would almost inevitably have meant an unpleasant albeit quick death. Many of them were not even aware that the 266 had a doubtful reputation. However, the 229 Squadron ORB notes that on 8 January 1945 'the Rolls Representative gave a talk to encourage the pilots to have faith in the Packard engines'. Perhaps indicative of some disquiet.

No. 453's Russ Baxter said:

> The Packard Merlin in the Mark XVI Spitfire did seem to run roughly compared with the Rolls Royce Merlins that I had flown previously in an RAF squadron before joining 453. We were told that the ignition plugs tended to oil up, so we were instructed to open up to full power for a short burst about every 30 minutes to clear the plugs. I was never told that there was any evidence of the Packard engine failing more often that the Rolls one . . .

Flight Sergeant Max Baerlein of 602 said:

> I had flown with Packard Merlins before the Spitfire XVI and I think it must have been in Mustangs. What, I think, made us concerned with them was the engine vibration, which was much greater than with the R.R. Merlin which had to all intents and purposes no vibration. As far as I was concerned I was always worried about flying over the North Sea, particularly as it was said that without a dinghy survival time was about twenty minutes! I used to listen to the engine noise and if the tone changed my heart did a little leap! However, I don't think this had anything to do with being Packard or R.R. Merlins. I do however think that the vibration made us more doubtful about the reliability of the Packards but I doubt whether there are any figures to prove this impression.

Pilot Officer Freddy van Dyck, a Belgian flying with 229 had this account:

The model I liked best was the Mark XVI with its clipped wings. It gave a little more speed and was quick to respond during low-flying or ground attacks. Crossing the North Sea was no concern for us. We knew that in case of ditching we could count on the Search and Rescue teams of the Royal Navy. Fortunately, we never had to call them up.

Warrant Officer Eric Mee with 229 Squadron thought that the Spitfire was 'a fine plane to fly – an extension of your body'.

After the war 602's Raymond Baxter said that of all the Spitfire variants that he flew, his favourite was the clipped-wing XVI. He found it a delight to fly, particularly at low level where it could be thrown about, and he considered that its armaments made it the 'most offensively optimized' aeroplane he flew. He had no concerns about the Packard Merlins but did recall one drawback – at a particular rev range, it did not run smoothly and as is the way of things, it was the range for long-range work that gave optimum fuel consumption. The only solution was to avoid that range, although he heard that subsequently a new carburettor was introduced to tackle the problem. No. 229's Flight Lieutenant Bob Sergeant recalled

A formation of clipped-wing Spitfires of 451 Squadron based at RAF Matlaske.
(Australian War Memorial Negative no. SUK14382.)

another drawback. The XVI's oil-pressure gauge sometimes iced up at altitude and showed zero pressure, but the pilots got used to it. Sometimes 'new boys' would want to turn back because of it but they were not allowed to! But on one point everyone agreed – the lavish tool-kit which came with each Packard Merlin delighted the engine fitters and many of the kits 'disappeared' along the way!

No. 453 had no qualms about them – as noted in the ORB.

> *To all intents and purposes the Spitfire XVI is merely a cleaned up version of the Spit. IX with a Merlin Packard engine, bomb racks to carry a 250 lb bomb under each wing and .5 machine guns instead of the .303s. All have the modified pointed tail and have clipped wings. The pilots are quite happy about their performance against that of the Spit. IX's.*

By the end of November they had eighteen – SM255 FU●A, SM249 FU●B, SM194 FU●C, SM184 FU●D, SM281 FU●E, SM230 FU●F, SM243 FU●J, SM185 FU●M, SM187 FU●N, SM233 FU●P, SM193 FU●Q, SM207 FU●R, SM188 FU●S, SM256 FU●W, SM282 FU●Z and SM244, SM278 and SM250.

No. 453 did not fly its first operational sorties in the XVIs until Tuesday, 21 November; before then, the armed recces in the IXs continued and there was another change of airfield. Bad weather posed a problem for the squadrons in keeping their pilots occupied. In their early twenties, these young men were fighting a war which no doubt satisfied the urge for adventure common in males, but in more peaceful times it should have been an age for finding their feet in the sparkling new world and, of course, finding out about girls. Most days had some activity programmed – armed recces, Jim Crows, defensive state or flying training – and often these were not cancelled until take-off was due. The pilots had to deal with the anticipation of the operation which suddenly came to naught, and there is nothing worse than hanging around a bleak, wet dispersal in the winter trying to keep warm. Sometimes the squadrons were 'released', at other times there were lectures, training and tests. And the ground crews needed to be kept informed. During this particular spell of bad weather, the 602 ground staff gathered to learn about just what the operations were trying to achieve and how the new XVIs were going to help. The CO, Squadron Leader Max Sutherland, gave the pilots a talk on ground-strafing and dive-bombing tactics. Such lectures were not unusual and usually finished with a debate about the best way to carry out whatever was being discussed. On this occasion, they concluded that the techniques developed for dive-bombing the V1 sites should be maintained for the V2s. (Of this more later.)

The day after the 'brainstorming', 14 November, with weather still not allowing flying, four Spitfires spent the morning at defensive state without being called, then in the afternoon camera gun films from previous operations were shown and analysed. Then they were released. The next day the release came at 10.30 and included the whole wing. On the 17th, the ground at Matlaske had become such a quagmire that the defensive state which 602 should have been doing had to be taken on by 303 at Coltishall – although conditions there were not much better. They were released at midday.

No. 229 faced a similar situation. On the afternoon of the 16th, Flight Lieutenant Tommy Rigler, one of the flight commanders, arranged a visit to Norwich for the pilots, but it fell through when the transport ordered did not appear because of some misunderstanding. On the 17th, released early again, the pilots occupied themselves constructing a stage in the building used as a theatre. The same weather stopped 303 Squadron at Coltishall carrying out any operational sorties too. Although operating from a better-quality base with the same mission, 303 began to become slightly isolated from the centre of gravity of the campaign, which was at Matlaske and the three squadrons based there.

The heavy rain over these few days made the airfield conditions at Matlaske even worse than it had been: 'Persistent rain and ground mist appeared to have taken a permanent lease at Matlaske. The aerodrome surface is gradually becoming a swamp.' The various undulations in the ground filled with water and became small lakes. It was so bad that 229's Intelligence Officer, Pilot Officer H. Cooper, had to wear Wellington boots because the water being blown into his office by the strong winds reached a depth of a couple of inches! With the rain blowing in every time the door opened, the maps and charts became soaked. Flight Sergeant Michael Francis found that the clinging mud caused real problems for the Spitfires. Taking off meant that the pilots had to open the throttles to at least half flying speed on the perimeter track before swinging on to a drier part of the aerodrome for the actual take-off. Then the throttle was opened and the tail kept down until, at just the right moment, the Spitfire would 'unstick'. Clearly, when the rain eventually eased, the ground would have to drain and dry out before it could be used operationally again.

To solve the problem, the squadrons based there received instructions that for the foreseeable future they were to fly out of another nearby airfield, Swannington, but remain billeted at Matlaske. If Coltishall is at 'one o'clock' to Norwich, then Swannington is a similar distance from the city at 'eleven o'clock' about 7 miles due west of Coltishall. Rather like Matlaske, Swannington's history is unremarkable. Construction began in November 1942 and it became operational on 1 April 1944 as part of 100 Group. Nos 85 and 157 Squadrons arrived there the following month and they remained there, more or less for the rest of the war. Both flew Mosquitoes of one variant or another whilst based at Swannington. In November 1944, the station was home to 133 officers, 144 warrant officers and senior NCOs and 963 other ranks. If the airfield conditions were better than at Matlaske, the domestic conditions were much the same, with the leaking Nissen huts awash. In hosting the three Spitfire squadrons, it was only obliged to provide essential accommodation and facilities, and the use of the airfield. Responsibility for rations, medical care, intelligence, signals etc. remained with RAF Matlaske. The arrangement was temporary until Matlaske either dried out or more substantial runways were constructed – concrete or Sommerfield tracking – but they were there for the long term.

The three squadrons made the move in the late morning of the 20th, but the weather did not allow much in the way of operational flying other than a Jim Crow in the afternoon by two 453 Spitfire IXs who reported that the weather over the Netherlands was as bad as over Norfolk – more or less complete cloud cover at about 2,000 feet and rain. The new arrangements at Swannington did not inspire them; they were described as 'inadequate huts surrounded by mud in a corner of the "drome"', but the men had little option other than to cope. Nos 602 and 229 shared a single unfurnished Nissen hut and two field telephones, which represented their sole means of communication with Matlaske, Coltishall and 12 Group. No. 453 had their own hut. A routine developed. Each morning the daily servicing ground crews left Matlaske at about 07.00 to drive to Swannington with the pilots following at about 09.00. Both groups returned to Matlaske in the evening once operations ended for the day – usually by about 18.00.

Notes
1. The village that the aerodrome was named after is spelt 'Matlaske', but the RAF Station seems to have been to refered to as 'Matlask' in some official documents, as well as 'Matlaske'. The latter spelling will be used for references to the station.
2. No. 316 Squadron flew Mustang IIIs.
3. The RAF Matlaske ORB records 229's arrival as 26 October.
4. The Dutch spelling changed after the war and the Haagsche Bosch is now Haagse Bos. For this account the language employed at the time is used.
5. Letter FC/S 39039/AIR AOC-in-C Fighter Command 17 November 1944 to Air Ministry (AIR24/632).
6. *All the Fine Young Eagles* by Lieutenant Colonel David L. Bashow, p 313.

CHAPTER FOUR

Shortening Days

The ability of the Spitfire XVIs to operate from Norfolk with two 250-pound wing-mounted bombs brought about a change in the way the armed recces were flown. Together with the list of known rocket sites drawn up by Hill's staff and an identification number, a map pinned to a wall of the Intelligence Officer's office showed these as well as photographs of the targets themselves. The Spitfires would patrol over the

Armourers of 602 Squadron preparing 500-pound bombs – one of a series of probably posed pictures. It also shows the 250-pound bombs on the wing strongpoints and a general impression of the bleak aerodrome behind.
(Courtesy Imperial War Museum. Negative no. CH14808.)

Netherlands as before, but if nothing better was seen – e.g. the launch of a missile – the bombs would be dropped on a specific target area at the end of the armed recce as the Spitfires prepared to leave. No. 229 Squadron awaited these new operations 'with keen enthusiasm' and a rather plaintive concern that 'so far no Spit. XVI's have arrived'.

On 21 November, the day that Hill's new rules came into effect, the weather at last relented and dawn brought clear blue skies, but also a drop in temperature, making it chilly to say the least. A full day of flying commenced, notable because it marked the first use of the XVIs against the V2s. No. 453 and its XVIs flew three operations, the IXs of 602 two, 229 three and 303 only one, but all directed against two main areas, Wassenaar Raaphorst and Wassenaar Rust-en-Vreugd in the north-west part of The Hague.

No. 453 blazed the trail in their Spitfire XVIs. Four took off at 08.04 to bomb the storage area at Rust-en-Vreugd: Squadron Leader Esau led with Pilot Officer H.D. Aldred in SM282 FU●Z, Flying Officer N.K. Baker in SM230 FU●F and Warrant Officer J.D. Carmichael in SM184 FU●D. Aldred took off late and had to jettison his bombs in the sea 18 miles off Great Yarmouth before returning early to base. The remaining three continued, crossing the coast of the Netherlands at Egmond and turning north to have a look at the port of Den Helder but finding nothing of interest. Swinging south, they flew to The Hague which they patrolled. They found it obscured by fairly heavy cloud but managed to identify their target, which they bombed south to north, diving down from 8,000 feet to about 4,000. Esau's bombs were seen to hit the aiming point, with the others exploding within the general target area. The 'boss' then strafed the target area with his guns, again on a south–north line, and they returned to base, landing at 10.05. Generally they reported good weather conditions with mixed cloud cover.

It was a good, if perhaps not outstanding start for the XVIs.

No. 602 followed, four Spitfires lifting off from Swannington at 09.05 led by Flying Officer F.W. Farfan in ML270 with Warrant Officer D.T. Menzies, a Kiwi, in MK464, Flying Officer F.J. Farrell, a Canadian, in MJ441 and Warrant Officer J. Toone in MJ522. Menzies ran into problems with the overload tank and returned to base almost immediately, leaving the other three to continue. After patrolling the general area of The Hague, the Spitfires strafed likely-looking target areas in Wassenaar without any obvious result being seen. They did manage to stir up the Germans, who retaliated with light flak, hitting Farfan's aeroplane. Because of this, the Spitfires recovered to Antwerp. Farfan returned to Swannington on the afternoon of the 23rd.

Then came 229. The pilots arrived at Swannington at 09.00 and four Spitfires took off an hour later to attack Rust-en-Vreugd, led by Flying Officer Walker in 9R●V. Accompanying him were Warrant Officer Hayes in 9R●S, Warrant Officer Cookson in 9R●O and Flight Sergeant Wally Haupt in 9R●U. They crossed the Dutch coast at the island of Schouwen at 10.34, turning north towards The Hague. Six minutes later, at a height of 7,000 feet, they spotted a large and rather unusual vessel in the Rotterdam Canal. They described it as being long and slender with a small superstructure amidships, black and brown in colour, riding high in the water and with several small tugs around it. They circled over it for a couple of minutes maintaining their altitude but suffering moderate flak from the nearby town of Maassluis. Then on they went to have a look at the various wooded areas in the north-east of The Hague, but saw nothing. The section found two small (possibly 15-hundred weight) trucks on the The Hague/Amsterdam road which they all attacked several times, leaving the vehicles smoking and one actually on fire. After this, they flew north-east to Leiden but returned to Wassenaar Rust-en-Vreugd. Nothing of interest was seen, although they encountered some intense light-flak which they think damaged the tailplane of Haupt's Spitfire.

Just before the 229 section crossed in over the Dutch coast at 10.34, a second armed recce from 453 was taking off back at Matlaske. Led by Flight Lieutenant W.R. Bennett in FU●H, the others were Warrant Officer C.A.M. Taylor, Flying Officer G.J. Stansfield in SM249 FU●B and Warrant Officer 'Frog' Lyall in FU●T. They crossed into the Netherlands over Westhoofd at 11,000 feet, then flew north to The Hague, passing to the west of Rotterdam. The target area at Langenhorst was obscured by cloud so they decided to attack Huis te Werve on the south-eastern side of The Hague in Rijswijk. As one of the 229 Spitfires was about to start a second strafing run, they spotted the 453 Squadron Spitfires in the distance preparing to start their bombing, so they pulled back and headed for home, crossing out over Katwijk to land at Swannington at 12.15.

Huis te Werve was an estate with a villa and a small lake, owned at the time by the *Bataafsche Import Maatschappij* and used as a recreation facility by their employees. The German rocket troops used it as a barracks and a storage area for V2s. Whilst some literature has it as a launching point, the soil was too soft for this and launches were made from a nearby tree-lined lane – an ideal site. There is a needle monument – the *Laantje bij de Naald* – and a statue in the grounds. During the afternoon of 27 October, a V2 went out of control and crashed onto an orphanage run by the Order of St John. Seventeen people were killed and twenty-four injured. After this the Germans ceased the launches, not because of fears for the safety of the Dutch, but in case another stray V2 exploded on a nearby ammunition dump.

The 453 Spitfires bombed from a height of 9,000 feet, pulling out at 3,000 in a north-west–south-east line. All bombs seemed to land in the target area and also on what looked like a stationary V2, but there was no explosion. Some of the pilots would later comment that a V2 they reported bombing might well have been 'a monument' – probably the *Laantje bij de Naald*. After this they set course for home, experiencing intense heavy flak on the way out over The Hague, which did not hit them. They landed back at Swannington at 12.30, by which time the second 602 armed recce of the day was in the skies over the Netherlands having taken off an hour earlier at 11.30.

Whilst still over the sea, 602's CO, Squadron Leader Sutherland in MK793, with Flying Officer Raymond F. Baxter, known to the Squadron as 'Bax', in ML244, Flight Lieutenant J.C.R. Waterhouse in MK999 and Roy Karasek (by now a Warrant Officer) in MJ457, saw two V2 contrails which they thought seemed to be coming from The Hague. Then as they crossed the coast south of Egmond they counted another five trails but were not able to pinpoint their origins. They patrolled over The Hague and were about to attack the Rust-en-Vreugd site when, just as they started to launch the attack, Squadron Leader Sutherland's engine started cutting out so he and Baxter left for Antwerp, where they landed safely, although at one point, Sutherland thought he might have to bale out. He returned to the squadron two days later with Flying Officer Farfan, who had had to make a similar diversion during the first of the squadron's armed recces of the day. 'Bax' Baxter did not return until the 25th. The others made their attack but saw nothing of any consequence. They landed back at Swannington at 13.16. At 13.00 602 took over the defensive state duty.

Only two V2s were recorded as landing in Britain whilst this armed recce was in the air, the first at 12.00 at Walthamstow and another at 12.03 at Little Waltham (possibly those spotted whilst they were over the sea).

As the 453 armed recce landed at Swannington at 12.30, the next 229 one took off led by Flight Lieutenant Patterson in 9R●K with Flight Sergeant Thomson in 9R●C, Flight Lieutenant McAndrew in 9R●B and Flight Lieutenant Sergeant in 9R●M; Rust-en-Vreugd once again the

target. They crossed in at West-hoofd, then headed north for Rotterdam. Cloud cover was 10/10ths, but clearer to the north. At 13.17, 8 miles from the port, they saw a V2 contrail heading towards the west, seeming to come from The Hague, one landed at Erith at 13.20. They took some desultory but

'Bax' Baxter.
(By kind permission of the family of the late Raymond Baxter and the Spitfire Society.)

accurate heavy flak from the west of Rotterdam then made for Rust-en-Vreugd, which they attacked through the cloud; they could not see the result of their attack, however. Near Leiden a canvas-covered vehicle was strafed by all the aircraft before they turned back to England, crossing out over Noordwijk, to land back at base at 14.50. The V2 that landed at Erith caused significant damage and casualties. It hit the Erith Oil Works as lunchtime was ending, with about seventy staff in the canteen. Nine of them died and most of the others were injured.

The next wave came from 453 again, taking off at 13.25, and led once more by Ernie Esau. This time the other three were Flying Officer Baker in SM230 FU●F, Flying Officer N.R. Adams in SM184 FU●D and Flight Sergeant McCully in SM193 FU●Q. They crossed in over Katwijk at 10,000 feet, observing cloud at the same height over The Hague. They patrolled the capital for some fifteen minutes before deciding to attack the storage area at Raaphorst, diving south-west to north-east from 9,000 feet to 5,000. They saw no results but returned to strafe the area with their guns before returning to base at 15.05. They reported flak from Leiden and Wassenaar. Cloud over the North Sea was 6/10ths.

The second to last operation of the day fell to 303 Squadron taking off from Coltishall at 14.30. Again, Rust-en-Vreugd and Raaphorst were their designated targets. The section leader was Squadron Leader Drobinski in RF●B, Sergeant K. Sztuka in RF●K, Warrant Officer A. Rutecki in RF●A and Sergeant Kucuc in RF●J. They crossed in at the Hook at 10,000 feet turning north for The Hague to patrol Rust-en-Vreugd and Raaphorst. They found nothing but at 15.17 saw a V2 launch which they thought came from Huis te Werve. The Poles reported some flak around Delft but not much else, and they were back at Coltishall by 16.15.

The final armed recce was carried out by 229 Squadron taking off at 15.15 and led by Flying Officer Walker in 9R●V, flying with Flight Lieutenant Welch in 9R●X, Warrant Officer Hayes in 9R●Z and Flight Sergeant Haupt in 9R●O and their target was Raaphorst. The crossed the Dutch coast at 15.45 hours over Westhoofd then made for The Hague, which they patrolled for half an hour. Nothing was seen but they attracted flak from the south-west side of the city, possibly Ockenburg or Bloemendaal, and the north-east – possibly Wassenaar. They proceeded to look at Leiden, attracting more flak, then returned to attack the Raaphorst site with their guns, but saw nothing to report. They turned north and crossed out over Katwijk at 16.20, landing at Swannington at 17.10.

No. 229 recorded a summary of the day's activities as they perceived it: 'Altogether today's operations have been fraught with more danger from flak than for a considerable period and it would appear that the dive bombing operations of 453 Squadron and the straffing of targets by other Squadrons has quite disturbed a hornets nest and roused all the

Ockenburg firing site in 2003.
(Author.)

opposition the enemy could muster.' Note that 'all the opposition the enemy could muster' did not include aircraft, which were few and far between over the Netherlands and were never a factor in the campaign against the V2s.

So what can be said about this flow of Spitfires shuttling back and forth, across the North Sea? They were taking off at roughly hourly intervals so that at any one time, there might be eight or twelve in the air at once, with four over the target areas and the enemy sites. But the constant activity did not stop the rockets being fired. If it was hoped that the pilots would be able to see rockets being prepared for launching and attack them, they were disappointed. Several rockets were seen being launched but the sites could not be pinpointed sufficiently well for them to be attacked. During an armed recce on the 26th, some 453 Squadron Spitfires saw a launch and were over the area only four minutes later, but still could find nothing to bomb. Even though an attack after a launch would only destroy the launching equipment and not the departed rocket, the launching troops would still have been at the location, packing up their equipment, even this never happened. The flak artillery deployed to protect the launches would not provoke an attack by opening up on a passing section of

Spitfires. Further, the dive-bombing descents started at about 8,000 feet and from this sort of altitude it would be very difficult to find the tiny target unless its location was known already. But having said that, the sight of sections of Spitfires constantly roaming about the skies over the The Hague with the realisation on that day that some were now carrying bombs, could only make the German troops more careful and nervous about their activities in case they were caught.

In total, on 21 November, no less than eight V2s landed in the London area, five of them in daylight hours whilst the Spitfires of 12 Group were active. During November, the number landing each day in southern England remained low and ironically, not many days suffered as many as eight. Firings continued during the nights which in November were long and still drawing out, and prevented operations by the Spitfires. Most pilots did some night flying as part of their training, but because Spitfires normally operated in daylight, their pilots only experienced a few night hours during their training and that really only to give them an idea what it was like in case they ever found themselves airborne in the dark. For the Germans, night operations of the V2s reduced the risk of attack considerably and this shift was one of the measurable consequences of the Spitfire campaign although its significance to the campaign to defend London is not particularly obvious.

After the 21st, the weather clamped down again for a few days, turning more and more wintry. Raymond Baxter, returning from Antwerp on the 25th faced a landing in heavy snow at Matlaske and 10/10ths cloud with a base of 1,500 feet. Some of the pilots started to realize that Matlaske was unlikely to be usable until the spring when it dried out completely. The unsatisfactory travel back and forward to Swannington was not likely to end. Despite the weather – and sometimes because of it – the monotony was occasionally broken. Spitfire XVIs continued to arrive at Swannington for issue to 229 and 602, who hoped that they would be able to fly them on the first occasion that the weather improved sufficiently to allow operations – although this was not to be. They needed to be air tested and although sometimes operations could not be flown, training could be continued. On the 25th, 303 Squadron practised full squadron formations. At lunchtime on the 23rd, 229, on readiness, received orders to have a section on fifteen minutes and another on thirty minutes for anti-Diver, or V1, patrols. Ten minutes afterwards at 12.20, the first four were ordered off. The second pair away had problems. The engine of Warrant Officer Grant's Spitfire would not start and then, once it did, as he went to take off, two of the XVIs being delivered 'got in his way' and he swung into a muddy patch. The aeroplane stuck fast. He hastily climbed into a different aircraft only to find that the other pilot, Warrant Officer Mackenzie, had R/T problems, so there was a further delay. It took them twenty-five minutes to get into the air. Cloud was 10/10ths in layers from 900 feet to

10,000. Various vectors were received and followed by the two pairs but only Warrant Officer Grant reported seeing what might have been a Heinkel, although in the heavy cloud, he could not be sure. (Heinkel 111s modified for the purpose were used to air-launch V1s.) They all landed back at about 13.30.

As discussed earlier, following the Prime Minister's announcement to the House of Commons on 10 November, the activities of the 12 Group Spitfires started to hit the headlines. In the evening after the operations on the 21st, the BBC *Nine o'Clock News* mentioned 453's dive-bombing activities and the newspapers picked it up as well. On the 22nd, 229's CO, Major Harrison, reputedly the only South African in Fighter Command in charge of an RAF squadron, made a four-minute broadcast to his home country. No doubt, the authorities felt that if the general population knew that the V2s existed, then they needed to let them know what was being done to counter them. Later, in April 1945, when the threat from the V2s had gone, Ernie Esau would make his own broadcast, and the attacks would be mentioned in the newspapers on other occasions. On the 26th, the 229 ORB records:

> *Today's newspapers again refer to attacks on Rocket sites . . . with special mention of 453 'City of Glasgow' Australian squadron's bombing attacks and mention 6 months special intensive training undertaken by this Squadron bombing replicas of the enemy rocket sites somewhere in this*

Aftermath of the New Cross V2.
(By kind permission of Local Studies, Lewisham Library Services.)

country. Neither 453 Squadron nor any one else has any knowledge of this training which must be a figment of some reporters imagination. This rocket site activity by fighters also took second priority on tonight's 9 o'clock news.

The less said the better!

On Saturday the 25th, the weather prevented any operational flying but it did not stop the rockets, and at 12.26 one fired from Wassenaar landed at Deptford. The resulting explosion could not have caused more death and destruction. It is reputed to have been the 251st rocket to be launched against the UK. It landed to the rear of a Woolworth's store in New Cross Road. Being a Saturday, many women and youngsters were shopping and it was full. Further, the store had received a consignment of saucepans, which were hard to come by at this stage of the war, and many women flocked there in the hope of getting one. The streets were crowded as well. One young woman recalled a sudden quietness, completely devoid of air, which seemed to take her breath away, then a sound that was so great it seemed to utterly overwhelm her faculties.[1] Her account is reminiscent of Rita Gathercole's 'disturbance in the air'.

Thirteen-year-old June Gaida remembered:

> *I was going shopping that morning for my mother, and suddenly there was a blinding flash of light, and a roaring, rushing sound. I was thrown into the air. There was noise all around me, a deafening terrible noise that beat against my eardrums and, when I fell to the ground, I curled myself up into a ball to protect myself, and I tried to scream but there was not any air. When the noise had faded, I picked myself up and I was coated in brick dust, with slivers of glass in my hair. Then I walked towards Woolworths. Things were still falling out of the sky, there were bricks, masonry, and bits and pieces of people. I remember seeing a horse's head lying in the gutter. Further on there was a pram-hood all twisted and bent, and there was a little baby's hand still in its woolly sleeve. Outside the pub there was a bus and it had been concertinad, with rows of people sitting inside, all covered in dust and dead. I looked over towards where Woolworths had been and there was nothing. There was just an enormous gap covered by a cloud of dust and I could see right through to the streets beyond. No building, just piles of rubble and bricks, and from underneath it all I could hear was people screaming.[2]*

Immediately following the explosion, the building seemed to bulge outwards slightly and then collapsed in on itself, releasing a cloud of debris and dust and giving those inside scant chance of escape. Next door was a Co-op which also collapsed. Buses, cars and lorries in the street were tossed around like toys, passers-by on the pavements and office workers in nearby buildings died instantly. There was complete destruction from

New Cross station to Deptford Town Hall and much of the surrounding area. Debris made the roads impassable. Most of the windows were shattered by the blast of the exploding rocket and shards of broken glass covered everything, creating more danger. People were in shock. Some did not move, others ran blindly to get away from what had occurred. The injured moaned as they lay on the footpath and the dead lay still, bloody and torn.

A hundred and sixty died and seventy-seven were seriously injured. It was a tragedy of epic proportions. An official report said: 'A temporary mortuary was established at the premises of Pearces Signs, to which bodies and fragments of bodies were taken. Identification was likely to cause considerable difficulty in view of the extreme degree of mutilation and/or dismemberment of many bodies.'[3]

If the Spitfire squadrons had any doubts about the value of their work, here was proof indeed that they were needed.

The night of the 25th/26th brought more rain and sleet and a severe drop in temperature, so that although the morning dawned brighter and clearer than for many days, with the possibility of operations, it left the ground covered with ice, as well as the roads. But this added another dimension. At 09.00 as usual the 602 pilots left Matlaske for Swannington in a truck with a WAAF driver. Near the Woodrow Inn, it skidded on a patch of ice and slid into a post at the side of the road, throwing Warrant Officer Ryan and Flight Lieutenant J.R. Sutherland out of the back and the driver out of her seat. She suffered two broken ribs, Ryan was concussed and Sutherland badly shaken, but the others were unhurt. A phone call from the inn brought an ambulance from Swannington for the injured and the journey eventually resumed. The airmen faced risks other than those over the targets. Despite this, the day saw another full programme of armed recces with Ockenburg Kliniek, Rust-en-Vreugd, Raaphorst, Bloemendaal and Langenhorst all receiving attention. But no fewer than twelve V2s landed in south-east England in the twenty-four hours from midnight.

Monday the 27th, dawned with fine weather over Norfolk; it was significant for 602 because it was the first day that the squadron flew their Spitfire XVIs operationally. Flying Officer Farfan in SM 234 and Flying Officer F.L. Farrell in SM 257 were up at 08.40 on an uneventful combined weather recce and Jim Crow. By the end of the day, as well as the two used on Jim Crow, 602 had taken delivery of SM235, SM254, SM276, SM287, SM288, SM296, SM301, SM307, SM341, SM343 LO●H, SM350, SM351, SM352, SM353, SM361, SM388 and SM424. All were Mark LF XVIs. Farfan and Farrell found the weather over the Netherlands to be so poor that they finished up having to fly at about 100 feet to keep themselves below the cloud base. Other attempts aborted because of the weather. No. 303 Squadron laid on an armed recce, taking off at 10.20, but reported 10/10th cloud, 1,500 foot base with tops at 6,000 and visibility under the clouds 2 miles over the northern Netherlands.

At 09.00 on Wednesday, four 602 Spitfire XVIs took off to carry out their first dive-bombing operation. Flying Officer Farfan in SM350, Warrant Officer H.G. Ellison in SM257, Flying Officer Farrell in SM341 and Warrant Officer Toone in SM288. Just after take-off, Farrell's R/T started to give problems and he returned to base, landing at 09.10. The other three carried on, each carrying two 250-pound general purpose nose and tail fused bombs on the wings. Their target was Rust-en-Vreugd, which they bombed as planned, but they could not see how successful they had been. They returned to Swannington at 10.45. Round about this time, a section of four Spitfire IXs of 229 Squadron led by Flight Lieutenant Patterson was over Leiden when they saw a V2 launching.

> *A flash followed by a dense cloud of smoke and dust from the woods some hundred yards west of the Hague racecourse which rose to about 200 feet. A red flame was seen rising from the explosion fairly slowly and wobbling as it rose. It was lost to view at about 10,000 feet to reappear at 20 to 22,000 with a white trail commencing and a little red flame. Both flame and trail weakened as it rose and curved at the top towards West.*

It looked as if the missile had come from Langenhorst, and Patterson went down on his own to have a look for the launcher but could not find it. A V2 landed at Sandon. The four gave the area a going over with their guns before returning to Swannington. Not long after 229 departed the area, a section of 453 Squadron Spitfire XVIs, also over The Hague was diverted to bomb it but they saw nothing and did not attack. The 'Hague race-course' mentioned in 229's report was at Duindigt and used by the rocket troops as a storage area.

Because the 229 pilots were reasonably sure that they could pinpoint the launch site area, 602 was tasked with bombing it later in the day – in fact their last armed recce, taking off at 15.00. They were accompanied by Wing Commander T.B. Fitzgerald DFC, the Wing Commander Flying, and Flight Lieutenant McAndrew of 229 in Spitfire IXs to observe the bombing. Although the attack went in as planned, no significant results were noted. No. 303 Squadron also completed an armed recce of the same area in the early afternoon.

The events of the day are significant because it was the first time that such clear co-operation and co-ordination of the attacks occurred: the initial sighting of the launch by 229, the diverting of the 453 section whilst in the air over the area to see if they could bomb the site, and the attack later in the day by 602 accompanied by the Wing Commander Flying to observe. Whatever the difficulties of operating out of the airfields back in Norfolk, the system worked.

(opposite)
A launching site near the Duindigt racecourse. A rocket surrounded by
fuelling vehicles can just be discerned at Point 'A'. The big craters were
caused by the premature explosions of rogue V2s and the large loop at
the bottom is a turning track for the rocket launching convoy.
(Australian War Memorial Negative no. SUK 14252.)

(above)
Another PRU photograph of the top part of the previous picture but
taken some time later. The effect of the Spitfires' dive bombing is
easily seen.
(Courtesy Imperial War Museum. Negative no. C5239.)

229/603 Squadron's Flight Lieutenant Bob Sergeant as a young sergeant pilot. *(The late Bob Sergeant.)*

The 30th brought another full day of similar operations, although 303 Squadron acted as escort for bombers on Ramrod 1384 attacking a synthetic oil plant at Bottrop. On the way back, the CO, Squadron Leader Drobinski, brought his section into Bradwell Bay, where unfortunately Sergeant J. Kucuc crashed and was badly hurt. He was taken to Ely Hospital at Cambridge. Three 229 pilots flew mid-morning to RAF Yeadon, from where they were to provide an escort for a Dakota carrying Air Chief Marshal Sir Charles Portal and his entourage from Yeadon to Northolt. They returned to Swannington at 17.00 'much to Flight Lieutenant Sergeant's great relief he having been apprehensive that the VIP's might have noticed his "very operational" hat.'

Bob Sergeant brought a wealth of experience to 229. Born near Hull, on leaving school he joined the family joinery and undertaking business and was a committed Christian and a lay preacher in the local Methodist church. He joined the RAF at the beginning of the war and fought with 249 Squadron during the siege of Malta in 1942. In February of that year, to try to alleviate the desperate situation on the Mediterranean island, several experienced pilots were flown there in a Sunderland. They included 'Laddie' Lucas, Stan Turner and Sergeant. Constantly bombed and with the air strips pockmarked with bomb craters, the flying was hard and not for the inexperienced. In May, he received a head injury which ended his time on Malta and returned him to the UK on 11 May 1942. He was an enthusiastic man – very 'can-do' by nature.

No. 249 flew out of Ta Kali and the officer pilots from the station lived in the Xara Palace on high ground overlooking the airfield a few miles away. When not on duty, the pilots sat on a balcony, from where they watched the airfield being attacked. This particular morning, Sergeant was in the dining room below having his breakfast when a raid developed. Bounding up the stairs to the balcony, he felt something hit his head and then blood on his face and hand. It transpired that a stray incendiary round from a German aircraft above had fallen on him – hitting his head and lodging in the back of his hand. He was very fortunate that it did not kill him. He eventually recovered from his injuries and kept the stray round for the rest of his life.

As far as the hat goes, he had a good one for wearing around the station, and an old one that he stuffed into a corner of the windscreen for use if he was landing away from base. It had been with him for a long time and by now was battered and comfortable – hence his concern!

Although now a Flight Lieutenant, Bob commented that 229 seemed to be well endowed with senior pilots and later, when a new CO arrived from another squadron (602) a number of them queried why one of their own flight lieutenants had not been promoted from within. Flight Lieutenant 'Tommy' Rigler was another experienced pilot on 229, but a flight commander. It was whilst undergoing pilot training at RAF Sealand earlier in the war that Bob Sergeant first came across Rigler, at that time a Leading Aircraftman (LAC). Sergeant was under the impression that Rigler came from Canada, believing he had been a lumberjack, and recalled that he had the enviable reputation of being able to drink 'pints of everything'! Balding and round faced, Rigler perhaps did not have the appearance of a dashing fighter pilot – one of his pilots said that he looked more like an all-in wrestler – nonetheless he was an accomplished airman with eight confirmed kills, one probable and three damaged. Awarded the DFM as a sergeant pilot in 1941, the promulgation in the *London Gazette* read: 'This airman has carried out 82 sorties since March 1941. He has displayed outstanding keenness to destroy the enemy in combat and to harass him on the ground. Sergeant Rigler has destroyed at least seven hostile aircraft (three were destroyed in one sweep) and has damaged a further two.'

During 1941 he flew with 609 Squadron from Biggin Hill with accomplished airmen like 'Sailor' Malan, Paul Richey, Jean Offenburg, Jamie Rankin and many others. The incident during which he brought down the three Bf109s mentioned in the citation for his DFM illustrated his courage and perhaps even foolhardiness. Separated from the squadron over France, he saw some aircraft in the distance and went to join them, assuming them to be Spitfires. Approaching from the rear, he realized that they were 109s, but rather than turn away he decided to 'have a go' and took a shot at the rearmost one in the formation, which promptly went down. As the German formation broke, two others collided and fell out of the sky, at which point 'Rig' turned away to set course for home with all haste!

Friday, 1 December 1944 saw more subtle changes in the operational methodology. With 229 now taking delivery of its XVIs and already having used them operationally, orders came for 453 and 602 to lay on a combined dive-bombing operation against the Haagsche Bosch with each aeroplane carrying 1,000 pounds of bombs – an additional 500-pounder on the fuselage centreline strongpoint replacing the jettison tank. But without the extra fuel they would not be able to make the return flight across the North Sea so the plan was for them to stage into airfield B65/Maldegem in Belgium. Maldegem is a few miles to the east of Bruges, near the border with the Netherlands, and had been used by the *Luftwaffe* in previous years. Being a relatively short flight from The Hague, the arrangement allowed the Spitfires to be refuelled and rearmed with another 1,000 pounds of bombs, which they could deliver on to a target in The Hague on their way back to Norfolk – or they could go back again to Maldegem. And ideally, they could do this several times a day. Eventually, this would become a routine way of working using several different airfields, and occasionally the pilots overnighted on the Continent.

At 09.00 on the 1st, 229's Tommy Rigler and Flight Lieutenant Johnny Welch took off on a weather recce to find that, whilst not ideal, it should be acceptable for the planned operation – 10/10ths cloud covered the whole area at 11,000 feet with a 10/10ths layer at 4,000 feet stretching eastwards from Utrecht. Having delayed take-off from 09.00 to give time for the weather over the target to improve, at 11.53, six of 453's Spitfires took off from Swannington, followed a few minutes later by seven of 602's. Both squadrons were led by their respective COs. They crossed in over the Netherlands at 6,000 feet above 10/10ths cloud with tops rising to 6,000. Over The Hague, they could see the city through small clear patches but these were not large enough to allow the attack to proceed so they headed out to sea to jettison the bombs, then made for Maldegem. Unfortunately, 602's Flight Lieutenant Dickie Pertwee hit a jeep crossing the runway, damaging the starboard mainplane of his Spitfire (SM257). Fortunately, neither he nor the driver of the jeep was hurt. They then returned to Swannington. It was no doubt a disappointment, but at least it demonstrated that if space could be found on the crowded continental airfields for them, more effective use could be made of the operations.

Nos 229 and 303 attempted their own armed recces but these came to little because of the cloud over the targets. In the evening, 229 added Pilot Officer Freddy van Dyck and Warrant Office Beckwith to its strength but learned, to the dismay of many of the pilots, that the CO, Major Harrison would be leaving them on the 15th to take up a post at the Central Flying School. This news certainly cast a cloud over the men.

The next day, Saturday, 2 December, started off with poor weather and an early-morning weather recce by Bob Sergeant and Pilot Officer Bill Doidge found 10/10ths cloud down to sea level off the Dutch coast, Flight Lieutenants Barrett and Johnnie Welch on a Jim Crow to Den Helder found the cloud base at 4,000, but it was still too low for dive bombing. At 11.45 Warrant Officer Cookson and Flight Sergeant Tommy Thomson left on another weather recce, this time to see if the conditions around The

Hague were suitable for an attack by the Spitfire XVIs of 602 and 453 Squadrons. They were not, so the planned combined dive bombing operation was called off.

Cookson and Thomson returned to Coltishall and not Swannington because the squadron had only just found out that they were moving there from Matlaske/Swannington. Now in the process of changing over to the XVI, the move probably could not have come at a worse time and at such short notice. According to the Squadron ORB, it had forty-two aeroplanes on strength – twenty-three Spitfire IXs, seventeen Spitfire XVIs, a single Spitfire V and a Magister – and they all had to be ferried across to their new base. With no operational flying, but the weather allowing the ferrying, the majority of the aircraft moved over during the afternoon, with help from half a dozen of the Australians of 453. Seventeen Spitfires – a mixture of IXs and XVIs – took off from Swannington at 15.30 to make the short trip to Coltishall. It must have been quite a sight, worthy of a twenty-first century air display at Duxford! Although not all of the aircraft were moved across on the 2nd, the intention was that the squadron would be ready for operations at 10.00 the following day – which it was.

Some of the XVIs issued to 229 were SM198, SM340, SM348, SM356, SM357, SM360, SM385, SM401 and SM405 – clearly all of the same batch as the other squadrons had already received.

Although the weather on the Saturday over the Netherlands would not allow dive bombing, strafing attacks could be made and 602 laid on an armed recce over the Haagsche Bosch by four of its remaining Spitfire IXs. They were flown by Flying Officer Farrell, Flight Lieutenant G.Y.G. Lloyd, Warrant Officer Toone and Warrant Officer Roy Karasek in NH150 LO●N. This would be the last operation flown by 602's Spitfire IXs. Farrell had to return early, but the three remaining aircraft crossed in over Katwijk and headed straight for the target area, which they attacked without any obvious results. Then they made for Overmeer, where they found a bowser truck towing a bowser trailer, which they attacked. As they completed the first pass, Karasek called up on the R/T to say that he was in trouble and the others watched as the Spitfire made what seemed to be a normal approach for an emergency belly landing in a field about ½ mile away from the scene of the attack. A few seconds later, they saw the Spitfire on the ground in flames. They attacked the bowser again twice, then turned back to base. Quite what had caused Karasek to crash was a mystery and they could not understand what had happened to him. They could not know that the problem began with the Spitfire's overload tank slung under the fuselage. Karasek recalled that they were not popular with the pilots, particularly once they reached about half full because the petrol would slosh about and affect the handling, but they did allow them to reach the target areas.

After spotting the vehicle,

... the section leader advised over the R/T that we would go down and attack. As the basic rule was not to go into action with overload tanks, I selected the main tank and then tried to jettison the overload tank – there was a lever in the cockpit to do this. The lever however would not budge. Everything seemed to be in order, so I decided to carry on with the attack. I dived down with the others and strafed the vehicles. Then, when I was more or less at the bottom of my dive, the engine cut. I don't know why this happened – there was no anti-aircraft fire. Possibly a lucky rifle bullet but somehow I doubt this; I'd heard or felt nothing. I realized I had no height to bale out and I had no choice other than to crash land. I struggled like mad to try to get the wretched jettison lever to work, but all to no avail. A brief call on the R/T to say I was in trouble; check the wind direction; turn ignition switches to 'off' (probably a bit unnecessary under the circumstances, but set procedures die hard and it would certainly do no harm!); and tighten the seat belts until they hurt. (I had had a previous crash landing, and hit my nose very badly on the gunsight due to the straps not being tight enough).

I now had to concentrate on the landing itself. The field was not all that big and surrounded by some trees. I think I made a reasonable judgement in this, as I remember hearing the tick tack *of the tops of the trees hitting the leading edge of the wing so I could not have been any lower.*

After that I remember nothing.

He woke up lying on his back on the ground with no idea what had happened to him. As he lay there trying to understand what was going on, he heard strange noises and turning his head, saw the Spitfire about 20 yards away engulfed in flames, with the ammunition 'cooking off'.

The moment I saw the Spitfire, all memory returned – up to the aircraft hitting the trees. From that moment my memory is a complete blank, and I often wondered what actually happened. There was nobody around who could have dragged me out. I presume that the aircraft must have exploded on impact, but how could all those four powerful Sutton harness straps have snapped? It has remained a mystery all these years.

I was still wearing my parachute which could have cushioned my spine but I was too weak to hit the release box. After a while I heard voices and two or three people arrived. I can remember pulling my map from out of my boot giving it to them and saying 'Fire' – it had the front line marked on it every day. One man lifted my head and gave me a drink of schnapps or brandy from a small bottle which was most acceptable. And I somehow got someone to release the parachute. I suddenly felt incredibly weary and passed out.

Karasek vaguely recalled being lifted and carried but passed out once more. He came to lying on a small bed on the ground floor of a farmhouse

– minus his boots, which he never saw again. He was tired and shocked and said that he could not care about anything. Every now and then he passed out or fell asleep. Then he recalled that a woman came over and knelt down beside him asking 'Do you want to escape?', which suddenly brought him back to life and alertness. And then as he says,

A wonderfully dramatic bit – straight out of a cheap comic – the woman said 'There is one person you must not trust . . .' But just at that moment there was a crash, the door was kicked in and in came German soldiers with rifles and bayonets. My stomach turned over but the Germans seemed to ignore me and my 'couldn't care less' attitude came over me again. At one point I heard a woman screaming from upstairs, which upset me rather, but then I soon returned to my coma.

He was moved from the farmhouse in a horse-drawn cart and then transferred to an ambulance which took him to hospital in Amsterdam, where he was examined by three doctors. By now he had pains in his spine and knees and a 'most fearful' headache. He recalls that they pointed to a bed. 'I staggered towards it and fell on it, but I'm sure I was asleep before my head hit the pillow.'

He was more or less back to normal the next day but found himself wondering just what had happened and how lucky he had been to survive. He tried unsuccessfully to escape – suffering solitary confinement in prison in Amsterdam as a punishment – but survived to return home after the war ended.

Karasek's story demonstrates quite vividly the shock and disorientation that a shot-down airman would experience and have to deal with. Only a couple of hours before, safely back at base, he had perhaps been arranging to go for a pint in one of the locals once the squadron was stood down for the day. He may only have been called for the operation shortly before it took place. Max Baerlein who joined 602 Squadron a few weeks later said that he did not remember there being rosters for the various operations. His recollection is that the CO or Flight Commander would come into the dispersal hut and call the pilots who would be flying. From safety and normality, the new circumstances were frightening, uncertain and difficult. Instead of waking up in his own bed at Matlaske on the Sunday morning, Karasek was waking up in hospital bed in a strange city as a prisoner, not knowing what was in store for him. The fear of torture and even death must have crossed his mind.

For those back at Matlaske, his loss would have come as a shock too. Many of the younger pilots on their first operational posting regarded it all as a bit of an adventure. Few of their friends or colleagues were being killed, unlike other campaigns, where pilots failed to return on a regular basis, as in the heavy fighting of 1940 over the south of England when front-line squadrons regularly lost several pilots on a single operation and those left had to learn to cope with losing close friends on a daily basis. The failure of Roy Karasek to return that day must have been a sobering reminder for those left behind despite them being told that the chances of being hit by German flak were so slight they were not worth bothering about, there still remained the chance of something unpleasant happening to them and they could not allow themselves to become complacent. In particular, as nobody knew whether Karasek had survived or not, or perhaps been injured, many would be concerned for him – concern tinged with fear for themselves.

There are several intriguing points in Roy Karasek's account, but one in particular is the screaming that he heard after the Germans forced their way into the farmhouse. Did they come from the woman who was trying to warn him or someone else? Why was she screaming and what happened to her? He is unlikely ever to find out.

The weather on Sunday, 3 December was marginal and another combined operation by 453 and 602 was laid on. However as the dozen or so Spitfires neared the Dutch coast, the cloud closed in and the formation broke up. After jettisoning their bombs into the sea, they made their way to Maldegem for refuelling, then returned to Swannington. No. 453's Norman 'Swamp' Marsh noted in his log book 'Weather bloody terrible – jettisoned bombs – landed at Antwerp – considered staying but when V2 landed close by decided to beat it to Maldegem.'

By now, 229 was settling into their new quarters at Coltishall, and at muddy Swannington 453 Squadron moved into the hut being used by 602 and recently vacated by 229.

No. 229 Squadron's first operation using the XVIs took place on 5 December – an armed recce with two 250-pound bombs each to The Hague but with the almost predictable failure to bomb because of the weather. The four pilots who made the flight were Major Harrison, Pilot Officer Doidge, Flying Officer Walker and Warrant Officer Cookson. For the next few days, 229 continued to fly a mixture of operations some using the XVIs and some the IXs. The final flight of the IXs took place on the 9th – a camera gun practice by Pilot Officer Freddy van Dyck and Flight Sergeant Snowy Wheatley, an Australian who no doubt felt at home with 453 Squadron nearby.

Although the 229 operation had to be aborted, four Spitfires from both 602 and 453 Squadrons managed to bomb Rust-en-Vreugd with little in the way of results to report.

Air Marshal Hill wrote:[4]

From the 21st November onwards the four squadrons in 12 Group which were assigned to this duty took every opportunity of attacking them [the listed objectives] *with bombs and machine-gun and cannon fire. The general prevalence of bad weather made these opportunities few, especially in November and the latter half of December. As a result, these squadrons had plenty of time for intensive training in pin point dive-bombing of which they took full advantage.*

Notes
1. *Hitler's Rockets* by Norman Longmate.
2. *London at War* ©1985, Joanna Mack & Steve Humphries, p146. Quoted by kind permission of London Weekend Television and Pan Macmillan.
3. Incident at New Cross Road. Report by Casualty Services Officer HO186/2381.
4. Supplement to the *London Gazette* of Tuesday, 19 October 1948, 'Air Operations by Air Defence of Great Britain and Fighter Command in Connection with the German Flying Bomb and Rocket Offensives, 1944–1945'.

CHAPTER FIVE

A Hard Winter

odern-day visitors to The Hague might very well visit the
Gemeente Museum, an art museum, and its neighbour the *Museon*
– science – situated a few miles to the west of the Haagsche Bosch
on the corner of Stadhouderslaan and what is now President
Kennedylaan. The museum buildings are low, rectangular and long, built
after the war, sandstone in colour with two large rectangular pools at the
front along their length up Stadhouderslaan. The visitor might stop for
coffee or lunch in the café and whilst sitting, glance across the wide avenue
at the dark houses on the other side which have the appearance of having
been built around the beginning of the twentieth century – large but not
walled off or standing in their own grounds, more like little blocks of un-
remarkable but vaguely picturesque flats. On a closer inspection, one of
these buildings is slightly different to the others – a later design and
construction – but the passing of time and the mellowing of the materials
makes the difference quite subtle and not particularly noticeable. Coming
out of the museum, turning right and walking up Stadhouderslaan,
within a few hundred yards, the visitor reaches Stadhoudersplein, its
junction with Willem de Zwijgerlaan and what is now called
Eisenhowerlaan. The junction is wide and open, not quite rectangular in
shape and crossed by steel tramlines set into the road and round a tri-
angular area of grass. To the south-west are houses.

It was here that, early on the morning of 8 December 1944, German
rocket troops set up the launching platform for a V2 and fired it off at
05.45.[1] Unfortunately, it was one of many rogues which, immediately on
lift-off, careered out of control, turning over on itself and exploding on the
house opposite the museum, destroying it completely and killing the
occupants as well as anyone who happened to be passing. This is why the
house is different in appearance from the others along the street. Having
fired their missile, the Germans packed up and left. All in all, twelve V2s
exploded in this way, killing Dutch civilians, and the new buildings in

112

Indigostraat, Westduinweg and Riouwstraat are there because of unplanned explosions of V2s.

This mirrors the experiences of Jan van't Hoff. The Germans seemed deliberately to fire the V2s from places that they knew were near to Dutch civilians in the hope that the RAF would hesitate to attack them – which of course they did. The RAF found itself faced with having to attack very small targets with high levels of accuracy and ever since aeroplanes started to bomb ground targets, the problem of avoiding unwanted damage around the target has never been resolved. Of course the concern about this was not so great when it involved Germany, but when the civilians of an occupied country – the Allies – were under the bombs the reasons for taking more care were obvious. The problems would be tragically illustrated when 2nd TAF eventually sent in some of its medium bombers to help attack the V2s, but this was some way down the road. Fortunately, with The Hague and the rest of the Netherlands within range of the single-engined aeroplanes based in Norfolk and on the Continent, Hill had an option not available to the heavies of Bomber Command and the 8th Air Force; dive-bombing – much more accurate than area or low-level skip-bombing and resulting in fewer collateral casualties.

It says much for the brilliant design of the Spitfire that what started off as a day fighter in the 1930s, could be adapted to become a dive bomber in the 1940s. But as well as having the right equipment, the techniques for dive bombing had to be developed. Pierre Clostermann, a Free French pilot, flew with 602 Squadron from the autumn of 1943 until 1944, but had been posted elsewhere by the time it returned to England to attack the V2s. He was, however, with 602 when in March 1944 it spent a week at RAF Llanbedr in Wales at 12 Armament Practice Camp learning a methodology for dive bombing using a Spitfire. The squadron flew their Spitfire IXs to Llanbedr from their Detling base on 13 March 1944, having only arrived there from Orkney a few days before. According to Clostermann, they were there to experiment and develop a dive-bombing methodology, although the 602 ORB makes no mention of this aspect and suggests that the objective was training and practice in dive-bombing and ground-attack methods rather than to develop them.

On the face of it, dive bombing seems quite straight forward, but like most activities, it is not as easy as it seems. At too shallow an angle, aiming is difficult; too steep and a bomb coming off a Spitfire centre line will pitch through the arc of the propeller. The optimum is somewhere in between. Bombs on the centre line of the *Luftwaffe*'s Ju87 *Stuka* were in a cradle that swung the bomb out beyond the arc of the propeller allowing the aeroplane to go down in a very steep dive. They also had a mechanism to pull the aircraft out of the dive in case the G-force imposed on the pilot made him black out – as they often did. The Spitfires had neither of these, so the pilot had to get it all 'just right' to be successful. Unlike modern 'smart' bombs, with their sophisticated electronics and guidance systems, those used by the Spitfire squadrons had none of these advantages so once the bomb was released, if the aim was wrong, there was no correction, and factors like the wind at ground level and the angle of release could easily affect the trajectory and whether or not the bomb landed on its target and the operation was a success.

Clostermann says that Squadron Leader Sutherland evolved a method for delivering a single 500-pound bomb from the fuselage centre line whereby the aircraft in the section approached the target area in 'close reversed echelon' at 12,000 feet. When the leader saw the target appear behind the trailing edge of the wing, he dived at an angle of 75 degrees, followed closely by the others, with the target in their gunsight and at full throttle. At 3,000 feet, they would begin to pull out, count three and release the bombs. Eventually, with practice, the pilots could place them within a 450 yard circle.

Raymond Baxter's recollection was slightly different. He remembered that the approach was made at about 8,000 feet (depending on cloud height) but never below 5,000. On final approach to the target, with the speed reduced to 200 knots, the formation leader would call 'Echelon starboard (or port)' and overfly it so that it passed out of sight under the wing, outboard of the flaps (which were retracted, not lowered) and just inboard of the roundel. After it reappeared, and after a count of three, the Spitfire was rolled to reveal the target, which would be lined up in the centre of the unlocked gyro-gunsight. The Spitfire would be throttled back and trimmed into what was effectively a 'hands-off' dive at about 70 degree. He said:

> Of course an attack at this angle made you feel as if you were diving at the ground vertically, which was made worse if you were not quite steep enough and you had to push the nose down even more! Once trimmed, and with the throttle pulled back, the Mk XVI held very steady when hurtling ground-ward, which allowed you to make full use of the excellent Mk II gunsight, and thus achieve impressive levels of accuracy. We never really monitored our dive speeds during these attacks – I think 360 mph was a typical maximum velocity achieved. The gunsight graticule was brought to bear on the target, and all instrument readings and flak bursts ignored for the duration of the dive. One had to avoid side-slipping, skidding to dodge the AA or turning whilst in this phase of the attack as they all adversely affected your aim.[2]

The bombs were usually released at 3,000 feet – no lower than 1,500 feet – and the aircraft was then pulled out to escape at low level. An experienced pilot could bomb accurately to within 25 or 30 yards.

Flying Officer John Moss flew with 603 later in 1945, although not against the V2s. However, he did the training and remembered that the Spitfire was trimmed into the dive. This was because it was inherently stable and would try to return to more level flight left to its own devices. He also remembered that on one of his first practice attempts at dive bombing, he pulled out by winding in a sudden large nose up trim which made the aeroplane swoop into a climb and caused him black out with the high induced G-force – not unlike George Pyle's experience when testing the Spitfire IX or many of the pilots in action who might black out for ten or fifteen seconds on the way up. Raymond Baxter remembered:

> We adopted the tactic of flattening out the bottom of the dive into a 5'g' pull by continuing to go down after we had salvoed our bombs at 2500 feet – the lowest altitude at which bombs could be released in a dive was 1500 feet but that meant a high-g pull-up straight after your bombs had gone. We would level out at about 100 feet and make our escape at tree-top height. The great temptation of course was to climb out from the attack to see how accurate you had been in delivering your ordnance, but the German gunners knew their stuff so this manoeuvre was discouraged. On several occasions Spitfires from other squadrons broke up or shed wings in diving attacks, but that was usually when the bombs failed to unstick, and the 'g' force exerted on the flying surfaces during the pull out exceeded the design's maximum wing loading. Unfortunately, you only discovered that your bombs had 'stuck' once you pulled the stick back to level out.[3]

This happened to Eric Mee of 229 Squadron on one operation. Completing the dive, when he toggled to release the bombs they did not go and the extra mass created a much greater G-load on both the pilot and the aeroplane as it pulled out. Then Mee had to deal with a tricky landing back at base with live bombs on board. Afterwards, the Spitfire received a thorough inspection and Mee's fitter called him over to see the bolts which held the mainplanes to the fuselage. They had bent with the stresses imposed on them during the pull-out – an indication of just how robust the men and their machines had to be. Sometimes pulling quickly out of a high speed dive created such stress on the wing surface that it deformed into ripples requiring the mainplane to be replaced.

With all that the pilots had to do, their co-ordination needed to be good. As well as just flying the Spitfire, the graticule on the gyro-gunsight was controlled by a twist grip on the throttle, and the bomb-release button was on the end of the throttle lever. And on the control column there were two buttons, one for firing the cannon and the other for the machine guns.

Originally dive bombing the V1 sites in France meant running the gauntlet of intense flak with the risk of *Luftwaffe* fighters coming along. So these attacks were limited often to a single section whilst the others kept guard above, but by the time of the V2 attacks, the risk of interception had

Tom Hall, Aussie Typhoon pilot with 2nd TAF.
(From 'Typhoon Warfare' by kind permission Tom Hall.)

reduced to almost nil, so sometimes more than just four Spitfires went down one after the other – their main problem being flak. To protect the launching operations, the Germans included 3.7 cm anti-aircraft guns mounted on half-tracks as part of the launching units and they also installed fixed guns along the coast to attack Spitfires crossing in or out. The Resistance passed information about these fixed positions back to Britain. Clearly, the Germans only opened up once an attack had started – there was no point in drawing attention to the sites before – but once the firing started, it may have given some pilots cause for concern. Bob Sergeant said later that he thought flak could be quite pretty with its black bursts and fiery red interiors, but lethal nonetheless. Diving into a carpet of flak called for extra courage, as Eric Mee had discovered on his first operation. It was not unusual to encounter flak on the way over the coast, but quite another thing diving through it over a target. The leader might have nothing to contend with, but for those following him down, the carpet of white puff-balls seemed solid. Paddy O'Reilly recalled that it made him flinch when he reached it.

Radar-predicted flak posed a real threat. Tom Hall, the Aussie Typhoon pilot whose squadron had shared the ALG at Deurne with 453 and 602 recalled that the German radar, usually associated with the much-feared 88 mm guns, caused a distinct 'click click' sound in the pilots' earphones so that they could tell when they were being tracked. The trick then was to jink – contantly changing speed, height and direction so that the aeroplane was not in the same bit of sky as the shell when it arrived. Raymond Baxter also remembered that crossing into enemy territory ran the risk of predicted fire from German 88s and that avoiding it was easy – the Spitfires flew in climbing or diving turns and it gave the pilots a glow to see the flak bursting where they would otherwise have been. Clearly this was an added strain on the airmen, and the constant changes used fuel.

Jack Batchelor joined 229 Squadron at the beginning of 1945. He said that he used to try mentally to note the position of flak batteries and return to have a go at them later – presumably either after the attack or on later operations. Sometimes during the dive, pilots reported feeling little bumps, as if their aeroplane was being hit by something, even if there was no flak. Eventually it was decided that this was likely to be caused by empty shell casings from Spitfires in front firing their guns.

Usually having finished the attack, the Spitfires exited the target area as fast as they could to rendezvous somewhere safe, often out to sea. But sometimes they returned or roamed the countryside looking for targets. Max Baerlein found himself diving to strafe a German vehicle near a village and realized that the Dutch population had gathered to watch, in two groups on either side of his strafing run! They were not at risk from his shells, but certainly were from ricochets. Another time, he saw an elderly Dutchman working in his garden, seemingly oblivious of the lines of bullets kicking up the ground around him.

The Germans realized that horse-drawn carts were not being attacked by the marauding Spitfires and they started to use them for their own transport. The Allies let it be known to the Dutch that to overcome this they would 'buzz' the carts first so that the occupants could jump off and into safety. Raymond Baxter remembered going down to attack a line of horse-drawn vehicles and seeing the Dutch drivers jump for the roadside ditches – waving cheerfully at him nonetheless! Once they started doing this, the Germans soon stopped the practice.

The Dutch were very much with the British pilots in what they were trying to do, even if it meant that there were Dutch casualties. For Han Borsboom the days could be filled with air-raid warnings. Once, he hid in a house on Bezuidenhoutsweg whilst a Spitfire flew down the street spraying bullets along the ground. After it had gone, the youngster ran out into the street to collect the spent cartridge cases, which were still hot. He and his friends collected many cases and splinters over the weeks and months of the attacks. Jan van't Hoff said that the sight of RAF Spitfires overhead encouraged them hugely and gave them the feeling that they were not forgotten and alone and the Dutch were quite selfless. An exploding V2 or a stray bomb which might kill or injure them was regarded as a sacrifice which might help the Allies release them from their occupation – even following 2nd TAF's disastrous attack later in the campaign when many innocent civilians perished during a daylight raid on The Hague that went wrong and incidents like that at Stadhoudersplein. The loss of an RAF Spitfire was a tragedy for the Dutch as well as the British, and the ordinary Dutch civilians endured their hardships stoically and with enormous courage.

No. 602 Squadron remained at Llanbedr until 20 March 1944, when they returned to Detling to take the fight to France. The training was intense – many short flights each day – and they lost one of their pilots, Flying Officer Don Hale, in an accident on 15 March. Just before starting an air-to-ground firing exercise on the Dyffryn range, Hale made a tight

A probably posed shot of a 602 Squadron briefing at Matlaske or
Ludham. The board is interesting, with detailed maps of the
Netherlands and The Hague, as well as PRU target photographs of
likely V2 launch sites.
L to r: ?, Flight Sergeant 'Tommy' Love, Squadron Leader Max
Sutherland, Flight Lieutenant Z. Wroblewski, Flying Officer F.J. Farrell.
(Courtesy Imperial War Museum. Negative no. CH14809.)

turn at very low altitude and struck a tree. The Spitfire crashed and Hale
was killed, much to his comrades' sorrow. On that particular day, the
squadron completed sixty-seven training sorties and dropped 135 practice
bombs.

Clostermann gave Squadron Leader Max Sutherland credit for
developing the dive-bombing technique. And both he and 453's Squadron
Leader Ernie Esau get credit for developing the V2 attack methods using
the Spitfire XVI. Pierre Clostermann thought Sutherland to be 'a typical
English public school product' – whatever that means. Sutherland sported
a small pencil moustache and dark hair brushed back. Before joining the
RAF he had been a London policeman and no mean boxer. One of his
pilots is sure that Sutherland acquired the nickname 'Max' because he had
been a sparring partner of Max Baer, the famous heavyweight boxing
champion. Clostermann described him as being slightly immature with
an inclination to be moody and capable of extreme obstinacy. But on the
other hand he was extremely generous; sometimes serious and quiet when

on duty, exuberant and boisterous in the mess. Another pilot also recalled the unpredictability. On one occasion, Sutherland tore an enormous 'strip' off two new WAAFs who had not saluted him – something that he was quite entitled to complain about, although the reaction seemed overly harsh at the time. But he was a fine pilot and a respected leader in the air. He often flew Spitfire LO●R.

Ernie Esau, 453's CO, who was orphaned at an early age, is remembered as an exuberant, flamboyant sort of man – constantly working away at things, chattering in the air over the R/T, cajoling, pushing, always in at the first and out at the last. His men nicknamed him 'Screaming Ernie'. He had a beaming, infectious smile and a driving enthusiasm for what had to be done to end the war. One of his pilots, Brian Inglis, commented: 'Ernie was a colourful character and I think he would be pleased to be remembered as flamboyant. He was a competent squadron commander, full of energy and action, but his *modus operandi* was to use "break through" techniques at high volume which gave him something of a swashbuckling reputation.'

Another pilot, Russell Baxter, joined 453 after the V2 campaign ended but he recalled:

> *Ernie had the reputation of being rather brash and noisy, but frankly I liked and respected him during the short period that I served under him. Some of our pilots certainly did not like him because he was not slow to dress them down if they stepped out of line. Possibly because I, along with Brian Inglis, had been educated at a private school, I found the mild discipline of the RAAF to be like a Sunday school picnic by comparison. Therefore I found Ernie to be the kind of man I expected to have as my CO – firm but fair, even if a bit noisy. I was sorry when he was posted home to Australia.*

He seems to have been consulted frequently by Group as to the best tactics to employ against the V2s.

Attached to Air Marshal Hill's letter to the Air Ministry of 17 November is an appendix listing targets which had been allocated to 2nd TAF on 16 October, including the goods station at Leiden and billets with a vehicle park at the Hotel Promenade in The Hague. It will be recalled however that 2nd TAF (and Bomber Command) had not been as active as Hill would have wished against other targets and on 10 December the Spitfires turned their attention to these other targets – the station at Leiden and the Hotel Promenade. Leiden is about 12 miles to the north-east of The Hague, roughly a third of the way to Amsterdam and the station is towards the north-west edge of the town. Until now, the Spitfires had been directed primarily at the launching and adjacent storage sites – now they were tackling some of the infrastructure.

The V2 campaign was three months old.

On Sunday, 10 December, the weather at Coltishall started off with visibility between 2 and 4 miles and increasing upper cloud. By the afternoon, visibility was down to 2,000 yards, with the cloud base at 2,000 feet and the first spots of rain starting to fall. Light at first, it gradually increased to become continuous and interspersed with snow. At 08.15, whilst many of the folk living nearby would be having breakfast and thinking about going to church, four Spitfire XVIs of 229 Squadron were taking off, heading for Leiden. Pilot Officer Bill Doidge led the section in 9R●B supported by Flight Sergeant Snowy Wheatley in 9R●S, Flight Lieutenant Bob Sergeant in 9R●E and Flight Sergeant Paddy O'Reilly in 9R●L. The station had been attacked by Typhoons of 2nd TAF and the Spitfires were to assess the damage and if necessary drop their bombs to finish the job. They crossed the Dutch coast at 09.00 at 11,000 feet and found Leiden without any problems, although the 5/10ths cloud obscured the target somewhat. They decided that the Typhoons had not completed the job, so they attacked it too, diving through gaps in the cloud from south-east to north-west, pulling out at 4,000 feet. Paddy O'Reilly and Snowy Wheatley both reported seeing four bombs bursting on the station and possibly another four as they pulled away. They were safely back at Coltishall by 09.55, after an apparently successful operation.

During these attacks, some of the bombs missed the target and hit houses, killing about eight Dutch civilians, although Paddy O'Reilly is certain that 229's attack was accurate. The raid on the Hotel Promenade followed soon after. At 10.00, 602's Flight Lieutenant J.C.R. 'Scotty' Waterhouse took off from Swannington in SM388 LO●W, together with Flight Lieutenant J.R. Sutherland in SM350, Flight Lieutenant G.Y.G. Lloyd in SM301 and Flight Sergeant Michael Francis in SM424 LO●U. They crossed in over The Hague and found the target relatively easily. Bombing from 11,000 feet down to 3,000, they reported two bombs exploding just to the north of the building, with two others to the east. Cloud prevented them seeing much else as they pulled out from the attack dives. There was no flak. They made their way over to Leiden and then Amsterdam but saw nothing of any note and the four landed back at 11.45.

No. 453 Squadron did not carry out any operations during the day but the others flew armed recces in addition to the operations to Leiden and the Hotel Promenade. At 10.30 four Spitfires of 229 took off to attack Wassenaar/Langenhorst, then at 12.35 602 sent a section to attack Wassenaar/Rust-en-Vreugd. Meanwhile 303 completed two armed recces, not specifically targeting the V2s but of a more general free-ranging nature, from Westhoofd to Amsterdam – perhaps illustrating their somewhat different status to the other three squadrons. By the afternoon, with the weather clamping down, operational flying stopped. Three V2s landed on Britain that day – two in the darkness of the early morning and one late in the evening, but none during the hours of daylight. These raids made the newspapers – but not until much later in December – as part of the effort to reassure the Londoners that the V2s did not have it all their own way.

On 11 December, an improvement in the weather allowed operations to resume with all four squadrons active over the more usual targets in and around The Hague. No. 602 attacked the Hotel Promenade again and the Staatspoor railway station where it was believed that liquid oxygen was transferred from trains to motor tankers. Squadron Leader Sutherland led the operation and although they found the Dutch capital covered by cloud, they managed to find a hole in it and drop their bombs accurately. They reported that four dropped on the east end of the station, from which a dense cloud of white smoke arose as well as debris. Another four fell in the centre of the station and more on trucks, other buildings and the railway lines themselves. After his attack and rather against good advice, Squadron Leader Sutherland climbed back up to about 2,000 feet to observe the results of the attack. He professed that 'it was the finest piece of Dive Bombing I had ever seen'. They encountered no flak.

Both on the 10th and the 11th, the squadrons were generally reporting heavy flak when they attacked – on the 11th during their second sortie of the day, 453 attacked a train that turned out to be a flak train. On their previous operation, the flak had been noticeably greater than usual – Brian Inglis recorded in his log book ' "The hook" of Holland. Flak!' In the afternoon of the 11th, at 15.00, four 229 Spitfires took off from Coltishll – led by Flight Lieutenant Patterson, the pilots were Flight Lieutenant McAndrew, Pilot Officer Doidge and Flight Sergeant O'Reilly. The ORB describes the operation:

> *The 3rd. Armed Recce of the day with bombs was led by F/Lt. Patterson and took off at 15.00 to bomb Wassenaar Rust en Vraigd* [sic]. *Crossing in near Westhoofd at 11,000 feet they flew to the target to find it obscured in mist. A hospital could be seen in very close proximity. They orbited at 10,000 feet waiting for the mist to clear and then 'peeled off' in a steep turn to dive from more or less E to W. from 10,000 feet to 4,000 feet. F/Lt. Patterson's bombs fell about 5 yards from the corner of a very tall and large 5 storey building about 100 yards North of the suspected site. All the rest fell on the pinpoint which was North of and along the side of the road. They were met by the heaviest flak yet, a very intense carpet of light flak, very accurate and from the woods about 1 mile round the pinpoint. It burst in white puffs and P/O Doidge thought it was mist. F/Lt. McAndrew fired into it and F/Sgt. O'Reilly, flying No.4 had to decide whether to dive straight in against what looked hopeless odds, or pull away. He did the former and dived straight*

*into it. Nobody was hit although they were still followed by heavy accurate
flak and light from the coast off Hague and Katwijk. They crossed out North
of the Hague at 4/6,000 feet at 15.45 hours and flew South to Hook where
they reformed and set course landing Coltishall at 16.40 hours.*

*This was perhaps the most opposition yet and called for great courage
from all the pilots.*

There is no explanation for the sudden apparent increase in the flak
defences as perceived by the pilots.

But the squadron celebrated that night.

*At 6.0pm. the Squadron dinner and dance on the occasion of the presenta-
tion of the Squadron crest, a boar's head pierced by a sword with the motto
'Be Bold'. This crest has taken a considerable time to acquire but after final
arrangement by the 'Chester Herald' and approval by the King. At 18.00
hours the officers of the squadron foregathered in the bar to meet the AOC,
AVM Henderson . . . Dinner was served at 20.00 hours. Major Harrison
was at the head with Gp. Cpt. Donaldson and the AOC on either hand. F/Lt.
Patterson was at the foot of the table. Dinner was excellent and a thorough
success . . .*

*At 21.00 hours everyone proceeded to the dance held at the airmans' [sic]
mess where the AOC made a speech which was followed by a farewell speech
by our very much respected CO, Major Harrison. Then the dance continued
and beer flowed freely, the CO was frequently toasted and men of all ranks
came to wish him every good wish. The dance lasted until midnight when
everyone again set course for the bar at the officers' mess.*

Two days later, command passed
to the promoted 'Pat' Patterson.
He was remembered as a bit of a
'loner' and not a great deal is
known about him. It is perhaps
ironic that having just received its
badge and a new CO, 229 would be
disbanded a few weeks later. On
the 16th, Flying Officer Leslie Trail
and Warrant Officer Eric Mee
joined 229. Another of Mee's
'memoirs' gives an insights into life
on 229.

Warrant Officer Eric Mee.
(The late Eric Mee.)

I was ordered to report to RAF Matlaske and arrived there at 2am in the early hours of the morning. Presenting myself at the guardhouse, I was directed to a hut by a grumpy duty guard. Dog tired, I made up my bed and was dead to the world until 10.30 the following morning.

Due to report that morning I asked for, and was given directions to the flight lines. Tramping the considerable distance, lugging my kit bag of course, I thought everything seemed strangely quiet, no sounds of aircraft engines being run up and no sight of aircraft taking off. However all was made clear when I went into the control tower and asked where I could find 229 Squadron. I was told 'They haven't been here for some time, they moved to Coltishall a while ago.[4] By the way, we've already got them to send over a truck top pick up an Aussie pilot who has been posted there and he went a while ago.' This Aussie, it transpired was Johnny Green, who had arrived earlier the day before and had had a good night's sleep. Another phone call went out from flying control Matlaske requesting transport for another somewhat bewildered pilot. I gathered from remarks made on the phone that the squadron were not at all pleased at having to send out another truck. Eventually it arrived and I was transported to Coltishall. First stop was the squadron CO's office where I met the 'boss' – S/L Patterson. He studied my log book and asked why I was late arriving, so I explained what had happened. Whilst answering his questions I could not help but stare fascinated at the wall above his head. It had a Spitfire's windscreen on it. The windscreen had been hit right in the centre by a bullet which had however not penetrated the two inch thick toughened glass but had starred it into an opaque mess. It must have saved someone's life – but I never did hear the story behind it.

Next I was introduced to my Flight Commander, F/L Rigler. He started off my squadron career by administering a right rollicking to me for being late reporting for duty, the fact that I had been sent to the wrong airfield was made to appear my fault entirely. Somehow he had got the idea that I had arrived at Matlaske at 2pm the previous day, not 2am that morning. It was quite a while before he and I really got on together but we did in the end.

We had solid brick combined mess and living quarters including toilets and bathroom with unlimited hot water on tap. There were two to a room which had a wash basin with hot and cold water. I was to share a room with Tommy Thomson who was to become a very close friend. Tommy had already done a few ops and his help and advice was a great help to a new boy like me. We had a comfortable, centrally heated lounge with leather armchairs just right for sleeping in. The food was excellent and outside the mess were landscaped flower beds and shrubs.

Until Christmas Eve, the bad weather set in and curtailed operations greatly. Some armed recces were undertaken but generally flying was limited to training flights over England. The numbers of V2s landing in Britain varied: on the 15th there were seven, on the 16th none, on the 17th and 18th only two, on the 19th five. Although many came in the hours of darkness, daylight did not necessarily bring relief. On the 24th, though, good weather returned and a significant operation, Big Ben Ramrod 16, was laid on in the morning against a block of flats in the Marlot area of The Hague right in the centre of the V2 activity – Duindigt racecourse to the north-west, Beukenhorst to the north, Langenhorst to the north-east and the Haagsche Bosch to the south-west. Also, to the north lay the estate at Wittenburg, a large country house and stable block used by the Germans to store and prepare V2s for launching (see Appendix 2).

The Germans used the flats at Marlot as a headquarters and billets for their troops. The block was around a square courtyard, described as being 80 yards by 100 yards and, by one Dutchman, as of an 'English' style. It provided comfortable living accommodation very much within the operational area for firing the rockets. Freddy van Dyck is sure that it also served as an HQ for the Gestapo, with papers concerning the Resistance kept there, and that the attack was asked for by the Resistance. The Ramrod had been planned for several days but consistent bad weather brought successive postponements.

Dawn found Coltishall white with a hard frost but with clear blue skies, and just as the sun lifted above the horizon the pilots and ground crews at the dispersals saw several V2 trails in the distance. The three Spitfire XVI squadrons would all be involved so it was a big operation, starting with a weather recce. Flying Officer Carter and Warrant Officer Carmichael of 453 Squadron took off from Swannington at 08.25 and headed out at 10,000 feet, making landfall at The Hague. They found haze over the North Sea rising to 500 feet but clear air above, and over the Netherlands unlimited visibility. They described the conditions as 'perfect' and returned at 09.40 having radioed back their observations, so allowing the Spitfires to be appropriately bombed up. In the meantime, four of 303 Squadron's Spitfire IXs took off at 08.30, just after 453's weather recce, to strafe Rust-en-Vreugd and Huis te Werve. They could not see whether their attacks were successful and ran the gauntlet of accurate light flak whilst attacking Rust-en-Vreugd. They were back at 10.30 and must have passed the other aircraft on their way out. Although 303 would not be bombing, they had a small role in the attack in that they were tasked to provide escort to two PRU Mustangs of 26 Squadron, who were to photograph the results of the attack. They were first off. Flight Lieutenant K. Bartys in MA528 and Sergeant Sztuka in BS281 took off at 10.00 to meet the two Mustangs, one of which returned early with engine trouble.

The plan called for 229 Squadron to bomb first, then 602 and then 453, but with the slightly different distances from the two airfields 602 was actually off first at 10.05. They supplied ten aircraft, led by Flight

Lieutenant Waterhouse. The others were Warrant Officer L.T. Menzies, Flight Lieutenant J.R. Sutherland, Warrant Officer Toone, Flying Officer Farrell, Flight Lieutenant Banton, Flight Lieutenant Pertwee, Flight Lieutenant Pullman, Flying Officer R.H.C. Thomerson and Flight Lieutenant G.D. Stephenson. They were armed with two 250-pound bombs on the wings and a 500-pounder on the fuselage, and would refuel at Ursel after the attack. Freddy van Dyck said that the need for accuracy was made very clear to them, mainly to avoid civilian casualties. At their briefing he said the CO promised a bottle of Scotch to the pilot who put all his bombs in the centre of the target.

Five minutes later the first wave, 229 Squadron took off from Coltishall; twelve aircraft in all led by the CO, Squadron Leader Patterson. The others were Pilot Officer Doidge, Flight Sergeant Wheatley, Flight Lieutenant McAndrew, Pilot Officer Grant, Flight Sergeant Thomson, Flight Lieutenant Kirkman, Pilot Officer McConnochie, Flight Sergeant Haupt, Warrant Officer Cookson and Pilot Officer van Dyck. At the same time, Bob Sergeant also took off but he would be acting as No. 2 to Wing Commander Fitzgerald and they would return directly to Coltishall after observing the attack. Needing more fuel, they carried two 250-pound bombs and a drop tank whilst the others had the same load as 602 with the aim of refuelling at Ursel as well.

Bill Doidge in 9R●H, did not get far. Whilst in the circuit and waiting for the squadron to form up, his engine cut. With quick thinking, he decided to try to put the aeroplane down on the extension strip at the dispersal, which meant that he had to make his approach steep and fast, and at right angles to the runway in use. He managed to touch down successfully but just then the undercarriage collapsed and the Spitfire slid on its belly for about 100 yards before coming to a stop. But the contact with the ground shook the 500-pound bomb and one of the 250-pounders loose and they both bounced across the ground scattering onlookers. The 229 ORB described it as, 'a signal for general panic among the onlookers. The word "bombs" coupled with a suitable service adjective being freely used. Most of the crowd ran away from the crash but the usual half dozen "mad types" ran to the rescue.' Fortunately, the bombs did not explode and Doidge sustained no injuries, although he was a bit shaken. Nonetheless he managed to 'give a quiet discourse on technical details concerning angle of dive etc.'.

Another pilot also returned shortly after with what he thought was engine trouble when he found that it kept cutting out as he tried to switch over to the drop tank. Of course, on this operation the tank was replaced by a 500-pound bomb in place of the tank! He landed successfully.

At 10.25, 453 took to the skies over Swannington, led by Ernie Esau. The other pilots were Flying Officer 'Swamp' Marsh in FU●W, Flight Lieutenant Bill Bennett, Flight Sergeant McAuliffe, Flying Officer Grady,

Freddy van Dyck. This was taken in June 1945 after transferring to 349 (Belgian) Squadron based at Wunstorf.
(*Freddy van Dyck.*)

Warrant Officer Stewart, Flying Officer Clemesha, Flying Officer Wilson, Pilot Officer York, Flight Sergeant Lynch, Warrant Officer Peters and Pilot Officer Brian Inglis in FU●F. Once formed up, they turned to the east.

Meanwhile, the 229 formation crossed the enemy coast at 10.55 south of Zandvoort at 10,000 feet and shortly after turned south towards The Hague and straight to the target, which they managed to identify without any problems in the gin-clear air. The sight of the formation of Spitfires must have been quite special, especially bearing in mind Jan van't Hoff's comments that even just seeing the Allied aircraft over them boosted the civilians' morale. Wing Commander Fitzgerald and Bob Sergeant went down first to open the raid at about 11.00. They pulled out at 3,000 feet then re-formed together to the north to watch the rest of the attacks. The rest of 229 went down at 11.04. They hit the south-west corner of the building and in towards the central courtyard and reported seeing a fire breaking out and a lot of smoke and dust, which eventually stopped them seeing more. However, they seemed to think that they had bombed successfully. The Germans replied with medium and light flak, which the pilots reported as being 'moderate'. Freddy van Dyck remembered that there were machine-guns on the roof and the Germans included tracer rounds in the flak, which he found particularly disconcerting. 'It came very fast and seemed to be heading straight for you.' He said there was a 'lot of it about', and he had to concentrate hard to keep the Spitfire going down at the right angle and did not have time to pay attention to anything else. After dropping his bombs, which he is sure hit the building, he eased back slowly on the stick to avoid blacking out then turned east towards the rendezvous over the Zuider Zee. 'Arriving there I couldn't see any Spitfires and after waiting for ten minutes I dived down and at low level went back to the target for a quick look at the damage.' The 229 Squadron Spitfires headed for Ursel without van Dyck.

No. 602 went in next, bombing south-east to north-west from 9,000 to 2,000 feet. Apart from two overshoots and an undershoot, they reported all their bombs landing on the west corner of the flats and on the ground nearby. They thought that they must have caused considerable damage judging from the amount of smoke. Following their attack, the squadron re-formed and followed 229 to Ursel.

Finally, came 453. They made landfall at 10,000 feet at The Hague and flew straight to Marlot. They bombed at right angles to 602 – south-west to north-east – pulling out at 3,000 feet. Half their bombs landed on the flats and half undershot. By now the Germans were wide awake and the diving Spitfires were subjected to withering flak. Bill Bennett in SM187 FU●N seemed to take a direct hit. The aeroplane disintegrated in mid-air but Bennett managed to get out at about 1,000 feet – quite low. His parachute opened but being near to the ground it soon disappeared in the forest between the target and the Duindigt Racecourse. There was hope that Bennett had survived and indeed he had, although he became a POW. He returned to the squadron on 17 May 1945 after being released at the end of the war. Russell Leith recalled Bennett as 'an aggressive pilot and leader'.

The remaining eleven Spitfires turned south for Ursel, where they landed at 11.55, a quarter of an hour after 229 and at much the same time as 602. After all the attacks had finished, Wing Commander Fitzgerald and Bob Sergeant continued to orbit the flats to try to estimate the damage,

Flight Lieutenant Bill Bennett.
(Australian War Memorial Negative no. UK2204.)

then they turned for home, crossing the coast at 11.15 and landing at Coltishall at 11.55. As well as these two, the whole attack was witnessed by the two 303 Squadron Spitfires and the remaining PRU Mustang, which arrived over The Hague at 10.45. Following the bombing, the Mustang took its pictures and at 11.30 the three aeroplanes turned west once more. They too found intense flak directed at them and reported some R/T problems which they attributed to interference. The Mustang retained its escort until 20 miles from Felixstowe, when the Spitfires peeled off for Coltishall to land there at 12.25, having been airborne for almost two and a half hours.

As we have seen, 229's Freddy van Dyck returned by himself to have a look at the building after 453 had finished. 'The place was surrounded by a lot of German soldiers and smoke was rising from the building. I then fired a long burst to keep things lively before heading south.' He also recalled seeing the tail of Bill Bennett's Spitfire sticking out of some rubble. He made his way to Ursel on his own.

The photographs and the reports from the pilots suggested that considerable damage had been done although it was always difficult to be precise in this sort of attack. Some photographs showed 'extensive damage to the clock tower and buildings and smoke pouring from the courtyard'. Interestingly, there are suggestions that the Germans knew of the attack and few of them stayed around to be under it. It is also suggested that this is one of the instances when the Germans might have infiltrated the Resistance groups and could intercept radio messages. The inference is that because they knew of the raid before it happened they pulled their people out and possibly strengthened the flak defences. But according to Roderic Hill, 'the building was so badly damaged that the Germans had to leave it'.

No. 453's 'Swamp' Marsh's log book notes: 'Attacked billets near Hague – bags of Flak – Bill Bennett bailed out.' And Brian Inglis made the cryptic note in his log book 'V2 "Boffins" home.' Freddy van Dyck of 229 wrote, 'Attack on V2 H.Q. by 30 a/c. Heavy flak. 1 Spit shot down. Drop my bombs on building in La Hague.' Ursel had run out of bombs that day, which meant that on the return leg of the operation, the three squadrons had to be content with strafing the targets in The Hague rather than bombing them, but 303 and elements of the Spitfire XVI squadrons continued their more normal attacks against the usual targets in The Hague and its environs. This attack 'hit the press' as well. One paper produced a stylized and overly dramatic impression of the day's activities.

Back at Coltishall while the raid took place, the Spitfire brought down in an emergency landing by 229's Bill Doidge had to be dealt with. First the unexploded bombs had to be defused by the armourers, Sergeant Arthur Inch being one. He recalled an occasion when a Spitfire flown by Snowy

Wheatley crashed on take-off with a 500-pound bomb on the centre line and a 250-pounder bomb on each wing. It overshot the runway, landing on its belly and gouging a furrow in the mud before coming to a stop. The pilot was out of it in a flash and ran for safety. Then came the question as to what was to be done with the bombs, still on the Spitfire and dug into the mud. Arthur Inch was a sergeant armourer and he recalled that all of the other airmen around turned to look at him, waiting for him to sort the situation out. Taking his courage in both hands, he cautiously approached the crashed Spitfire then crawled carefully underneath it. Each bomb had to have its tail fin removed and the fuses unscrewed and gingerly set aside, then the detonators. It was only then that he could declare the aeroplane safe and let the other airmen get on with their recovery work. This illustrates the sort of challenges and dangers that the ground crews faced and overcame. The pilots could not have flown the sorties without them and most will freely acknowledge this.

Years after the war, Freddy van Dyck had an interesting encounter with a Dutchman who had seen the attack. Freddy and his wife were visiting the tulip fields in the vicinity of The Hague. The tour completed, he decided to drive back to the city to find the location of the building that was the target in 1944. An elderly gentleman came over and told them how to get there. He then asked for the reason for Freddy's interest, and on being told, he took Freddy's hands and informed him that at the time of the attack he had lived near to the building and added 'I was most impressed when a lone Spitfire came back later and fired at the Germans – there were a lot of casualties. You must remember that we were starving and hated the Germans. Seeing them being cut down was pure joy. After this attack the plane flew low over our city and for us it was quite a boost

for our morale.' Later whilst driving home, Freddy's wife said 'About that pilot who went back after the bombing – don't you think he was a little crazy?' Freddy replied 'You should know – you married him!'

Three V2s landed in the UK on Christmas Eve.

Pilot Officer Brian Inglis flew on

Brian Inglis of 453 Squadron. His father's Air Corps wings from the First World War can be clearly seen on his left breast.
(*Sir Brian Inglis.*)

the Marlot raid with 453 Squadron. Known as 'Bing' to friends on the squadron, he was born in Adelaide in South Australia in 1924 so at the time of the Marlot raid was a week or so short of his twenty-first birthday. Educated at Geelong Church of England Grammar School he successfully matriculated at the end of 1942, aged 17. In peacetime, the next step would have been university, but with the war well under way, and having already been 'called up' in April, instead of a campus his next destination was the RAAF. It was a natural choice for the young man, whose father fought the Germans in the skies above France in the First World War with the Australian Flying Corps (AFC) in SE5A scouts. The younger Inglis wore his father's AFC wings on his battledress 'for luck'. He was a confident young man, who survived the war and went on to have a highly successful career in business and engineering.

No. 12 Group conducted no operations on Christmas Day, not because of the festival but because the weather clamped in with heavy fog. The very early morning started off fine but by 09.00 the developing haze became a mist and soon after visibility fell to about 50 yards[5]. No. 602 made their way across to Swannington from Matlaske as usual and 229 at Coltishall were down at the flights expecting to be flying but eventually the release order came in time for both to enjoy a decent Christmas dinner in the evening. In the British and Australian air forces Christmas dinner was traditionally served to the airmen by the officers and senior NCOs and this tradition continued. Warrant Officer Eric Mee kept the menu for his dinner; it included cream of celery soup, roast turkey with parsley stuffing, roast and creamed potatoes, Brussels sprouts, Christmas pudding and cheese and biscuits washed down with beer and 'minerals'! Cigarettes were also supplied. He clearly enjoyed his meal and afterwards 'succumbed to the lure of the leather armchairs in the mess'!

No V2s landed on England on Christmas Day.

The officers and NCOs of 453 Squadron enjoyed their meals in their respective messes on the evening of Boxing Day. There were decorations aplenty at Coltishall, and the festivities included dances and parties. There were two sittings of Christmas dinner with a musical interlude. The Concert Party laid on a pantomime, 'Cinderella of Stratton Hall', which got excellent reviews.

Rusty Leith spent Christmas 1944 with the Dickson family in Orpington, Mrs Dickson being a distant relative. Having experienced several Christmases in the UK, a winter December (rather than the Australian warm summer ones he had been used to) was no novelty, but a white Christmas was. 'We had the coldest Christmas for fifty years. The frost was terrific, so much so that all the leafless twigs looked like white coral. Strangely enough, along with the cold came a succession of thick fogs. On Christmas Day in Orpington we couldn't see twenty yards.' He returned to Matlaske on the 27th.

In the Netherlands, the population starved, froze and died. By now, most men between the ages of sixteen and forty-five had been rounded up and sent to Germany for forced labour. Jan van't Hoff was fifteen just under the critical age. The effects of the freezing weather and the *Hungerwinter* took their toll. The waterways froze over and snow lay on the ground. Life was an absolute struggle. The constant search for food and fuel meant that much of the family's possessions were bartered away. A couple of potatoes or a handful of grain brought some relief. With the city's trams removed to Germany, the people's bikes confiscated or stolen by the occupiers, no electricity or gas, life could not be much worse and many succumbed. In December, the weekly rations amounted to half a loaf of bread for the family, perhaps a few potatoes and a small amount of degreased cheese. By February, the van't Hoff family would be reduced to eating tulip bulbs and raw sugarbeet to survive. And as for Christmas, there was little to celebrate with so much misery.

The only ornaments for a virtual Christmas tree were the strips of silver paper ('window') dropped by the Allied bombers in order to disturb the enemy radar. Riet and I kept ourselves busy trying to find a tree but to cut it to pieces for our stove to try to keep warm and not to decorate. Sometimes the Spitfires helped us when they accidentally knocked down a house nearby so we tried to get hold of doorposts or whatever would burn.

An aerial view of the damage caused at the Prince of Wales explosion on Boxing Day 1944.
(Courtesy Imperial War Museum. Negative no. CH15115.)

Jules Borsboom developed an ingenious way to make soup. Han rememberd that his father used to leave small pieces of food in the hallway of the house to attract seagulls in. Then he would shut the door to trap them then catch and kill them. So the people's agony continued with no end in sight.

On Boxing Day, at 21.26, a V2 landed at Islington, north of King's Cross, and killed about seventy people. The explosion centred on Mackenzie Road, a few yards from the Prince of Wales pub, which was full – more than usually so being Boxing Day and because the pub down the road had run out of beer. The bar floor gave way and took the customers into the cellar with it, as well as masonry from the roof and walls. Rescue efforts were hampered by a thick mist, making it difficult for rescuers to find casualties, and the cold meant the injured ran the risk of exposure. Divisional Fire Officer Cyril Demarne recalled:

> The glow of a number of fires could be seen through swirling fog as a trailer pump operator set his suction hose into an emergency water dam. He attempted to draw water without success. A horrible thought entered his mind; surely it was not empty? He shone his torch through the door and saw that the water was frozen with the suction strainer lying on the ice. He smashed the ice with a large axe and soon the water was flowing and the men were bringing the fires under control.[6]

The weather did not clear until the 28th, which saw a full day's worth of operations, including attacks on the Hotel Promenade target area by both 303 and 229 Squadrons. Other targets hit included Rust-en-Vreugd, Langenhorst and the Haagsche Bosch. The generally poor weather prevented operations on the 29th, but in a slight change of tack on the 30th, 453 acted as escort to thirteen Lancasters of 617 Squadron carrying out an attack on U-boat pens at IJmuiden. Twelve of their Spitfires took off at 15.25, and at 15,000 feet met the Lancasters. The formation then flew straight to the target, to find it covered with patches of cloud. The bombers circled the area once, and then headed back to base without bombing. The Spitfires landed back at 16.50. For 229 the day turned into a bit of a shambles. Eight aircraft took off on a training flight in the morning but the weather closed in unexpectedly and although two (one being Eric Mee) managed to get back in at Coltishall, the others finished up at various stations – Wittering, King's Cliffe and Wenting. 'Both Met. and Ops. were blamed for this fracas and both indulged in some "passing of the buck" to each other.'

In the evening, the BBC *War Commentary* broadcast an account of the dive-bombing of the V2s by 229's Tommy Rigler and Johnny Welch, which seemed to get approval from the squadron, although the two involved expressed some disappointment that much of their account had been edited out. Another highlight that evening was the WAAF Gang Show, made even more interesting for 229 because one of them was Flight Lieutenant McAndrew's sister, who 'gave an excellent display of ventriloquism in very short skirts' which was clearly much approved – the only down side being that Flight Lieutenant McAndrew was on leave!

Then came New Year's Eve, Sunday. The squadrons wakened to hard overnight frost and after some initial cloud, the skies cleared, but there was a covering of ice on the roads and the runways at Swannington so that it seemed at first that no flying would be possible from there. However, it quickly melted and all four of the squadrons flew operations, although they were curtailed, particularly by poor weather over the Netherlands. No. 229 carried out a particularly interesting Ramrod in the early afternoon targeted on the Haagsche Bosch. Twelve aircraft, each carrying a 500-pound bomb with .025 second delay and two 250-pound bombs fused for airburst, took off from Coltishall at 12.55 led by the CO, Squadron Leader Patterson. Reports had been received of six V2s in one part of the wood and a total of twelve in two others. The formation made landfall at Katwijk at 10,000 feet and flew south, following the main road until at 8,500 feet they reached The Hague. As they were about to attack, Squadron Leader Patterson's R/T failed, which created some uncertainty amongst the pilots as to when they should start their bombing dives. Nonetheless, they bombed successfully and with the exception of one bomb which they reported falling on houses, they thought that all of the rest landed on the pinpoints. Some reported seeing a particularly vivid red flash which might have been a direct hit on one of the rockets. The ORB continues:

> *The target was covered in a curtain of intense accurate light flak at 4,000 ft. and the last pilots went in with some trepidation. The only handicap of the whole effort, was that the last 2 sections turned to dive upon the objective from too far away, making the dive at too small an angle which had to be rectified and somewhere impeded accuracy of aim. S/Ldr. Donovan's aircraft received slight damage in the spinner from flak and he now covets the same to keep as a war relic for 'line shoots'. They crossed out over the Hague at heights varying from 3,000 feet to zero feet at 13.40 hours encountering very intense very accurate flak from the coastal area (sanddunes) F/Lt. Kirkman reported seeing some Jerries chasing to the guns as he crossed out. Other pilots reported seeing light flak guns on roof tops. The fire followed them 2/3 miles out to sea and F/LT. Sergeant appears to have had a particularly bad time with flak all around and behind following him with persistency as he crossed out. The squadron reformed 3 miles out to sea N.W. of the Hague at 1,500 feet and set course for Ursel (B.67) landing there at 14.20 hours. P/O Van Dyck failed to reform as he climbed into cloud to avoid flak and found himself alone in emerging. He returned*

to the target and set course independently for Ursel. F/Sgt. Wheatley who said he was remaining behind to report on the bombing became very alarmed when he found himself alone and after 'asking' for a vector landed at Knocke (B.83) Le Zoote. The Squadron took off from Ursel after refuelling at 15.35 hours and all landed safely at base at 16.45 hours.

It is interesting that the Ramrod was laid on because of reports (possibly from the Resistance) of the storage of the V2s. Also interesting are the reports of the 'vivid red flash' and the possibility of a direct hit on a rocket, the flak which seems to have been unusually heavy and finally the problems caused by the CO's radio becoming useless and the problems of control that seem to ensue. Freddy van Dyck, on his own again, wrote in his log book 'Attack on V2 site in middle of La Hague. 12,000 lb dropped. Bombing not so good.'

Whilst this was going on, 453 completed three armed recces over The Hague. No. 602 started one operation but were recalled. No. 303 completed only two operational sorties escorting a PRU Mustang to The Hague, probably taking photographs of the 229 Ramrod target.

Eight V2s landed on Britain that day, all in the hours of darkness – the first at 00.35, the last at 23.40. So 1944 drew to a close; the first V2 of 1945 exploded at Laindon at 01.55 on 1 January.

For the pilots and ground crews there were celebrations. Coltishall held an 'all ranks' dance, at which the 229 officers and ground crews happily mixed. No doubt similar gatherings took place at Matlaske. Perhaps more than Christmas, it was a time of reflection. The war in Europe was almost over. There was the possibility of an end in sight, albeit a fearsome Japan still had to be defeated. For the Australians this might mean a move to the Pacific and nearer to home. For the Poles, there was a growing sense of betrayal. As the others contemplated victory and a return to a world without war, they must have seen that Poland was unlikely to get the freedom they had fought for. If the British and Australians drank that night in celebration, the Poles must have been drinking in despair.

No. 602 being a Scottish squadron – and Glaswegian at that – the high-spirited pilots cheerfully and enthusiastically embraced the festival of Hogmanay. The station would surely have resounded to at least a few choruses of 'I belong to Glasgow' which, according to Max Baerlein, tended to be sung with gusto, even although many of the pilots had never been to Glasgow!

In his account,[7] Air Marshal Hill suggested that a fifth phase of the V2 campaign started on 1 January, based on his analysis of the effectiveness of the Spitfire attacks until the end of December. A hundred and fifty-four V2s landed on British soil in November and 134 in December. Hill noted that at the end of November, the average daily number was seven but that it reduced to four in mid-December and slightly less at the end of the month. But why should this be? Was it the divebombing or were there other factors? Hill concluded that the apparent reduction could not be attributed solely to the Spitfires, although it would be easy to draw this conclusion. He was complimentary about the accuracy and skill of the Spitfire pilots, likening them to 'the picked crews of No. 2 Group in some of their spectacular attacks on buildings used as headquarters by the Germans'. Clearly the pilots were carrying out their duties admirably. But he stated:

> *The chief factor in limiting the scale of the attack was almost certainly the rate at which supplies could be brought to the firing areas; and this in turn must have been mainly determined by the frequency and success of the armed reconnaissance and rail interdiction sorties flown by the Second Tactical Air Force over the enemy's lines of communication.*

He also suggested that preparations for the German attack in the Ardennes diverted some of the missiles that would otherwise have fallen on the south-east corner of England to Antwerp. On the face of it, he appears to be saying that the effect of the divebombing was perhaps not as significant as he would have liked, but he did make the point – borne out by the records – that over the period, the timing of the launches tended to move into the hours of darkness, presumably to avoid the attentions of the marauding Spitfires. And why would this be significant? Because, he postulated, 'casualties were generally lower after dark, when most people were at home, than in the daytime, when they were massed together in factories and offices and in the streets'.

He concluded that forcing the Germans to fire their rockets at night 'was definitely favourable' although the people who were caught up in the Prince of Wales pub blast on Boxing Day probably took a different view. He went on: 'Clearly, our fighter-bomber programme was not such an effective deterrent as we had hoped.'

He did however, acknowledge that without the divebombing attacks, the numbers of V2s being launched might have been greater. However, there remained the problem of how to force further reduction. During December, the Air Ministry asked the Foreign Office and the Ministry of Economic Warfare to look into the effectiveness of carrying out attacks on the factories producing liquid oxygen, the basic fuel of the V2s, and in that way, disrupting the launches. It will be recalled that the fuel was loaded only just before launch and that liquid oxygen needed to be kept at cryogenic temperature. They concluded that there were ten liquid oxygen factories in Germany and eight in the Netherlands. Three in the Netherlands invited particular attention, one near Dordrecht, another at IJmuiden and a third in a suburb of The Hague called Loosduinen. Attacks on the latter two would involve a heavy risk to surrounding buildings and civilians. (Some Dutch historians are sure that all liquid oxygen came from factories in Germany by rail and that no factories existed in the Netherlands.) In the meantime, Hill considered his options.

New Year's Day brought poor weather – at Coltishall low cloud at about 700 feet and visibility about 1,500 yards, reducing to 800 in fog. Operations resumed, however. On the Continent, the Germans launched two major assaults to assist the offensive in the Ardennes. The first, Operation *Nordwind,* started just before midnight south of the Ardennes in the Vosges and a few hours later at first light, Operation *Boddenplatte,* which involved hundreds of *Luftwaffe* aircraft attacking Allied airfields in Belgium and the southern Netherlands and catching many aircraft on the ground, destroying about 300. Whilst both operations created alarm for the Allies, they achieved little. *Nordwind* sucked enemy troops away from the Ardennes battles, where they might have been better employed, and although *Boddenplatte* cost the Allies dearly in terms of aircraft, the *Luftwaffe* lost a similar number – about 215 to the Allies and another 80 or so to their own 'friendly fire' – which in the longer term reduced their ability to defend the retreating German armies both because of the aeroplanes lost and – perhaps more important – because of the loss of experienced pilots.

Amongst the airfields attacked were several that were used by the squadrons: Ursel, Maldegem and Deurne. Over the next few days, the weather interfered with the operations. The targets by and large were the usual ones, the Hotel Promenade being attacked again, but on the 3rd a major operation came along against a new target, the tram sheds at Loosduinen, which Air Marshal Hill thought was one of the liquid oxygen factories. He had decided that although civilian areas adjoined two sides of the sheds with a canal basin opposite, the accuracy of the dive bombing could allow the target to be attacked with a minimum of civilian damage. He decided to attack it both because of the Air Ministry's request that more could be done to attack the infrastructure supporting the V2s and because of his 'desire to leave nothing undone which offered a chance of hampering the enemy'. He went on: 'In order to reduce the risk to civilian property to a minimum, the pilots chosen for the job were instructed to use methods which can be best described as "trickling their bombs towards the target".' Quite what this means is not clear and some of the pilots involved in the attacks did not understand it either! Presumably it meant that they aimed the bombs just to the canal side of the buildings and the following aircraft dropped theirs closer.

Hill must have made the decision to attack Loosduinen fairly quickly. It is interesting that some Dutch historians do not agree that it was a fuel factory, but rather, if anything, just a motor park and workshop. Nonetheless, for the Spitfire attackers, it appeared on the target lists as a factory and as far as they were concerned, this is what they were bombing.

Initially, on 3 January, the first order went to 229 and 602 Squadrons to provide twelve Spitfires each. The pilots were told that the building construction was brick and light metal with a glass roof, but that the walls were strengthened in case the liquid oxygen exploded. 'Heavy and accurate' bombing would be the order of the day, and the target should be destroyed in a single attack. Photographs would be taken by two Mustangs of 26 Squadron escorted by two of 303's Spitfires. But after all the preparation, this operation did not go ahead because of the weather. The attack was ordered and then cancelled a number of times before it finally happened for the first time on 3 February.

The weather clamped down; it snowed and there was mist. Sunday, 7 January saw an odd event at Coltishall which presaged a change for 229 Squadron. Fairly early on, and apparently unexpected, Wing Commander Christopher Foxley-Norris arrived at the railway station in Norwich with about twenty-nine aircrew and 264 ground crew of the disbanded 603 Squadron, the City of Edinburgh Squadron of the Auxiliary Air Force with whom 602 had a long-standing but friendly rivalry. They were all just off a troopship from Egypt, where the squadron had been flying Beaufighters. Foxley-Norris recalled that whilst chatting with him over a pint in the bar of the Coltishall officers' mess, the Sector Commander, Group Captain Arthur Donaldson, asked what the squadron code was so it could be painted on their Spitfires. Foxley-Norris, rather surprised, stammered out that they flew Beaufighters and no doubt it would be obvious that many

1990s gate guardian replica at RAF Turnhouse near Edinburgh, home of
603 Squadron.
(Author.)

of the aircrew were navigators! Many of them left shortly after to go to Banff near Elgin in Morayshire to fly as part of the Banff Strike Wing whilst the groundcrew element, 6603 Service Echelon, found themselves billeted at Matlaske. But rumour abounded. On 10 January, the 229 Squadron ORB was noting that, although there was no confirmation, it was believed that 229 Squadron had become 603 that day, and they made the diary entry 603. The compiler said that in 1942 603 Squadron had disbanded to become 229 and that this latest change merely changed things back to the way they had been – although they had none of the 1942 records to confirm this of course. It was not until 24 January that official notification was received that it was indeed 603 Squadron. In the interim, they had referred to the unit as '229/603 Squadron' or '603/229 Squadron', a solution which caused a little embarrassment in administration circles!

Officially, the switch seems to be taken as having happened on 10 January. It marked a quirky aspect to the change that happened in Malta in August 1942 when 603, then flying Spitfire Vs and commanded by Squadron Leader Bill Douglas, disbanded to become 229. Now the reverse happened – 229 disbanded to become 603, although the pilots flew the same aircraft from the same airfield carrying out the same operations. Like 602, 603 formed in 1925 as the Edinburgh Squadron of the Auxiliary Air Force, basing itself in a 'town headquarters' – what had been a large private house in the centre of Edinburgh – and flying out of what became RAF Turnhouse (and eventually Edinburgh Airport) to the west of Scotland's capital. Like 602, it started off as a bomber squadron but by 1939 it had also turned to the fighter role and been equipped with Spitfires. Along with 602, it took part in the action on 16 October 1939 when the first German aircraft, a Ju88, was brought down over the UK. Although 603 and 602 shot down one each at more or less the same time, it seems that 603 and Flight Lieutenant 'Patsy' Gifford could claim the first – although only by minutes. It fought valiantly in the Battle of Britain but in 1942 it moved to the Mediterranean, where it disbanded to become 229 Squadron on Malta, then re-formed in early 1943 flying Beaufighters operating in the maritime strike role. It is interesting though that 602 and 603 should be ending the war fighting alongside each other as they had been when it started in 1939 – and both flying Spitfires.

The squadron's badge reflected its origins, portraying the three-towered David's Castle, symbolic of Edinburgh Castle which dominates the city and the motto *Gin ye Daur* – 'If you dare'. No. 603's identification code was XT but it would be some weeks before they replaced 229's 9R – not until March. No. 229 never re-formed. Only a month after getting word of the approval of their new crest, the number became history.

It is a tragedy that the first casualty of the new 603 occurred the following day, the 11th, and all the more so because the individual concerned, Flying Officer Leslie Trail, was engaged to be married on his next leave. He and Flight Lieutenant Bob Sergeant were tasked with a Jim Crow to Terschelling and Den Helder, to the north of The Hague, which was a major port. They took off from Coltishall at 09.20 flying Spitfires 'E' and 'C' (SM306) from a frozen surface into a cloud-covered sky from which light snow fell from time to time. With the cloud base at about 700 feet, they flew low across the North Sea, arriving about a mile off the island of Texel at about 10.00. Sergeant eased up to allow Trail to make the crossover turn below them that would put them on a course for Den Helder, but as he watched for his No. 2 to reappear below him, he glimpsed Trail's Spitfire diving into the water and blowing up. He circled a few times to see if the other pilot had survived but saw nothing other than some flak, which was coming at him from the shore. As he circled, the flames and smoke gradually reduced until there was nothing but an oily patch on the water and no sign of life. They were flying as 'Green 1' and 'Green 2'.

Sergeant continued his Jim Crow, looking at Den Helder then flying up the seaward coast of Texel before returning once more to the crash site to check again whether Trail might have survived. Once again all he could see was the oily patch on the surface. With a heavy heart he turned back towards the coast of Norfolk, still flying low – the weather over the Netherlands was much the same as over eastern England. He tried to inform Coltishall what had happened but the altitude prevented this. Halfway across he managed to make contact with a squadron above him (possibly 303) and asked them to relay the news but to instruct that no search mission should be attempted. He landed back at about 10.55. Some of his fellow pilots were standing by to carry out a search, but after Sergeant made his report, it was decided that it would be pointless and the young flying officer was assumed to have been killed. He had only been with the squadron a matter of weeks, and his death seemed so futile. It is notoriously difficult to judge altitude against the surface of the sea and it may have been that Trail misjudged his height or fed in a bit too much slip and hit the water. He was twenty-one and came from Wandsworth in London. His name is to be found on Panel 268 of the Runnymede Memorial. This sad little incident demonstrates that the six squadrons did not operate exclusively against the rockets, but attacked other targets as and when the opportunity presented itself.

Six days later, on the 17th, everything was being made ready for another attack on the Loosduinen tramsheds but the plan was swiftly shelved when an 08.30 Jim Crow to Den Helder by two Spitfires of 602 Squadron spotted a number of ships in and around the harbour, two of them being merchant ships of about 6,000 tons. The opportunity could not be missed, and an attack was hurriedly planned, using thirty-two Beaufighters from a Coastal Command strike wing based at RAF North Coates a few miles down the coast from Grimsby, escorted by Spitfires of

602 and 603. The attack was fast and low and fiercely defended, but all the Spitfires returned safely, with 602 landing at Swannington at 15.00 and 603 at Coltishall five minutes later. The Beaufighters straggled back, touching down at North Coates between 15.12 and 15.47 hours. Two of them, one from each squadron, landed at Donna Nook on the coast. One whose undercarriage would not come down had to make a belly landing. Five Beaufighters from each squadron were found to be damaged on their return, but six were lost, three from each squadron. The strike was considered to be a success. If nothing else the operation showed that the pilots had to be flexible and that each new day brought with it the possibility of new challenges.

Round about this time, when 229 became 603, Squadron Leader Patterson fell ill. He seems to have developed problems associated with stress and exhaustion after a long period of operations, and he apparently flew his last flight on 7 January – and that was an air test. He went into hospital at Ely in Cambridgeshire on the 12th, expecting to be there for about two weeks, but he did not return to 603. A new 'A' Flight Commander arrived as well: Flight Lieutenant Jack Batchelor. He came from 1 Squadron and brought considerable experience and skill. He wore sunglasses almost permanently to protect an eye damaged by a stray

Clearly posed – aircrew very rarely looked at their bombs! 602 Squadron
at Matlaske or Ludham; possibly Flight Sergeant Stan Gomme and
Flight Lieutenant Pertwee.
(Courtesy Imperial War Museum. Negative no. CH14807.)

splinter of metal during a dogfight with a 109 some time before. His sight was saved but he took to wearing an early type of contact lens, which left the eye red, raw and uncomfortable. The sunglasses served two purposes – to reduce the glare, which could be painful, but also to prevent others seeing it.

Poor weather in January severely disrupted flying. On the relatively few days that operations were possible, the pilots were fully occupied with attacks on the now familiar targets in and around The Hague, but the bald statistics illustrate just how much the conditions had affected the campaign by the end of the month. No. 453 completed 113 operational sorties, 602 flew eighty-one, 229/603 only seventy-four and 303 sixty-three. On many days, some consecutive, preparations for the Ramrod against the Loosduinen tramsheds by one or other of the squadrons came to nothing. No. 229/603 called it the 'yo-yo' state because the bombs were constantly being hoisted up on to the aircraft then lowered to the ground again! On some days the flying could not go ahead because of mist and rain, but later in the month heavy snow and the weather prevented movement on the airfields. Sometimes, if it was suitable for flying over Norfolk, over the Netherlands heavy cloud cover prevented target identification and meant bombs being jettisoned into the sea. But the weather did not stop the V2s coming over. Over 220 of them landed during the month – on the 3rd there were seven, the next day thirteen, on the 5th seven, on the 20th sixteen on the 26th eleven. It is noticeable that as the month went on, and as the number of operations undertaken by the Spitfires reduced, more V2s arrived, many of them launched during daylight hours, but there is no direct correlation to show that on the days the Spitfires operated their activities stopped the rockets being fired. On some days when the Spitfires could not fly, few rockets arrived, and on others when the Spitfires flew, many came. The wind might affect the flight of a V2 but mist, rain and snow did not. Areas already hit were hit again and the location of the explosions reads like a directory of London districts or Underground stations: Potter's Bar, Clapham, Ilford, Croydon, Woolwich, Battersea, Willesden, East Ham, Greenwich, Willesden (again), Rainham, Hendon, Barking, East Barnet.

The Station Commander of RAF Matlaske, Squadron Leader P.G. Ottewill GM, aware of the strains and inconvenience that operating from Swannington entailed for all concerned, including those at Swannington, tried to improve matters at Matlaske by arranging for Sommerfield Tracking to be laid to provide a 'stripway' in the hope that the airfield might become operational again, although its orientation became the subject of debate, with HQ Fighter Command specifying 120°/300° but those at the airfield deciding it should be 050°/230°. In addition to the 'stripway', it seemed that an alternative could be identified over firmer ground. Ottewill acknowledged that the tracking, 'although a step in the

The site of the Ilford V2.
(Courtesy Imperial War Museum. Negative no. CH15108.)

right direction, is not the answer'. It would take at least a month and a half to make the sodden airfield usable. As the cold weather set in during January, various measures to deal with it came into play. Braziers were lit in the ablutions and lavatories to prevent the pipes freezing, vehicles were fitted with chains and resources diverted to clearing snow. This part of Norfolk can be beautiful in good conditions, but it is flat and can be bleak and exposed in bad weather. Life must have been pretty miserable in such conditions. The misery of getting up on a dark morning and washing in the freezing temperatures of a cold ablutions block can probably only be appreciated by anyone who has experienced it!

With limited flying, the pilots had to be kept occupied with ground training, lectures, sport and visits, some for training and some not. If the weather over the targets was bad but suitable over Norfolk, training flights took place. On the 6th, after a hard frost, dawn brought a heavy fog. No. 229 Squadron was on sixty-minute readiness, but orders came releasing it at 10.30. Someone organized a visit to the GCI (Ground Controlled Interception) station at RAF Neatishead, to be followed by a 'liberty run' into Norwich.

At Neatishead, Pilot Officer Cooper, the Intelligence Officer, witnessed an interesting but tragic intercept involving a ditched Mosquito. When the morning mist eventually cleared four Spitfires of 453 Squadron took off at

13.40 to attack the Haagsche Bosch, although the operation had to be aborted when they were only a few miles off the Dutch coast because of the weather. They landed back at Swannington at 15.00. Fifty minutes later two of their Spitfires, flown by Rusty Leith and Warrant Officer Stewart, scrambled to search for a PRU Spitfire which had apparently gone into the North Sea. Neatishead guided them towards the area where the aeroplane was thought to have ditched. Whilst they were on the way, it became known that the aircraft in question was actually a PRU Mosquito from RAF Benson and not a Spitfire. A Mosquito of 68 Squadron also scrambled. Leith and Stewart reached the site relatively easily to find it being orbited by the Mosquito. They could see a parachute in the water and what appeared to be a fluorescene stain under and around it, suggesting that the pilot's body was underneath it. At this time of year with the cold, he would have been unlikely to have survived, although the two Spitfires continued to circle for the best part of an hour until they were recalled. They landed at 17.15. Rusty Leith's log book records: 'Scramble – ASR – Mosquito in sea. Parachute in sea.'

The 229 visitors to Neatishead made their way to Norwich for the evening and eventually back to Coltishall. On other days the pilots attended lectures and films on security matters, various operational activities – daily inspections, air sea rescue, night flying, and combat films. On the 12th, the Coltishall Armaments Officer spoke to the 229/603 pilots about the use of rocket projectiles, as there was talk that they might be used against the V2 sites. On other days, they took the Fighter Command aircraft recognition tests. One lecture at the end of the month attended by pilots of both 603 and 303 covered the handling of the Spitfire XVI. It was primarily for the benefit of 303, who it had been decided would now get the later mark to put them on a similar footing to the other three.

For straightforward recreation, football matches were laid on and later in the month, 603 and 303 competed in target shooting with pistols and clay pigeons. Clay-pigeon shooting in particular helped the pilots 'keep their eyes' because of the speed of the targets and the need for accurate deflection judgement, so it was not just an interesting diversion but a training aid as well. Wing Commander Lardner Burke organized a visit to nearby Bullard's Brewery, which was heartily enjoyed by a full turnout of aircrew, who enthusiastically sampled the product. Eric Mee found it interesting but thought that the grinding boredom of some of the jobs he saw people doing there – putting the tops on an unending parade of bottles for example – difficult to accept. Even with the risks involved in flying, he knew where he would rather be. Norwich Cathedral provided another afternoon out – some of the pilots even went inside! Local pubs were favourite spots in the evenings – the Recruiting Sergeant in the village of Coltishall being one. There was a club at Sutton Staithe. Bob Sergeant remembered returning to it many years after the war and finding his and other signatures still in the Members' Book. Another favourite spot was the NAAFI Club in Norwich. Eric Mee recalled it with some affection. He said that it had superb facilities which included showers, a barber, an information point for train and bus times, a comfortable lounge with armchairs and settees, newspapers and magazines to read and a radiogram. The building had three floors, the top one being a cafeteria which produced excellent meals at very reasonable prices – all in all a fine place to relax.

But first the airmen had to get to these places. Perhaps the pilots of the six squadrons were reasonably fortunate because their airfields were not too far from Norwich unlike some of the wartime aerodromes in the fens which were quite remote. Some had motor cycles and some cars. Flight commanders had access to transport and would often organize trips in the evenings. Warrant Officer Johnny Green progressed from a motor cycle to a second-hand car, a Ford Eight. Eric Mee bought himself a car as well, another second-hand one which cost him the princely sum of £60. Of course he had not got a licence or had any driving lessons when he picked it up and drove it back to camp! Tom O'Reilly had a big black Armstrong Siddeley which they called 'O'Reilly's Hearse'. They would also do silly things. Tommy Thomson had an Austin Seven, and whilst he was flying an operation his friends pushed it up the steep slope of one of the air-raid shelters so that when he came back, he found it perched on the top like a sore thumb.

Relationships were strong – Snowy Wheatley had Paddy O'Reilly as best man at his wedding – but behind it all was the thought of death or injury. There were different views about the wisdom or otherwise of having children. Some men thought that it was wrong, if they died the child would be fatherless and the widow left with having to bring up a child on her own. Others felt that if there was a child, it was a bit of them to carry on should they be killed. Both views were perfectly valid. It did not do to look forward too far; live for the moment seemed to be the best philosophy. The Australians at Matlaske passed the time in the same way. Sometimes they went out to local pubs, sometimes into Sheringham near Cromer to see a film sometimes into Norwich if they had enough time off, where they might have a meal. Pilots on the different squadrons did not mix very much and first loyalties seem to have been to flights rather than squadrons. There was some rivalry, although friendships were struck in the various messes.

Heating for the flimsy huts came from the cast-iron pot-bellied stoves familiar to many ex-British servicemen before the days of central heating. They had a chimney poking through the roof and occasionally members of another flight, seeing their colleagues settled in the warmth, climbed surreptitiously onto the roof and dropped a Very cartridge down the chimney. Of course it exploded in the stove, sending hot embers and

Senior NCOs of 451 Squadron. Front l to r: Flight Sergeant F.S. Moran, Sergeant Fred Wigley, Flight Sergeant H.H. Osborne, Warrant Officer J.A. Lenney, Flight Sergeant L.J. Townsend, Sergeant L.W. Butcher. Behind: Sergeant R.C. Archer, Sergeant A. Sneddon, Sergeant R.F. Baker, Flight Sergeant A.A. Clark and Flight Sergeant K.W. Phillip. The photograph was probably taken after the V2 campaign had finished, but it illustrates the cast-iron stoves, the main source of warmth in the accommodation during the bitter winter of 1944/45.
(*Australian War Memorial Negative no. UK2398.*)

the heavy circular lid spinning round the hut. The results of this can only be imagined and it is probably a miracle that nobody was hurt!

There does not seem to have been any rivalry or ill-feeling between the different nationalities – each group respected the other. The Poles are recalled as having a serious temperament and rather lacking in humour, keeping to themselves. Perhaps this is understandable, with the way the war was going. Many of them just wanted to kill Germans. One pilot recalled that often the Poles introduced a seriousness into a conversation that the British and Commonwealth men would not have seen – sometimes a political angle – although individual Poles on the squadrons did not act in quite the same way. Max Baerlein of 602 recalled being on an operation with one of the Poles leading. Coming across a 109, the Pole pursued it relentlessly down to ground level, with Baerlein following unwillingly, thinking they would both crash.

At the end of the month, the weather relented a little. For the 25th, 603's ORB records: 'The airdrome still u/s and snow covered. Weather conditions have remained static for almost a week and the snow has made no signs of disappearing.' Then on the 26th, 'In spite of more snow falling last night and during today, the first signs of a thaw appeared.'

But still there were few operations. On the night of the 27th/28th about 5 inches of snow fell, and on the 29th/30th another 2–3 inches. Then on the 31st a quick thaw set in, getting rid of the snow but making Coltishall unusable because of flooding! Ironically, the two squadrons based at Matlaske were able to fly from Swannington and they both undertook limited operations.

Notes
1. One source dates this incident to 2 February 1945.
2. From *Spitfire Flying Legend* by John Dibbs and Tony Holmes, p153. © Osprey Publishing Ltd.
3. From *Spitfire Flying Legend* by John Dibbs and Tony Holmes, p153. © Osprey Publishing Ltd.
4. Of course there were no aircraft at Matlaske because of the ground condition – the Matlaske-based squadrons still flew from Swannington.
5. Interestingly, the 229 ORB states that the weather was good, unlike those of the other three squadrons.
6. *Doodlebugs and Rockets* by Bob Ogley, p.170.
7. Supplement to the *London Gazette*, Tuesday 19 October 1948, 'Air Operations by Air Defence of Great Britain and Fighter Command in Connection with the German Flying Bomb and Rocket Offensives, 1944–1945'.

CHAPTER SIX

Liquid Oxygen

O n 1 February, command of 603 passed to 'Tommy' Rigler and Squadron Leader Patterson was posted to Station Headquarters Coltishall with effect from 26 January. He had not responded to the treatment he was receiving in hospital at Ely. Sadness in the squadron greeted his departure, which he marked by writing a letter of farewell to his erstwhile colleagues. He would be missed, although Rigler would prove to be more than capable of taking on the job of CO. On the 2nd, 453 and 602 received orders for a Ramrod against the Loosduinen tramsheds

A 602 Squadron Spitfire IX taken at one of the continental ALGs whilst part of 2nd TAF.
(Courtesy Imperial War Museum. Negative no. CH12890.)

147

but it was postponed yet again because of poor weather. The following day, however, conditions allowed the attack to go ahead as Ramrod 20. The morning brought clear skies and sun to Coltishall and the warmth of the day dried the airfield out. The day's activities started with two of 602's Spitfires carrying out a weather recce over The Hague and finding that it was suitable for the Ramrod. It was not a complicated operation, calling for the two squadrons to form up together, fly to the target, bomb it and then recover to Ursel for refuelling before returning to Swannington. No. 602's twelve took off at 09.50 with another twelve from 453 five minutes later. Flying Officer Farfan of 602 returned early with mechanical problems, landing at 10.25. The two groups flew across the North Sea crossing in at the Hook at a height of 12,000 feet and descending to 9,000 as they approached the target, which they seem to have found without much difficulty. All the aircraft carried two 250-pound bombs under the wings and a single 500-pounder on the fuselage centre line. But the pilots were very aware of the need to avoid civilian casualties – a concern that went all the way up the chain of command to Roderic Hill, and above.

The sheds lay on the east side of a sweeping bend in a street with houses on the west and the north; to the south and east there was a canal basin,

The Loosduinen tramsheds taken in 1951. The canal basin is at the top of the picture, with civilian houses in the foreground. This is looking in the direction from which the Spitfires would be bombing.
(Courtesy Haags Gemeentearchief. Photo no. 0.86865.01.)

which made identification of the target area reasonably straightforward. No. 453 bombed from south-east to north-west, and presumably 602 did the same. This meant that any undershoots would hit the canal basin and avoid the houses. Overshoots would hit them, of course, but with the pilots being told to 'trickle their bombs in' the idea would be to gradually move them up from the canal to the top of the target. They pulled out at about 3,000 feet, both squadrons reporting intense, accurate light and medium flak from the target area. Both squadrons' bombs undershot, although some landed in and around the sheds. Michael Francis' log book states 'Dive bombing. Most bombs undershot.' They crossed out south of The Hague and took accurate, heavy flak as they did so. After landing at Ursel, they returned to Swannington as planned.

After the attack, two of 303's aircraft escorted a pair of Mustangs to photograph the results, although one of the Spitfires had to divert to Ghent in Belgium with engine trouble. The results were disappointing. The target was not hit as severely as had been hoped, but in defence of the pilots, their concern to avoid overshoots and Dutch casualties probably meant that they would release their bombs slightly early. Rusty Leith's log book noted cryptically: 'Bombing of liquid oxygen factory at Loosduinen – fair. Intense light, medium and heavy flak.'

Whether it was preplanned or a consequence of these disappointing results, Ramrod 21, an almost identical operation to Ramrod 20, was ordered, and once again twenty-three Spitfires of 453 and 602 Squadrons took to the air with two 250-pound bombs each at 14.50. Many, but not all, of the pilots who flew in the morning were flying again in the afternoon. This time one aircraft from 453 and two of 602's aborted the mission, one of the 602 Spitfires acting as escort for the other. The remainder crossed in again over the Hook at about 13,000 feet, from which they dropped down to 10,500 to pinpoint the sheds. All aircraft bombed east to west, pulling out at 3,000 feet, and were once again targeted by intense and accurate flak. This time, both squadrons reported that more of their bombs seemed to hit the target. They noticed bomb craters from the morning's attack and concluded that it might have been more successful than first thought. Instead of diverting to Ursel, the squadrons went straight back to Norfolk. Rusty Leith said: 'Same as morning. Bombing better – Intense flak.'

No. 603 was in the air too, flying several armed recces against fairly specific targets which seemed to be associated directly with the rockets rather than the usual wooded areas. They reported some successful hits on buildings, vehicles etc. Their third armed recce of the day took off at 14.55, and as they crossed out at Gravezande after delivering their attacks, they saw the smoke rising from the tramsheds. Later, at the end of the fourth and final armed recce of the day, Squadron Leader Rigler crossed over to look at the sheds and took cine pictures of the damage, although the pilots said that they could not see any damage at all. The Poles of 303

Squadron found themselves in their Spitfire IXs back to escort patrols for a 100 Group aircraft, this time a Halifax which was very likely on Big Ben duties.

Sunday, 4 February brought with it poor weather that was considered to be 'unsuitable for operations'. Nonetheless 602 and 453 attempted armed recces, but the only attack was against the Hotel Promenade area by four aircraft of 602. It brought only limited success, partly because of inaccurate bombing and partly because four bombs 'hung up' and had to be jettisoned into the sea.

The Loosduinen tramsheds became a priority, as the attacks on 3 February clearly had not achieved their objective of forcing the Germans out. A similar operation planned for the 6th had to be postponed. On the 8th, despite marginal weather, 453, 602 and 603, with thirty-six aircraft, attempted another attack, Ramrod 24. Nos 453 and 602 took off more or less at the same time from Swannington – 453 at 09.20 and 602 at 09.25. Flight Lieutenant Rusty Leith led 453 with Squadron Leader Max Sutherland leading 602 and the Swannington group. They found themselves having to fly at 9,000 feet between more or less complete (10/10ths and 9/10ths) layers of cloud – the lower rising to 1,000 feet with the base of the upper layer at 10,000 feet – arriving over the target to find it completely obscured. After orbiting the area several times looking for a gap, 602 turned south to the Hook looking for their secondary target but could not find that either. Meanwhile, 453 had found a small break above Loosduinen which allowed four of the Spitfires to bomb. After that, the Australians flew over to the Staalduin Bosch which they managed to see, and the remainder bombed successfully, bar for one which had R/T trouble and was also running short of fuel; he jettisoned his bombs into the sea. No. 602 returned and through the break, ten of their Spitfires bombed the sheds. They reported hits on the target although some bombs landed on the canal basin area. The combined group headed for Ursel.

The final twelve Spitfires from 603 tookoff at 10.00 led by Squadron Leader Rigler and flew to Loosduinen between the same cloud layers as the others, but by the time they arrived, the break in the cloud had covered over and they could not see the sheds at all. Accordingly, they also headed to the Staalduin Bosch, which was clear, and all twelve bombed it before following the others to Ursel. In the afternoon, all three squadrons returned to Norfolk after strafing 'transportation targets'. For the Loosduinen attack 453's 'Swamp' Marsh's log book says baldly, 'Liquid Oxygen Factory Bombed Through Hole in Cloud. Weather very grim from target to Ursel. In amongst balloons near Antwerp.'

The next attack on the Loosduinen sheds, Ramrod 25, took place the next day, the 9th, this time by 453 and 603 Squadrons. It took until lunchtime for the almost complete cover over the Netherlands to disperse to the east, leaving about 40 miles from the coast inland completely clear and allowing the Ramrod to be laid on. Both COs led their respective squadrons, taking off at more or less 14.30 – twelve from 453 and ten from 603. They each carried a full load of 1,000-pounds. They found the sheds without difficulty and carried out their attacks as planned. No. 453 reported: 'Many near misses both target buildings. Several large explosions observed from tramsheds.' 603 noted: 'Bursts were seen over the whole of the Northern half of the target area, buildings at H.051 V.078 and H.055 V.075 being seen to be hit. One building was seen to be smoking badly and on the other after the first section had Bombed occurred a large orange flash and a mushroom of orange smoke shot up from it.'

The Spitfires flew to Ursel for refuelling then returned to their respective bases – 603 to a new dispersal on the other side of the airfield at Coltishall. Following the raid, two PRU Mustangs flew across in the afternoon just after the attack to take photographs of the results. They were escorted by two 602 Spitfires flown by Warrant Officers J.P. Ryan (Red 1) in SM257 and Stan Sollitt. Ryan was brought down whilst at about 5,000 feet altitude. Sollitt said later:

> *The weather that day was such that although the ground was quite clearly visible, the horizontal visibility was poor, so that Ryan and I, being spread out to cover both sides of the Mustangs, could not see each other except when we were turning to reverse direction. It was on one of our turns that I did not see him. I thought I'd heard a vague radio call earlier which was unreadable, but when he did not appear during the cross-over turn, I put two and two together. I saw no flak or enemy activity so thought he'd maybe had an aircraft problem. I continued with the escort until I parted company with the Mustangs over the English coast.*

Sollitt returned to Swannington but there was no sign of Ryan, who was posted missing. They did not know that he had made a good forced landing and survived the war as a POW.

On St Valentine's Day, 603 carried out two other raids on the sheds, this time on their own, following other operations in the morning which found them at Ursel for refuelling and rearming:

> *At 12.10 they were airborne again to attack the liquid oxygen factory at Loosduinen, flying direct from Ursel to the target and attacking it from 10,000ft in dives down to 4,000ft at 12.30 with cannon and machine guns on an E/W course. Aircraft crossed out over the Hague and returned to base landing at 13.25.*
>
> *Immediately the aircraft were seized for re-fuelling and rearming as yet a third show was laid on for 16.00. While taxiing out for this F/O McConnochie in T had the misfortune to run into a tractor drawing a bomb trolley which had remained in the peri-track despite the movement of*

aircraft. The bump was gentle and little damage seemed to have been done on cursory examination and as the driver of the tractor baled out in time no one was hurt, but only 11 aircraft took off on the recce led by F/Lt Batchelor, which was airborne at 16.00 to attack Hague/Loosduinen. 2 aircraft developed mechanical trouble and were forced to return early landing at base at 16.40. 9 aircraft however went on to bomb the target attacking in dives from 8,000ft down to 2,000ft on an E/W course. All bombs fell in the target area at least 10 being within a hundred yards of the aiming point . . . Another stick was observed to burst on the road leading through the target area. Moderate accurate flak was observed from the target area and meagre but accurate heavy from the Hook of Holland. The weather over the target was good but cloud 10/10ths at 8–9,000ft forced the pilots to begin their dives lower down than usual.

The Spitfires did not attack Loosduinen again. Roderic Hill stated: 'After the last attack on the 9th we judged that the target had suffered enough damage to be left alone in future.'

He considered the operations[1] to have been successful on two counts: the sheds had been severely damaged and the bombing had avoided the feared civilian casualties. For the pilots, the attacks seem to have been unremarkable – just more of the same dive bombing. Sixty years on, Rusty Leith had little recollection of them. They knew they were bombing what was believed to be a liquid oxygen factory but probably did not appreciate the significance of the change in strategy that it represented or that it could only go ahead because of their undoubted skill at placing their bombs accurately. They did not appreciate the debates that Hill and his staff must have had to come to the decision to allow the attacks to go ahead and their relief when the objective was achieved. It is clear from the post-operation reports that the pilots did make great efforts to ensure that the civilian houses to the west and north of the site were not hit. The many under-shoots were probably the result of their efforts to 'trickle the bombs in' towards the target, but nevertheless the tactic seems to have worked and the buildings were left damaged.

At the end of January, Air Marshal Hill found himself under pressure from the Air Ministry to step up the attacks on the V2 storage and launching areas, although they were still unwilling to allow Bomber Command to divert any of its resources to the fight against the rockets. However, the Defence Committee decided to request that the light bombers of 2 Group be used to attack certain selected targets. Both of these were changes that Hill had been pressing for and he 'negotiated' an arrangement with the 2nd TAF that 12 Group's Spitfires would in future operate further east to Amersfoort and that on the days when the weather would not allow attacks on the storing and firing areas, the Spitfires would have a go at railway targets. The significance of Amersfoort was that it was a hub or bottleneck for railway traffic from Germany, and the arrangement would allow it to be raided by Hill's Spitfires. At the same time, when their operational commitments allowed, 2nd TAF light and medium bombers would attack rocket targets identified by staff at Fighter Command. In this lay the seeds of a tragedy to come. As a further change in response to the pressures being exerted on him, Air Marshal Hill drew in two other Spitfire squadrons to assist in the campaign – 124 and 451, the latter being a sister Australian squadron to 453. No. 124 still flew Spitfire IXs whilst 451 had XVIs. On 10 February, the day following Ramrod 25 on the tramsheds, 124 Squadron moved to Coltishall from Manston. It would be several weeks before 451 entered the fray.

No. 124 (Baroda) Squadron formed initially in March 1918 at Old Sarum, training in the day-bomber role using DH4s and then DH9s, but it disbanded five months later, having never become operational. It re-formed again just over twenty-three years later in May 1941 at Castletown on the north coast of Caithness in Scotland, just to the east of Thurso, with Spitfire Is. Its main role there was the protection of the fleet at Scapa Flow in the Orkney Islands just a few miles north across the Pentland Firth. It then spent much of the war operating from the south of England across the Channel, and moved to 12 Group and Coltishall on 10 February 1945. Its identification code was ON. The squadron badge showed a mongoose passant, with the motto 'Danger is our Opportunity'. The Maharajah of Baroda in India sponsored the squadron, hence the mongoose in the badge.

No. 124's CO was Squadron Leader G.C. Scott. Their first operation against the V2s took place on 14 February, the day that 603 carried out the final attack on the Loosduinen tramsheds. Jan van't Hoff recalled that there seemed to be a routine with the Spitfires coming over first thing and attacking the Haagsche Bosch out of the rising sun from the east. Whilst the attacks were generally accurate, stray bombs did damage houses in Bezuidenhout from time to time – a mixed blessing in that there might be casualties, but if not the ruined buildings became a source of fuel for the freezing, scavenging civilians. Many would leave their houses at first light in case of stray bombs then return at dusk to see if their house had survived the day's attacks. He also recalled seeing a Spitfire being shot down whilst he was queuing for bread. About half a dozen Spitfires tipped over to dive on the Haagsche Bosche when suddenly one just blew up in mid-air, the pilot had no chance of escaping. Jan said that he felt bad about it despite the hardships that he and his family were enduring – he considered the loss a tragedy.

No. 124's first operation was against the Haagsche Bosch – twelve Spitfire HFIXs led by Squadron Leader Scott as part of Ramrod 26, which included 602 and 603 as well. It would be costly. The weather across Norfolk was fair with clouds and some light rain; over the Netherlands it was fine. On their first Big Ben Ramrod, 124 took off first at 08.55 followed half an hour later at 09.25 by twelve from 603 commanded by Flight Lieutenant Jack Batchelor and 11 from 602 led by Squadron Leader Sutherland. No. 124 found the target – the north-eastern corner of the wood – easily enough but were treated to 'intense, accurate non-tracer flak' which seems to have hit Warrant Officer J.F. Kelman on his dive. His Spitfire exploded and Kelman died instantly. He is buried in Westduin General Cemetery in The Hague. The others recovered to Ursel. Then 602, followed immediately by 603, attacked the area with much the same result. They too reported significant flak as well as some of their bombs 'hanging up' – a not unusual occurrence. They too recovered to Ursel.

After refuelling at Ursel, 124 returned to Coltishall whilst 602[2] and 603 returned to the UK via The Hague, where 602 carried out a strafing attack on the Hotel Promenade area and 603 reportedly strafed the liquid oxygen factory at Loosduinen. Presumably this was another occasion when no bombs were available at Ursel. As 602 arrived over Swannington, Sutherland ordered them into 'echelon starboard' and in carrying out the manoeuvre, Flight Lieutenant G.Y.G. Lloyd in SM538 pulled up underneath Flight Lieutenant Waterhouse in SM353 and the two collided. Lloyd's Spitfire immediately fell away then dived into a field beside the airfield, killing the pilot instantly. The propeller of Waterhouse's aircraft sustained damage but he managed to get it down safely and landed uninjured. Nos 124 and 602 flew other, similar operations later that day, as did 303.

For 124 it had been a costly start to their contribution to the campaign with the loss of Warrant Officer Kelman. They would lose another pilot, Flight Sergeant Allen, the next day as well. He was killed during a practice dive-bombing exercise. The loss of a colleague could be hard. No. 603's Bob Sergeant said:

> Losing one's mates was something we all had to deal with and we developed our own special way of doing this. The general consensus was that there should be no grieving, there was simply no time for that anyway. Many of the lads made known what they wished to be done with any special effects and of course the first drink without them was sunk in their honour.

Ursel had a single runway and was not a permanent base for any squadron. The unit based there was No. 424 Rearming and Refuelling Unit, and apart from the squadrons coming in daily for replenishment, some other squadrons flew there for a few days from their bases in England to help with the various operations being carried out by the Allied armies. For the men of 424 it was arduous, and some of the pilots flying against the V2s brought over newspapers and other things that were difficult to find on the Continent. Often, Belgian civilians gathered

at the perimeter fence to watch the Spitfires taxiing past and waved at the
pilots. A few of the more enterprising airmen noticed that many of
the civilians' bicycles had no tyres, or indeed inner tubes. Some ran on the
metal rims although this did not last long, and some used wooden blocks
as makeshift tyres. These pilots would fly the first operation of the day
swathed in tyres and inner tubes under their Mae Wests, and when they
arrived at Ursel, would nip out to the fence and sell them to the locals.
Occasionally, the Spitfires would overnight at Ursel or one of the other
airfields in Belgium and of course the pilots took the opportunity to visit
the local towns for entertainment. Some of them recall visits to the lovely
medieval city of Bruges not far from Maldegem.

By now, many of them flew in army khaki battledress rather than the
RAF blue tunics because of the similarity of the RAF blue to the *Luftwaffe*
blue/grey, which might mean a pilot on the end of a parachute being
mistakenly shot. Although Bob Sergeant had his old battered cap stuffed
into a corner of the cockpit, many of the pilots did not have a hat with them
and going into a local town in a khaki tunic (albeit with RAF insignia)
attracted the attention of zealous Army 'redcaps' (military police) who
found it hard to accept that they were RAF personnel and not under their
jurisdiction. Pilots were also issued with revolvers and 20 rounds of
ammuntion to protect themselves from any Germans or collaborators still
roaming the area but many felt that they did not really want them. They
thought that if they were about to be captured, they would not be too keen
to take on 'the entire German army single-handed'. Some saw them only
as a way of setting the aeroplane on fire to stop it falling into enemy hands.
In any case, the revolvers themselves were not accurate weapons and were
more likely to be of use shooting animals for food than anything else.
Some were of First World War vintage, .38 Enfields or .455 Webley & Scott
revolvers being common, although after D-Day American Colt .45
government-model automatics made an appearance.

Like most human activities, the days developed a routine. An early
task was to establish the weather over the Netherlands to decide if operations could go ahead. If the conditions over Norfolk allowed, the first
operation of the day would be a weather recce. Two Spitfires raced low
over the North Sea until they got to about a mile off the Dutch coast when
they climbed to 2,000–3,000 feet to look at the cloud cover over the target
areas. Paddy O'Reilly recalled that if the weather was good, the code
transmitted back was 'Bertie', which meant that they should expect to
arm the Spitfires with two 250-pound bombs and a 500-pounder. If there
was some cloud cover, the code was 'Roderick', which meant that conditions would only allow the two 250-pound bombs plus a 90-gallon tank
on the centre line.

One 'perk' of this duty were the 'aircrew breakfasts' the pilots could eat
on their return, which included luxuries like bacon and eggs. Sixty years

Another in the posed series of photographs of 602 Squadron. This time
another briefing, with the wall board used in one of the previous
photographs now on the table. Note the pilots' lockers with their names
at the top and the seat-type parachute on top of one of them. It also
shows clearly the 'mixed' uniform worn by the Polish airmen.
(Courtesy Imperial War Museum. Negative no.CH1484.)

on, some pilots do not recall there being formal briefings for each
operation, but others do. Eric Mee described a briefing for an attack on the
Haagsche Bosch:

> *We all studied blown-up photographs of the target, these clearly showing
> the missiles lined up along the paths and under the trees. We were given a
> target map showing the streets in The Hague and we marked our routes on
> our cross-channel maps. Also at the briefing we were issued with an escape
> kit in a plastic box containing emergency rations and currency of the coun-
> tries we might have to escape through if we had to bale out. We wrote down
> on the back of the hands the call signs and radio channels we would be using
> for that trip. Our radios were crystal controlled, the radio mechanics
> putting in the correct crystals in the radios for the frequencies we would
> operate on, the radio control in the cockpit having an 'on-off' switch and
> four channel push buttons. Channels were allocated to base aerodrome,
> operational control, emergency and a channel for the airfield on the
> Continent.*

The use of crystals in the radios and the resulting inability of the pilots to talk to other aircraft in the air at the same time and vicinity was a contributing factor in a tragedy that happened a few weeks later, at the beginning of March.

After briefing, the rest of the flying kit would be taken from lockers and put on – Mae West, parachute etc. – and then they would go out to the aircraft to ensure a prompt engine start and take-off. Sometimes pilots shared lockers. Ground crew were allocated to individual aircraft and a good relationship between the pilot and his ground crew was invaluable to create a team ethos. The ground crew took pride in their aeroplane, many of which had names. In 603, each had a name that was a form of transport: 'Batch's Buggy' or 'Jock's Trap'. Bob Sergeant's was called 'Bob's Slayer' and Eric Mee's 'Curly's Caravan'.

On the 19th, 602 moved to Coltishall where they were to remain for under a week pending a move to yet another nearby station, Ludham. The weather for the rest of February remained wintry and mixed. After the 14th, it was a week before any significant operations took place. But the 21st and 22nd were very full days again, with a slight change in emphasis ordered by HQ Fighter Command, which might not have been obvious to the airmen concerned. One of Hill's intelligence officers suggested that they should concentrate on a single target for several days rather than try to hit several, and this is what happened with the Haagsche Bosch. Some of the raids were against other targets, but by and large they did do as requested and concentrated on this particular area. On Wednesday, 21 February the Spitfires in the Coltishall sector, for example, flew 104 sorties most against the Haagsche Bosch. The 602 sections returned via Ockenburg, which they strafed on each occasion. No. 303 Squadron had ten aircraft on Halifax Big Ben escort duties during the afternoon, while 124 spent the day practising dive bombing. Two Australian pilots from 453 were brought down but survived. Warrant Officer Carmichael was hit by flak and baled out 12 miles north of Leiden. He made contact with Dutch farmers, who hid and protected him until Canadians liberated him on 11 May[3]. Warrant Officer Gadd had problems with his drop-tank not unlike those that brought Roy Karasek down in December and crashed. He too made contact with local Dutch who protected him until he was liberated by Canadians on 8 May.

A similar programme of concentrated operations against six targets in the Haagsche Bosch and Ockenburg took place the next day. No. 124 carried out ten sorties against the Haagsche Bosch and seventeen against Ockenburg. They also sent two Spitfires on a patrol looking for midget submarines. No. 603 completed thirty-five sorties against the woods, although six of these were directed at film studios north-west of the area used by the Germans as a storage area. No. 453 sent twelve Spitfires to dive bomb the studios, with the remainder attacking the Haagsche Bosch.

A PRU photograph of the film studios in the Haagsche Bosch after
bombing by the Spitfires.
(Courtesy Imperial War Museum. Negative no. C5241.)

The operations all reported large clouds of smoke rising from the studio
site. No. 602 made twenty sorties against the six targets in the woods and
strafed and bombed Ockenburg.

Roderic Hill seems to have been pleased with the results of these
attacks, and others on subsequent days. He concluded that the Germans
'had been driven from the Haagsche Bosch, at least for the time being' and
forced to alternative facilities at Duindigt racecourse. PRU photos of the
Haagsche Bosch on the 24th did not show any rockets. He also stated that
in the sixty hours after the attacks on the 22nd not a single rocket launch
took place. This was not quite accurate: the records of rockets landing in
England show that five fell on the 21st, eight on the 22nd, twelve on the
23rd, although only one fell on the 24th, timed at 07.40. None fell on
the 25th and the first of seven on the 26th landed at 09.10 – a gap of about
fifty hours. But none fell on the 27th and 28th. It is interesting that
following the attacks on the 22nd, poor weather severely curtailed Spitfire
operations on the 23rd, when twelve V2s landed, but the resumption of
concentrated operations on the 24th seem to have restricted launches that
day and on the following two.

Although this account concentrates on the activities of the six Spitfire
squadrons, the contribution to the campaign against the V2s of the

Typhoons of the 2nd TAF should not be minimized or ignored. These squadrons spent their days carrying out a variety of operations in support of the troops on the ground often under very difficult conditions. And sometimes they attacked the V2s as well. Mention has already been made of Tom Hall and 175 Squadron. During February, they were constantly being told to look out for V2s, either being transported west by road or rail or ready to be fired. They regularly saw V2s being fired and their brief-ings identified firing sites in the area of Heek/Coesfeld just inside Germany north of the Ruhr and south-east of Enschede in the Netherlands – an area known as a site for V2 launches. On the 21st, Hall led 175 on an armed recce of the Heek area looking for V2s. The operation started badly when one of the Typhoons suffered an engine failure on take-off but the pilot managed to make a good wheels-up landing. The others continued:

As we approached Heek we noticed that close to the railway line were some buildings and a short distance away in a cleared space was an upright V2 venting vapour. We were in a good position and we echeloned out to attack and as we came down out of the sun intense light flak started up from the buildings and the surrounding woods. Just as my number two and I came out of the attack I looked back to see a terrific explosion. [4]

During the whole of the campaign by the 12 Group Spitfires, no V2 was ever caught in the open in this way, and yet it could have happened. It all hinged on luck – whether or not the aircraft were over the launching sites when firings were taking place.

No. 175 continued to attack V2s. On the afternoon of 24 February they were briefed to look out for two trains in the Coelsfeld area, which had been reported carrying rockets. They found them stationary in a yard at Dulmen and attacked them, although one of their pilots went down, either from flak or from debris thrown into the air by the attack. Together, the Spitfires and the Typhoons made a formidable weapon.

On Friday, 23 February 602 Squadron moved to Ludham and 603 Squadron joined them on the 24th. Ludham was one of the airfields built and operated pretty much as a wartime facility, with a rather un-remarkable history. It was slightly to the west of the village whose name it took and about 11 miles north-east of Norwich, only a few miles from the coast. Built in 1941, unlike Coltishall and Matlaske, it had three concrete runways laid out in a triangle[5], typical of RAF airfields of the time. It became operational in November 1941, when it was used by the Spitfires of 152 Squadron on convoy patrol work, and saw a number of different units operating from it until August 1943, when it was taken over by the Ministry of Works to prepare it for occupation by the USAAF. But this did not happen and it remained virtually unused for about a year, which seems surprising considering that it had hard runways and good

Stan Sollitt and Cec Zuber of 602 Squadron.
(From 'Glasgow's Own' by kind permission of Prof Dugald Cameron)

facilities. However, in August 1944, possession passed to the Royal Navy, who commissioned it as HMS *Flycatcher* but remained there for only six months. On 19 February, Squadron Leader Ottewill, who had been the Station Commander at Matlaske, arrived to command Ludham and only four days later, 602 moved in. Although it was now an RAF station, for a few days many of the functions continued to be run by naval personnel – the airmen's cookhouse, the telephone exchange and the officers' mess – but on the 24th, the main party of 700 sailors departed first thing in the morning.

No. 602 arrived during the late morning of the 23rd, and as the Ludham ORB records, 'were comfortably installed by Lunch'. Certainly 602 seemed to like it – the ORB made the comment: 'It is a very fine airfield'. After the difficulties of operating from Swannington and being based at Matlaske, it is hardly surprising that it should be seen as an improvement. The pilots and ground crew spent the afternoon organizing their dispersal and were well pleased that they would be able to carry out operations the next day. Later in the afternoon, the weather had deteriorated to such an extent that 603 could not fly their Spitfires across from Coltishall, but Squadron Leader Rigler and the 6603 Service Echelon came across by road to prepare for the aircraft to arrive the following day, which they did on returning from an operation over the Netherlands. No. 603 had moved dispersal at Coltishall a few days earlier so that for both of the Auxiliary units, the transfer to Ludham represented a second significant upheaval within the space of a few days, during which they had also managed to continue operations. It is curious that having opened the war flying together over central Scotland and bringing down the first German aircraft over the United Kingdom, the two Scottish Auxiliary squadrons were now back to operating from the same airfield near its end – although by May, when the War in Europe did end, they were no longer together. By now, their Auxiliary origins were only being maintained by the ground crews, but the two squadrons were very aware of their heritage and their longstanding but friendly rivalry, which even the youngest and newest of pilots adopted with enthusiasm.

Flying Officer Farrell and Flight Sergeant Zuber of 602 made the first operational flights from Ludham. They took off at 09.40 on the 24th on a combined weather and armed recce over the Netherlands, returning at 11.15. The weather was better the day before and another very full programme of operations against the V2s took place. Moving to Ludham prevented 603 from flying any operations on the 24th, but 602, 453, 303

451 Squadron. Squadron Leader C.W. Robertson (on the wing) and
Flight Lieutenant M.A. Kemp.
(Australian War Memorial Negative no.UK 2753.)

and 124 were all busy, with 124 flying sixteen sorties against the Haagsche Bosch and Ockenburg, although most were aborted because of marginal weather over The Hague. No. 603's first operation from their new home was also the day after their arrival, on the 25th, an early-morning weather recce by Flight Lieutenant Staniforth and Flying Officer Burrows, who took off at 07.35.

The arrival of 451 Squadron at Matlaske marked another significant change, as one of Air Marshal Hill's measures to step up the pace of attacks with more aeroplanes. Another RAAF squadron, 451 formed at Bankstown, Australia for reconnaissance duties before travelling to the Middle East and Kasfareet in May 1941 where it equipped with Hurricane Is in the tactical reconnaissance role but manned mainly by RAF pilots. As the year went on, and the battle for North Africa swirled back and forward along the Mediterranean, it gradually replaced the RAF airmen with Australians, but continued to carry out the same tasks. In March 1944 it transferred to Corsica, where it flew fighter cover for the invasion of southern France but saw little action. By December 1944, it had reached

Matlaske. Pilots of 453 Squadron. From l to r: Flying Officer N.R. Adams, Pilot Officer R.A. York, Pilot Officer R. Peters, Pilot Officer W. Mace, Pilot Officer C.A.M. Taylor, Pilot Officer D. Johns and Pilot Officer R. Lyall.
(Australian War Memorial Negative no. SUK 14386.)

Britain, based at RAF Hawkinge with Spitfire IXs, then XVIs and on 11 February 1945 it moved to Manston. It was not allocated a squadron badge and identification letters at this time were NI. The CO was Squadron Leader Robertson. A week later, on the 18th, orders came in that it should move to Matlaske and on the 23rd the ground parties made the change, arriving there at 19.00. The following day, the 24th, the aircraft flew into Swannington.

No. 451 did not become operational until 4 March, but its arrival meant that at the end of February and beginning March there were six 12 Group Spitfire squadrons dedicated to the campaign against the rockets: 602 and 603 (the Auxiliaries) at Ludham, 451 and 453 (the Australians) at Matlaske/Swannington and 303 and 124 (both still flying Spitfire IXs) at Coltishall. The Australians came under the command of Wing Commander Don Andrews as their wing leader. Andrews had been CO of 453 in the past so his appointment meant a reunion of old and trusted friends. The campaign was hotting up with the addition of the fresh squadrons to 12 Group and with agreement at last that medium bombers of the 2nd TAF would take part, but against the backdrop of the sufferings of the Dutch civilians and the concern which went all the way from the pilots in their cockpits to Air Marshal Hill to the Dutch Government exile and even Winston Churchill that the RAF's attacks should not add to the misery of the families impatiently waiting for the Allies to come into western areas of the Netherlands. By now, thousands[6] of Dutch people had died of cold and starvation. Those who went foraging far and wide for food discovered that any that they managed to find was confiscated at checkpoints so that they returned to their starving families empty-handed. The foragers might manage to eat whilst on the move, but those depending on them still starved. People died in the streets. Any available wood had been burned and the only chance to keep warm was in bed, getting up only to try to get food or go to the toilet. Although there was still water, gas and electricity was but a memory. Everybody's sole concern was to survive the next day, then the next, then the next. But the daily sight of the Spitfires coming over made them feel that they were not alone and they knew that the end was in sight – but just how far away was it?

No. 303 Squadron lost more pilots. At 10.00 on 25 February, Flight Lieutenant S. Szpakowicz led four Spitfire IXs on an armed recce during which they attacked the Ockenburg site in The Hague. On the way back, they crossed out at 10,000 feet over the Hook but met heavy flak from the harbour there. Szpakowicz, who was call sign Blue 1, continued out to sea for about five minutes before realizing that his radiator had been hit. The four made for Ursel, with Szpakowicz' Spitfire gradually losing height until it ditched about 500 yards from the land near Schouwen. The three who were left orbited the position for five minutes and saw the aeroplane and its pilot sink into the water. Szpakowicz is assumed to have been killed; his body was never found. He was flying Spitfire IX EN367.

By now 303 was flying a mixture of IXs and XVIs with practice bombing carried out using Vbs. On the operation immediately before this, the section leader, Flying Officer S. Zdanowski was in a XVI with the others in IXs. On the 27th, two days after Flight Lieutenant Szpakowicz went down, Sergeant K. Prusak was taking off from an American base in Northampton in Spitfire MA814. The aeroplane was seen to roll whilst still at low altitude before it hit the ground and burst into flames. Prusak was killed. During February, 303 flew Big Ben patrols with Halifaxes and completed a number of anti-submarine patrols as well. There seemed to be enemy midget submarines operating off the Dutch coast and if they were not actively patrolling for them, the squadrons certainly were looking for them as they crossed the sea. They were probably assigned Big Ben patrols because of their use of Spitfire IXs, which were less suited to the armed recces than the XVIs.

During this period, the 2nd TAF had also been doing its part against the V2s. Its Spitfires and Typhoons were invaluable in attacking eastern launch sites and the transport infrastructure, disrupting the supplies of the rockets to the firing points.They attacked a liquid oxygen factory (if indeed it was one) at Alblasserdam near Dordrecht on 22 January, and no doubt this increased the problems of the rocket troops.

No. 12 Group was not operating in isolation. On 23 February, a conference convened at the headquarters of 2nd TAF in Brussels to discuss and agree methodologies for the co-operation of 12 Group and 2nd TAF. The various matters were confirmed in a letter issued by Air Vice-Marshal G. H. Ambler on behalf of Fighter Command on 25 February.[7] The main points noted:

(i)   Second Tactical Air Force are prepared to use 2 Group Squadrons to attack "BIG BEN" targets when effort can be spared from support of the land battle.

(ii)   Fighter Command will continue to issue a weekly list of priority targets to both 12 Group and Second Tactical Air Force. Whenever Second Tactical Air Force are able to spare effort for this purpose, they will select from the list the highest priority target, which they consider suitable for 2 Group attack.

(iii)   Second Tactical Air Force will send a copy of their Form 'D' to 12 Group, repeated to Fighter Command, and will inform 12 Group of any delays or postponements by telephone.

(iv)   Second Tactical Air Force will be responsible for all necessary escorts to 2 Group aircraft and for subsequent damage assessment after their attacks.

(v)   Fighter Command will forward to Second Tactical Air Force, all

relevant details and photographs of targets of which they are
not already in possession.

(vi)   12 Group will give way to 2 Group whenever it happens that
         both Groups have planned attacks which might interfere with
         each other.

Paragraph (vi) is significant because it shows that Fighter Command did
not have an absolute say in which targets would be attacked by 2nd TAF.
The problems of command faced by Hill have been discussed earlier, but
considering that the final responsibility for preventing V2s getting to
Britain lay with him and not 2nd TAF, it is surprising that 2nd TAF was
allowed such a degree of independence to the extent that their aircraft
would take priority over those of 12 Group once in the air. Of course,
it would be easier to divert a few Spitfires than a formation of medium
bombers (e.g. Mitchells and Bostons), but the very fact that two sets of
aircraft could be heading for the same target at the same time, each with
no knowledge of the other, does seem unusual. Eric Mee commented on
the use of crystals in the radios and of course this meant that 12 Group
Spitfires and 2nd TAF bombers flying in the same airspace were not likely
to be able to talk to each other – another factor in the forthcoming tragedy.
    The conference also considered the question of civilian casualties in the
proximity of any attacks and a note issued later[8] stated that the process
adopted by Fighter Command for the selection of aiming points had been
explained to those from 2nd TAF and 'pointed out the state of occupation,
or otherwise, by Dutch civilians of surrounding built-up areas'. In particular, this referred to those living near the Haagsche Bosch. It went on:

> The difficulties under which Fighter Command had been attacking Rocket
> Targets in Holland, because of the presence of Dutch civilians in many of
> the Target areas, were referred to in detail by Fighter Command represen-
> tatives and particular mention was made of the greater risk to Dutch
> civilian life involved in attacks by medium bombers. This consideration, it
> was concluded by the Meeting, practically ruled out any Target but the
> HAAGSCHE BOSCH for medium attack at that time. 2nd TAF. . . . would,
> of course, be fully alive to the need for avoiding civilian casualties.

And with regard to clearance distances to Dutch properties, as far as the
Haagsche Bosch was concerned, the aiming points would have to be at
least 500 yards away.
    On 1 March 1945, HQ Fighter Command issued an analysis of the
results of the attacks since 21st February. 12 Group and 2nd TAF were both
included in the circulation[9]. It noted that the concentrated bombing of the
wooded areas seemed to have driven the Germans to the Duindigt racecourse area and that it was suitable for attacking. However, around the

area of the film studios attacked on the 22nd by the 12 Group squadrons, there were still targets. Accordingly, for the week there would be three main target areas: Wassenaar/Rust-en-Vreugd, Duindigt and storage and maintenance areas in the Haagsche Bosch. If these could not be attacked, the secondary targets were to be railway related. But it looked as if the medium bomber squadrons would be getting into the fray at last.

Notes

1. The 12 Group ORB for 14 February reports 603 as attacking the Staalduin Bosch and makes no mention of Loosduinen. In his account, Hill mentioned only five operations – those on 3, 8 and 9 February – and does not mention the two attacks reported by 603 on the 14th. The comment from the 603 ORB that 'another stick was observed to burst on the road leading through the target area' suggests that it was one of the wooded areas being attacked and not the confined site of the tramsheds.
2. Two of 602's Spitfires returned to Swannington directly because of 'rough running' engines.
3. The war in the Netherlands finished officially on 4 May but it took some days before all areas were taken over by Allied troops.
4. *Typhoon Warfare* by Tom Hall, p. 127.
5. The runway orientations were 08/26, 02/20 and 14/32.
6. Estimated as 22,000.
7. AIR20/794.
8. AIR20/794.
9. AIR20/279.

CHAPTER SEVEN

The Bombing of Bezuidenhout

Saturday, 3 March brought generally fine weather to the airfields in Norfolk, although the day started with a thin mist which soon cleared and did not affect operations. No. 602 opened activities with an armed recce of the Haagsche Bosch. Four Spitfires took off at 07.15 and found so much cloud over The Hague that they aborted their first attack but took a second shot at it, which they reported as being successful. After re-forming, they swept the area to the south-west of Amsterdam, shooting up a staff car which they left blazing. No. 603 was next off at 08.30, six Spitfires led by the 'A' Flight Commander, Flight Lieutenant Jack Batchelor. Bob Sergeant flew this particular operation too. No doubt after forming up, as they crossed the North Sea, they eased out into the more relaxed formation employed to make the transit easier and conserve fuel. For the likes of Bob Sergeant, who had been flying Spitfires for many years now, it would have been a day to enjoy being in the air. Soon afterwards, they were told that medium bombers of 2nd TAF were on their way to bomb the same target and that they should divert to bomb their alternative target – the woods north of Haagsche Bosch. The Staalduin Bosch. This was not a problem but the use of the mediums was certainly new and unusual.

For the people living in Bezuidenhout, another day of starvation and chill beckoned. The utter cold of the depth of winter may have passed but without proper nutrition, any reserves of strength and energy had been used up long ago and life remained bleak. How would they survive this new day? It was Hans Borsboom's ninth birthday. The previous day, a British bomb fell near to the family house and his parents decided that it would be safer to leave; they had done so only thirty minutes before. For the young Jan van't Hoff, the unmistakable sound of the Spitfires' Merlins brought the usual crumb of comfort.

167

B25 Mitchells of 320 Squadron on 8 January 1945 being cleaned of snow
at B58 Melsbroek.
(Courtesy Imperial War Museum. Negative no. CL1775.)

Today, when 602 bombed, they came from the south-west and not out
of the sun, where the first attacks of the day often started – or so it seemed
to the boy. And of course like the Borsbooms, many of the people moved
away from the area in the morning in case stray bombs hit their houses,
as happened from time to time. Jan's parents, Pieter and Truus were away
on a foraging expedition leaving Jan to be looked after by his sister Riet.
By now the foraging meant having to go far from The Hague and into the
countryside to find anything, sometimes bartering with farmers. With the
whole population of western Holland searching, however, not much was
left. As on previous expeditions, Pieter and Truus pushed a handcart
which they loaded up with wood for fuel and any food they could find,
and hoped that they might be able to get it past any German checkpoints
they might encounter. On this occasion, the parents walked all the way to
Zwolle – 100 miles each way. At about 09.00, Jan, out on the street, spotted
aircraft in the distance. He remembered the skies as being clear, and saw
a large number of Mitchell bombers and several Bostons heading towards
Bezuidenhout. But he was sure that they were just passing over, heading
for Germany or some other target – definitely nothing to do with them.

*I knew every type of aircraft that came over, whether it was a Mosquito or
a Spitfire or a B25 Mitchell – I knew it. Then I saw them coming over*

heading in a funny direction, which turned out to be their bomb runs. They
turned round and I thought what are they doing? Then I saw things coming
out and thought they were parachutists – but from a bomber! Thought we
were being liberated you know but the black things were bombs and then
they were bursting all around. All at once hell broke loose.

He ran to find Riet, his sister, and the pair of them rushed in a blind
panic to get away from the deafening explosions. All around was death,
destruction and noise.

The six 603 Spitfires arrived over the area at the same time. There
seemed to be two waves of mediums and at about 9.15 the Spitfires made
their attack on the Staalduin Bosch, diving from the north-east from 10,000
feet to 3,000 between the attacks of the two waves of mediums. They found
the target area to be covered with cloud – 7/10th from 3,000 feet to 8,000
feet – although this did not stop them and they reported a successful operation. They could see that the Mitchells and Bostons were making a
dreadful mistake but they could only watch helplessly as the bombs whis-
tled down on the unfortunate Dutch because they could not contact the
bombers to tell them – the crystals in their radios were set to different
channels. They could do nothing. Bob Sergeant noted in his log book
'Armed Recco. Arrived as Mitchells were bombing – amazing! – bombed

The sight which greeted Jan Van't Hoff on the morning of 3 March 1945.
(This photograph was taken in April 1944, and is illustrative only.)
(Courtesy Imperial War Museum. Negative no. CH12842.)

Bezuidenhout, 3 March 1945. Smoke billows up from Dutch homes
accidentally bombed by 2nd TAF medium bombers.
(Courtesy Netherlands Institute for War Documentation image no.69676.)

crossroads then watched the mediums again.' Years later he recalled the
incident with horror, his memories still clear: 'We saw them going in and
knew it was wrong. It was atrocious.' They returned to Ludham at 09.55.

The Poles of 303 Squadron arrived next at about 09.45. Led by Flying
Officer Maksymowicz four Spitfire IXs attacked the Haagsche Bosch again
and reported 'black smoke . . . rising from buildings SE of HAAGSCHE
BOSCH to 8.000 ft and stretching to ROTTERDAM. Fires seen amongst
buildings . . .' Shortly afterwards, another four Spitfires of 124 Squadron
were overhead and they reported 'All houses to south-east of target seen
to be on fire.' And so it continued. No. 453's first operation of the day took
off at 10.35 again to bomb the Haagsche Bosch and they reported the
damage to the houses and the fires still burning. Rusty Leith's log book
records, 'Bombed through light cloud – OK. Mediums hit civvies.' The
usual conveyor belt of armed recces continued throughout the day, with
many of them reporting the fires in the houses and the destruction of the
area. No. 603's Eric Mee said that the pall of smoke could be seen for miles
for many days after the attack. No. 602's Max Baerlein was also over The
Hague later in the day and he said:

*We were not in the area when the bombing took place but the whole place
was a mass of flames and the bombers had gone. The significance was very*

obvious to us as on the bombing runs we had made, up until then, we had always taken great care not to touch any of the civilian buildings in the area, only releasing our bombs at the lowest altitude that would enable us to pull out of the dive. The mess we saw from the air was, in consequence, most distressing. We were shocked to see that all the efforts we had made to avoid houses had been to no avail.

Once the bombing stopped, Riet and Jan picked their way through the flames and destruction back to their house and to their joy found it had escaped serious damage. They were both unhurt, but their parents did not know this. On their way back to The Hague in the afternoon they heard stories that the city had been badly bombed, but as they got nearer, they heard that Bezuidenhout was the worst damaged. They rushed anxiously back to try to find out what had happened to Jan and Riet, and to their huge relief found them safe and well at home, albeit suffering from shock as they absorbed this latest disaster. The Borsboom family did not fare so well. Although they survived, the house that they had left less than an hour before was destroyed. They still had a horse and cart to allow them to get around and of course the family survived the attack, so they appreciated their good fortune on that score.

Bezuidenhout – the aftermath.
(Courtesy Netherlands Institute for War Documentation image no. 69722.)

Bezuidenhout – the aftermath
(Courtesy Netherlands Institute for War Documentation image no 69793.)

Most of those living in Bezuidenhout fled when the attack started and, characteristically, the occupying Germans did little to help, so most of the houses and their contents burnt to the ground. Once the bombing stopped, many feared to go back because of the sight and sound of the marauding Spitfires overhead, which they now associated with damage rather than succour. Those who did hurry back tried to help the injured and, fight the fires – although this proved difficult because of the number of water mains damaged and cut. Only on the edge of the area near the canals and the town drains could enough water be directed on to the flames.

Bezuidenhout was effectively destroyed – the medium bombers did their job well. The toll rose to about 535 Dutch civilians killed with over 3,200 homes and buildings totally destroyed. In addition, 432 people were missing and 235 seriously wounded. About 2,500 of the damaged houses could be repaired, but the total number of Dutch civilians who needed alternative housing after the attack was about 30,000 – 5 per cent of the total population of The Hague. Jan van't Hoff commented many years later that the raid had failed completely. Many of his schoolfriends died – the school had been hit by several bombs. This part of The Hague was destroyed but, he recalled, there had not been a single bomb on the wooded Haagsche Bosch. In fact, this is not quite correct because many bombs did fall on the other target aiming point in the Haagsche Bosch. However, the overriding result of the disastrous attack by the mediums of 2nd TAF was the more or less complete destruction of Bezuidenhout and the deaths of the innocent Dutch who had the misfortune to live there. The personal tragedies of those under the bombs can only be imagined. The hardships that they had endured under the German occupation since 1940 had seemed at last to be coming to an end. They had suffered brutality and fear, deportations, the deprivations of the *Hungerwinter*, and now this last ironic twist, the death and destruction meted out by their supposed allies. There was anger and the Germans stoked it up. 'Look what your "friends" are doing to you.' they would say, and the point had validity. Why had it happened? It may have been a mistake, one of the errors and tragedies that occur in all wars, but surely the people of the Netherlands were due some sort of explanation.

Despite the reports coming in from the Spitfires about the fires in the houses and the plumes of smoke, it took a few days for the details to percolate up to the senior levels of the RAF. Eventually, however, concern reached the highest political level and put the whole campaign against the V2s in jeopardy, almost bringing it to a premature end. Ultimately, the affair attracted the fearsome attention of no less a person than the Prime Minister, Winston Churchill who wrote a stinging personal minute, whose circulation included the Secretary of State for Air and the Chief of the Air Staff.[1]

Juliana van Stolbergplein in 1945 following the bombing on 3 March.
Compare this with the picture taken in 1935.
(Courtesy Haags Gemeentearchief. Photo no. 6.16434.)

[The incident] . . . *shows how feeble have been our efforts to interfere with the rockets, and secondly, the extraordinarily bad aiming which has led to the slaughter of Dutchmen. This matter requires a thorough explanation. We have had numerous accounts of the pin point bombing of suspected Gestapo houses in Holland and of other specialised points. But good indications are given in this account of the wood where the rockets are stored and of the railway lines which, if interrupted, would hamper the supply of rockets. All this ought to have been available from Air Intelligence. Instead of attacking these points with precision and regularity, all that has been done is to scatter bombs about this unfortunate city without the slightest effect on their rocket sites but much on innocent human lives and the sentiments of a friendly people.*

He finished with demands for reports and explanations with the promise to 'bring the matter before the Cabinet'.

Churchill's outrage is clear even if his comments are somewhat unfair. We have seen that great care had been taken to avoid Dutch casualties, but on this occasion something went drastically wrong. Because the aircraft concerned – Mitchells and Bostons – were US-made, many of the Dutch thought that they were from the USAAF, or that at least some of them were, and this is still believed by some. In fact, they were all part of the RAF's 2nd TAF from 2 Group, the squadrons involved being 98, 180, 320, 226 and 342. What is entirely ironic is that 320 Squadron was formed from a core of Dutch naval personnel who flew their aircraft from the Netherlands to Britain in 1940. Some of the Dutch airmen taking part in this raid might very well have been looking down on their home town. (342 was a Free French squadron.) Nos. 98, 180 and 320 were from 139 Wing stationed at Melsbroek and the others from 137 Wing at Vitry-en-Artois. The initial reports from the airmen taking part show little realization that a mistake had been made and give the impression of an attack that was assessed to have been more or less a success. A brief daily task report originating from 2nd TAF[2] recorded 'A large possibly petrol fire was started with columns of smoke and flame just South of target.' An almost identical statement is found in the 2 Group ORB for the day[3]. This report also stated that 'main concentration fell in target area, with bursts in western and southern sections of target and built up areas'. As far as they and 2 Group was concerned, it seemed to be a job well done and attention moved on to the next operation – this time not directed at the V2s.

Contrary to Jan van't Hoff's recollection, there was significant cloud cover. Some of the bombs were aimed using G-H[4] with the target area not seen at all, so that the airmen in the mediums would not be able to see where their bombs were heading, although many of the 12 Group Spitfire pilots over The Hague at that time, particularly 603, knew that a terrible

An aerial shot of Bezuidenhout after the damaged areas had been cleared. It gives a good idea of the extent of the damage caused. The Church tower at the bottom left can be seen in other photographs taken from ground level. The Haagsche Bosch is at the bottom edge of the picture.
(Reproduced by kind permission of KLM.)

mistake had occurred. But the realization of just what had happened appears to have been limited to them. The intelligence officers at the squadrons (both the bombers and the Spitfires) making up the Operations Record Books did not mention the mistake explicitly, even although the Spitfire pilots would have reported what they saw. It might very well have been noticed with regret as just another tragedy of war, but perhaps understandably at squadron level, there was no appreciation of the political significance of what had taken place. Weather permitting, the 12 Group attacks continued over the next few days with attention swinging away from the Haagsche Bosch. It had received a real pasting and once again, it seemed that the enemy rocket troops had moved their operations elsewhere. Life continued as usual.

The Resistance in the Netherlands appreciated the significance of the mistake and set in train a reaction, but it was not until Wednesday, 7 March that the waves of anger emanating from the Bezuidenhout incident reached the British authorities. Once they did, they got to the highest of levels, both military and political, very quickly. The Government of the Netherlands in exile had established an embassy at 21A Portman Square in London. They issued two notes on the 7th, four days after the incident, based on information received from the Resistance, one[5] from the Dutch Naval Attaché, C. Moolenburgh, addressed to Air Commodore F. Beaumont the Director of Allied Air Co-operation and Foreign Liaison at the Air Ministry. It includes the following direct quotations from the Resistance groups, first in The Hague: 'Command Interior Forces, district the Hague as well as independently operating illegal groups, stress catastrophical results to civilian population of bombing attacks during last weeks, especially on March 3rd. Bezuidenhout quarter and part of city center heavily damaged though no military targets in these areas. Many killed.' And from the Amsterdam Resistance: 'Bombing of the Hague March 3rd cost several hundreds dead and wounded, thousands roofless and great damage in densely populated Bezuidenhout quarter and historical town center. No military targets in immediate vicinity, which is proved by German refusal to give petrol to Amsterdam fire brigade for assistance in fighting spreading fires.'

Moolenburgh continued:

> *I have been instructed to point out that the Netherlands Government fully realise the importance of keeping the V2 attack down to a minimum. But they feel at the same time that the Allied effort against these enemy missiles endangers the life and possessions of the Dutch population to a great extent.*
>
> *In anticipation of [receiving a detailed account of what took place], my Ambassador has instructed me on behalf of the Netherlands Government to inform you that they expect an interruption of all attacks against the V2 sites situated in the built up areas of the Hague [Author's roman].*

In diplomatic terms this was strong stuff, and it is to be noticed that the demand for the attacks to cease does not limit itself to the medium bombers but to *all attacks* which presumably included the dive-bombing Spitfires. Neither the Prime Minister nor the Dutch authorities in exile differentiated between the attacks by the medium bombers and the dive-bombing Spitfires, lumping them together.

The second note[6] came from E. Michiels van Verduyen, the Ambassador, and was addressed to Anthony Eden. The language was polite and restrained but that made the contents even more devastating:

> *Your Excellency,*
>
> *I have the honour to draw Your Excellency's attention to the catastrophic results for the civilian population of the RAF attack against V2 storage sites in the Haagsche Bosch, The Hague, in the morning of March 3rd, 1945.*
>
> *Though Her Majesty's Government realize that bombing always entails certain risks to civilians, owing to inevitable deviations, they are of the opinion that the specific attack against a target, surrounded by densely populated districts, was highly irresponsible. In this particular instance,*

town districts more than one mile from the target were hit. If more thought had been given to the immense risks to the inhabitants of The Hague, the already sorely tried civilian population would not have had the terrible suffering inflicted upon them by those responsible for this raid.

I have been instructed and have the honour to launch a formal protest to Your Excellency for the manner in which the attack has been planned and executed and to urge Your Excellency to lend your good offices in order that a repetition will not take place.

> *I have the honour to remain,*
> *with the highest consideration,*
> *Your Excellency's obedient Servant,*

Two notes, one to the RAF and one to the British Government, which might very well have brought the campaign against the V2s to an end. It is interesting that at this stage, the Netherlands Government seemed to believe that the bombing had been carried out as planned and that the fault lay with the planners. But clearly an investigation was needed and it started pretty well forthwith. As far as the demand to stop the attacks is concerned, on 10 March the RAF's Director of Operations, K.B.B. Cross, wrote a draft response to Captain Moolenburgh's letter, in which he said that no such undertaking could be given as it would be obvious to the enemy that the attacks had ceased. This was echoed in a note dated 14 March from the Chief of the Air Staff (Portal) to the Secretary of State, Sir Archibald Sinclair.[7] His view was that the whole campaign should not be stopped because of what he called 'one gross error'. His note also commented on the reasons for the error and he noted that it was so large that it could not have been caused by a mistake in estimating the wind, as was now being suggested. He went on to say that such an error would not have occurred if the crews had been adequately briefed, but in the meantime it was mooted that the Dutch should be told that the accident was caused by a false estimate of the wind; the full facts not yet known.

Meantime, 2nd TAF was investigating. The suggestion that the error might have been caused by an incorrect estimate of wind came from a letter dated 10 March from Air Marshal A. Coningham, the AOC-in-C 2nd TAF to the Under Secretary of State for Air at the Air Ministry.[8] Coningham made the point that visual bombing 'checked by G-H was ordered' but also states that there was a strong crosswind which was underestimated by the crews and led to the bombs landing well away from their aiming points. He went on to say that there was 'no question that the crews were not properly briefed' but nonetheless instructions had been issued that no further attacks by medium bombers were to be made against targets in The Hague. Portal responded on the 16th. He started by saying that he was 'far from reassured by your report' and went on to point out that if the briefing was 'entirely satisfactory' then the bombing error was 'astonishing'. He agreed that the attacks should be halted mean-time, but asked that a thorough examination be undertaken to establish why the error had been so large.

Two days later, the answers began to emerge in a letter dated 18 March from Basil Embry, the AOC 2 Group to Sir Arthur Coningham. As always in such situations, a number of factors combined to create the final effect, but the key error had been quite simple. The 137 Wing duty intelligence officer, a flying officer, had transposed one set of co-ordinates placing the aiming point in the middle of Bezuidenhout rather than in the centre of the Haagsche Bosch. This is clearly seen on the target photograph in Appendix 2, where points 'A' (H037 and V043) and 'B' (H042 and V064) are the required target, with 'B1' (H064 and V042) the aiming point given in error for 'B'. An inspection of the vertical and horizontal co-ordinates at the left-hand and bottom edges of the photograph confirms the mistake. The intelligence officer was subsequently court-martialled for 'conduct to the prejudice of good order and air force discipline', and reprimanded.

But whilst his mistake was the root cause, other factors could have prevented the tragedy. On 2 March, HQ 2nd TAF ordered 2 Group to attack the Haagsche Bosch areas. Receiving the order, the AOC 2 Group noticed that there was a built-up area within 500 yards of the target area, and bearing in mind the need to minimize civilian casualties, telephoned the operations officer at 2nd TAF to find out if the houses were occupied or not. He did not know and the query was passed to Fighter Command, who passed it in turn to the Air Ministry – by now late into the evening at 22.30. The Air Ministry responded that no particular clearance was known but the message passed back arrived at 2 Group as 'Hague target area is clear of Dutch people'[9]. An extract from the 2nd TAF Duty Operations Officer's Log[10] records that at 23.10, 'General clearance has been given by A.M. for this target to be attacked. Houses within 500 yards of the whole target area have been cleared of inhabitants.' Having received the desired assurances, 2 Group issued their operations order at 02.30.[11] H-Hour was 09.00, with thirty Mitchells from 139 Wing opening the attack. Next at 09.05 were six Mitchells and six Bostons from 137 Wing followed by another six Mitchells and six Bostons at 09.10 with a further six Mitchells from 139 Wing finishing the raid at 09.15. The co-ordinates of the aiming point for the first thirty bombers were Point A on the target map (Appendix 2) and for the others (which included an elements of both wings) Point B. The four elements should have followed the same route to the target – Base to Noordenhoofd and to the target.

It was not until towards the end of March that the full circumstances became clear to the British but by then the European war was nearly at its end with the last V2 landing on England on 27 March and, so the debate about civilian casualties became academic. On 31 March the Assistant Chief of the Air Staff (Operations) noted[12] 'In any case it appears that we are now being overtaken by events, and I suggest that Fighter Command be left to carry on with their present policy.' This was echoed in Churchill's personal minute of 15 April 1945[13] 'The problem of attacking rocket bomb sites seems largely to have been solved by the movements of our Armies.' And he was right.

Roderic Hill makes only the briefest mention of the incident: 'Unfortunately, the bombing was not sufficiently accurate, in consequence of which casualties occurred among Dutch civilians and their property was damaged. After this unhappy experience, Air Marshal Coningham decided to make no more attacks on targets at the Hague.'[14] Considering the extent of the injury and damage and the furore it caused, both in the Netherlands and in Britain, his comments are remarkably understated, possibly because even in 1948, three and a half years on when his paper was published, the incident could inflame emotions still raw and tender. Or perhaps he felt the quicker it could be forgotten and the less said the better.

Air Marshal Coningham had little choice other than to order the cessation of the involvement of the mediums considering the reaction of his superiors in the air force and the withering comments made by the Prime Minister. He would have been a brave man to have risked repeating the tragedy at such a late stage in the battle. Understandable and regrettable it may have been, but the bombing of Bezuidenhout on 3 March 1945 was a low point in the RAF's and the 2nd TAF's prosecution of the war. Both then and in modern wars, it has often been the Americans who are usually blamed for 'friendly fire' incidents rather than the British, but the British do have their own 'blue on blue' accidents. Some army units fighting in the European theatre in 1944 and 1945 became very wary of ground-support strikes after a number of accidents to their troops caused by the RAF hitting the wrong targets; it was not only the Americans. Tom Hall, the Aussie Typhoon pilot, witnessed an incident involving Bostons and Mitchells just after D-Day in the Caen area, which is disturbingly similar. Having been 'softened up' by heavy bombers, the army found the large numbers of bomb craters a hindrance in moving forward and the support passed to the mediums.

> *It was a disaster. They dropped their bombs short of the targeted area and bombed our advanced troops, mainly Canadians who suffered heavy casualties. Because we had flown a lot of ops in support of the army in the Caen area, it was obvious to us from our vantage point, that the glint of the dropping bombs from the leading aircraft were seen they were bombing far too short. No more bombing raids took place.*[15]

It could have been Bob Sergeant speaking. And it has been noted already that many people involved in the incident – both Dutch and

British – thought that the Mitchells and Bostons belonged to the USAAF. Perhaps in some British minds there was a view that this perception should not be actively discouraged. It has to be said that nothing has come to light to suggest that the crews of the mediums were in any way at fault. They seem to have carried out the operation as ordered and the bombing seems to have been executed in accordance with the instructions they had received and was accurate. The feelings of the intelligence officer who made the transposition error can only be imagined, but he must have suffered agonies once the consequences of his understandable and innocent mistake became apparent.

On the face of it, the bombing of Bezuidenhout has little consequence for the activities of the Spitfires of 12 Group, but this is not so. At the very least, it might have brought the campaign against the rockets to a complete stop if the request made by Captain Moolenburgh had been accepted. Throughout the campaign, Hill wanted the medium bombers of 2nd TAF to become involved and when they eventually did, their first effort was a disaster. Few may have given much thought to it, but with the overriding concern about the potential for casualties amongst the innocent civilians it demonstrated that even if the Spitfires 'got it wrong', the consequences were far less grave. When the Spitfires did get it wrong – and we have seen that some of the residents of Bezuidenhout used to leave the area in the early morning to avoid any stray bombs – the collateral damage caused by errors in the Spitfire dive bombing never reached the scale of this one incident. It showed that the Spitfires and their techniques worked. The effect of the campaign on the Dutch civilians and their morale is an integral part of any account of the battle of the rockets. We know that for Jan van't Hoff and his family, the sight of 'their Spitfires' meant encouragement and help in the heart of their misery but the effect of the bombing could have destroyed this. In fact, although many Dutch people did feel very bitter about the destruction and casualties of 3 March, the majority eventually saw it for what it was – a tragic accident of war – and did not bear any long-term hostility towards the British and the RAF. And this must have been very hard on top of all the other miseries they had endured that winter.

The message for the Spitfires of 12 Group was that they were doing it right, although the pilots flying the operations and their superiors probably did not see it like that and realize what it meant. They had their day-to-day duties to carry out. The bombing of Bezuidenhout was a tragedy and it came only three weeks before the end of the V2 attacks. As a postscript to the whole sorry affair, on 20 December 1945, a Dutch woman whose house had been destroyed in the attack on Bezuidenhout wrote to 'His Majesty the King of England' asking for compensation from the RAF because she was destitute. All that she owned had been destroyed in the bombing. The appeal is quite moving and cannot have failed to elicit sympathy. She estimated that her goods were worth £58,000 a very significant sum still.[16]

The claim was rejected, the reason being that the destruction of her property was 'a hazard of war'[17].

Notes

1. Prime Minister's Personal Minute dated 18 March 1945 Serial D.75/5 AIR8/1225 206738.
2. 2nd TAF ORB AIR37/718.
3. AIR25/25.
4. G-H was a development of 'Gee' and 'Oboe' in that two ground transmitting stations were used to plot an accurate position for the bomber.
5. AIR20/795.
6. AIR19/432.
7. AIR8/1225.
8. AIR20/795.
9. AIR20/795.
10. AIR20/795.
11. AIR20/795 Operational Order AO.717 – 3 March 1945.
12. AIR20/794.
13. AIR20/794 Serial number M.336/5.
14. Supplement to the *London Gazette,* of Tuesday 19 October 1948, 'Air Operations by Air Defence of Great Britain and Fighter Command in Connection with the German Flying Bomb and Rocket Offensives, 1944–1945'.
15. *Typhoon Warfare* by Tom Hall, p. 42.
16. AIR2/7894 Letter dated 20 December 1945.
17. AIR2/7894 Letter dated 4 March 1946 from A Rumbold to MW Low at the Air Ministry.

CHAPTER EIGHT

'VII Kaput'

From 3 to 15 March, 12 Group's Spitfires continued to attack the old familiar targets in The Hague with the exception of the Haagsche Bosch, which was not targeted again. Roderic Hill believed that the damage to the woods was so great that the Germans had been forced to withdraw from them completely, and attention turned to the Duindigt racecourse area and Wassenaar Ravelijn although Ockenburg, Rust-en-Vreugd, Staalduin Bosch, etc. continued to receive their fair share of attention.

On 9 March, 303 lost another pilot, Wing Commander J. Falkowski DFC, apparently to flak after an attack by four Polish Spitfires on the Duindigt racecourse. On the return journey, not far from the Dutch coast, one of the other pilots noticed what seemed to be glycol streaming from the Wing Commander's starboard radiator and warned him of this. The four returned to the coast and headed for Belgium but just to the south of The Hague, at 2,500 feet, Falkowski decided to bale out. His parachute was seen to open but his landing was not seen because of cloud. He was taken prisoner but managed to escape and he survived the war.

Captain Moolenburgh's request that all bombing should cease may have helped bring the efforts of the mediums to an end, but it did not affect the dive-bombing operations and on the 14th a new target appeared on the lists – the headquarters of the *Bataafsche Import Maatschappij* in The Hague known to many of the pilots as 'the Shellhouse' and to many Dutch people as 'the BIM building'. This T-shaped building is clearly visible on the target map just a few blocks to the north-west of the Haagsche Bosch on the north side of Wassenaarseweg at co-ordinates V045 and H021. The second and third floors were commandeered by about thirty German personnel, including some of American descent, who acted as a central co-ordinating point for radio intercepts of Allied traffic *Nachrichtentruppe*. They positioned radio antennae on the roof and the 'Americans' listened in to radio transmissions from Allied aircraft. Some of the Spitfire pilots thought that the top floor housed the *Gestapo*, their records and Dutch

The BIM building in happier times. This is the side attacked by 602
Squadron using 'skip-bombing'. The nearness of the church and the
difficulty of avoiding damage to it on can easily be seen.
(Reproduced by kind permission of Shell International B.V., The Hague.)

Resistance prisoners but this is not borne out by research by local Dutch
historians. In December 1944, a Resistance group sent a message saying
that they believed the building to be the headquarters of the V2 troops
with control centred there, and that its destruction should have a priority.
Situated at the center of the V2 activities, it made an ideal location for the
technical and administration staff associated with the rockets.

Built in 1941 and 1942, it is a remarkable building. In plan long and
narrow, rising to six storeys in height, it is clearly seen from the air because
of its shape and pale concrete and brick finish. The main five floors are
faced with a series of wide and ample windows which give good views of
the surrounding area between vertical facing columns. Apart from its
significance to the fighting of the Second World War, the building is of
some importance to architectural historians. It was designed by a well
known Dutch painter and architect, Jacobus J.P. Oud, who has his place
in history as a founder member of the De Stijl group and the magazine
they first published in 1917. It is not regarded as one of his best, being
described by one commentator as 'rather formal and heavy-handed'.[1]
However, with its reinforced concrete structure, the proximity to a church
across Wassenaarseweg and nearby residential areas, it proved a

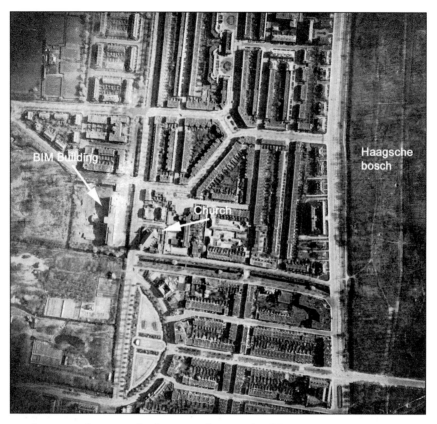

A target photograph showing the BIM building and the Haagsche
Bosch. Note how near civilian houses are to the target areas and the
problems they would cause for 602 Squadron carrying out its
'skip-bombing' attack.
(The late Bob Sergeant.)

headache for the Spitfire pilots of 12 Group trying to destroy it. According
to 'Bax' Baxter, the idea for the attack came from Squadron Leader
Sutherland and rather to his surprise was agreed by Group.[2]

The 12 Group ORB for 4 March records that four aircraft of 602
Squadron attacked 'BATAAFSCHE PETROL CO.' but according to the
602 ORB this raid was against the targets in Rust-en-Vreugd. Subsequent
information suggests that the BIM building did not become known to the
pilots until the middle of the month, so the 12 Group ORB is either wrong
or it refers to another of the company's facilities and not this building. On
the 14th, six 602 pilots attended a briefing for a low-level attack on the
building to be carried out in conjunction with dive-bombing attacks by

603 and 124 Squadrons but visibility over The Hague was very poor and it was cancelled. Pilots on a dive-bombing raid later that day against Duindigt found the racecourse difficult to find, despite their experience in bombing it and its unmistakable features from the air. The church on the opposite side of Wassenaarseweg, the H. Paschalis Baylon Church, made the BIM building a difficult target, hence the planned low-level 'skip-bombing' attack rather than the more usual dive bombing, and the need for excellent visibility.

We have seen already that dive bombing usually proved more accurate and resulted in fewer misses and civilian casualties. By now, eleven days after the bombing of Bezuidenhout, the last thing needed was another incident involving civilians and a church. As its name suggests, skip bombing required a fast and low approach with the bombs being dropped to 'skip' over the ground and into the target. George Pyle thinks that the idea came from the days of Lord Nelson and the Royal Navy, when cannonballs fired at enemy ships bounced off the water, rather like the 'Dam Buster' bombs. The fuses included a delay so that the bomb would not explode on first contact with the ground and underneath the aeroplane dropping it. A poorly aimed skip bomb could go some distance from the intended target, whereas a poorly aimed dive bomb should not go far, which made the proposed 602 attack quite unusual – almost unique for this campaign.

On the 15th, the operation was 'on' and six of 602's Spitfires, each carrying a single 500-pound and two 250-pounders lifted off from Ludham at 15.05 but poor visibility over the North Sea and the target prevented the operation going ahead and the aircraft returned to base after jettisoning their bombs into the sea. Flight Lieutenant Wroblewski pulled off a remarkable emergency landing when one of his colleagues spotted a bomb at the side of the runway as he made his approach at about 300 feet. He pushed the throttle forward, but the engine did not respond. He managed to land downwind on the runway in use although it was a near thing. Low cloud over The Hague caused a third cancellation on the 17th, but the afternoon of Sunday, the 18th proved suitable. After yet another careful briefing, the six pilots from 602 took off at 13.00 from Ludham.

Led by Squadron Leader Sutherland, the others were Flying Officer Baxter, Flight Lieutenant Stephenson, Flight Lieutenant Pertwee, Flight Lieutenant Pullman and Flight Sergeant Zuber, and they were armed as before with a single 500-pound and two 250-pound bombs. Their attack would be supported by diversionary dive-bombing and flak suppression attacks on the Duindigt racecourse by twelve Spifires each from 453 and 124 Squadrons. The Aussies led by Ernie Esau left first at 12.50 from Matlaske and made a normal attack, with little of note to report other than 'good' results. They landed at B67 to refuel, then returned to base. No. 124's dozen Spitfire IXs took off from Coltishall five minutes later at 12.55

The church across the road from the BIM building in 2003. 'Bax' Baxter almost hit the top of the spire, which gives an indication of just how low 602 was flying! (*Author.*)

to rendezvous with the six from 602 over Ludham and the formation of eighteen headed over the North Sea together. Nearing the coast, 124 flew directly to Duindigt, where four Spitfires attacked the racecourse and eight suspected flak positions. They recovered to Ursel, refuelled and re-bombed, then returned to the Netherlands to have a go at the railway line between The Hague and Gouda. They returned to Coltishall at 18.15 and, like 453, they reported successful operation.

As 124 made for the racecourse, 602 made their way to their target and at the appropriate moment, Sutherland took them down in an arc to flatten out about 300 yards from the building at very low altitude – below the roof level of the building, about 100 feet above the ground. Baxter recalled:

We let go with our 2x20mm cannon and .5 machine guns and released our 1x500lb and 2x250lb eleven-second delay bombs 'in our own time'. Then as I cleared the roof of the building, I looked ahead. And approaching me at eye-level and near enough 400 mph, was this black cockerel atop the weather vane on the Church spire. I can see it to this day. No space to turn, I could only 'tweak' the stick and say, in my head, perhaps two seconds later, 'Thank you God'. Maxie Sutherland pulled up to look at the result as the rest of us skimmed the centre of the Hague at rooftop height. The 'Boss' damn near got his tail shot off so at his request, I escorted him gently on to Ghent – at bale out height – while as planned he ordered the rest to press on ahead to land and refuel at Ursel. [3]

Zuber's aircraft also took a hit in the starboard mainplane just as he was about to release his bombs, and they landed 50 yards away on the left side of the building. He later commented to fellow pilot Stan Sollitt that it had 'been a bit hectic'. A young Dutch boy witnessed the attack from the western wing of the fourth floor. His family lived nearby. The boy turned sixteen in 1943 and being liable for deportation chose rather to try to avoid it by living a life in hiding. Despite the war and the firings of the V2s which he saw regularly, the youngster became bored and came into the building – presumably keeping out of the way of the Germans based there as much as possible – a risky pastime at best! Just as the 602 Spitfires arced down, he looked out of the window and saw them coming straight towards him in a line. Transfixed by the sight for a second or two, he threw himself on to the floor behind the window sill, where he hoped the outer wall would give him protection. No sooner had he done so than there came a tremendous banging from below, and in an instant it was all over and the aeroplanes had gone. He did not look out of the window to see what damage there was but clattered down the stairs to get away. Reaching ground level, he found his house totally destroyed, with no sign of the rest of the family. Then he heard his mother calling his name from a cellar under the main staircase of the building. Much to his joy, the rest of the family – father, mother and sister – were all there. They had all rushed to the cellar on hearing the air-raid warning, but had thought him dead.

Post-attack damage to the rear of the BIM building.
(Reproduced by kind permission of Shell International B.V., The Hague.)

They were fortunate to be alive, but their house and most of their possessions were gone. However, friends took them in until they could sort things out. They returned the next day to see what could be salvaged from the ruins of their house and found two wardrobes full of clothes undamaged despite the blast – a godsend indeed because there were none for sale in the shops and markets.

The 602 ORB reports:

Red smoke and flames were seen to roll from the eastern face of the building from bombs which must have penetrated inside the building and smoke and debris rose to a considerable height. White smoke rose from the Western side and the target was last seen enveloped in dense black smoke. The roof of the building however, appeared to be intact, but from the clouds of red smoke which were seen just after the attack and the heavy pall of smoke which later obscured the target it is considered that the inside must be totally destroyed.

Their assessment was optimistic, however; the damage was anything but total, and the Germans started to repair it. The starboard elevator of Squadron Leader Sutherland's Spitfire (SM351), holed by flak when he

pulled up just after the attack, needed replacing so he flew back to base in Flight Sergeant Zuber's aeroplane (which presumably had been repaired) leaving Zuber to bring the repaired Spitfire back later. The 124 Squadron ORB notes: 'Skip bombing was tried, but as results were not as favourable as those obtained by dive-bombing, the latter took precedence.' It isn't clear if this is a direct comment on the BIM building attack, or just a general remark. In the following days, there was no discernible reduction in the numbers of V2s landing on Britain – nine on the

Damage to the starboard elevator of Squadron Leader 'Maxie' Sutherland's Spitfire.
(Reproduced by kind permission of the family of the late Raymond Baxter and the Spitfire Society.)

18th, nine on the 19th, six on the 20th, eight on the 21st and sixteen on the 22nd. Another attack was needed.

Later on the same day, on another operation, Flying Officer Ernest Tonkin of 453 Squadron had to make a forced landing.

On the 3rd recce, Red 2 (F/O Tonkin), presumed to be hit by flak, was seen to force land in flooded country South of Gouda, approx pinpoint E.9075. The aircraft broke up on landing in a small Dyck. Red 3 (F/O Adams), stayed in the area but the pilot was not seen to get out of his aircraft. Flak was intense, light and medium from Gouda.

Tonkin survived. Once his aeroplane (FU●P SM233) came to a stop against the dyke, he found the cockpit filling with water and he had some difficulty getting out, but he did so eventually and made contact with the Dutch Resistance who hid him from the Germans for six weeks until the Allied armies found him. He returned to 453 on 16 May.

Over the weekend of the BIM building attack, the investigations into and consequences of the bombing of Bezuidenhout rumbled on and it was on the 18th, the same day as 602's raid on the building, that the Prime Minister sent out his withering note criticizing the RAF for the attack. It is, however, only coincidental that the 15th saw the last attempts to attack targets in The Hague; it had nothing to do with the anger of the Prime Minister or Captain Moolenburgh. The campaign was about to enter its final phase, although nobody knew it at the time. Fighter Command considered that the storage area at Duindigt had been so comprehensively destroyed by the Spitfires' dive bombing that attention could be concentrated on the mechanisms and infrastructure for delivering the rockets to the firing areas. From about 10 March, most of the rockets were being launched during the hours of darkness – often after midnight – and they concluded it was because the British air supremacy meant that the rockets could no longer be stored near the firing areas, but had to be brought there and fired immediately. On the 13th, 14th and 15th, relatively few rockets hit London and Fighter Command interpreted this as another sign that the concentrated attacks on the storage areas were having their effect. The last attack was on Ravelijn, carried out by four Spitfires from 603 Squadron over lunch. Although 303, 451, 602 and 603 attempted other armed recces after this, they all had to be aborted because of weather. The only exceptions were the diversionary attacks on Duindigt by 453 and 124 squadrons during the BIM building raid. From then on, the armed recces concentrated on the railways and the roads, and because of the weather, these did not start until the 17th. But the numbers of V2s arriving started to increase again, with no fewer than sixteen arriving in south-east England on the 22nd, as we have seen.

Group Captain Arthur Donaldson, the Sector Commander was leaving on Tuesday, 20 March, and he asked that the wing put on a maximum effort. They did so by flying 165 sorties in perfect weather but the day had other notable incidents. Nos 451, 453, 602 and 603 attacked a V1 launching ramp at the airfield at Ypenburg, south-east of The Hague (target code FC/520) – one of the rare occasions during the V2 campaign on which the 12 Group Spitfires came up against the other 'V' weapon. The Ramrod took place in the late afternoon after a very active day against railway targets. First over were six Spitfires each from 451 and 453 Squadrons led by 451's CO, Squadron Leader Robertson. They left Coltishall at 15.55, crossing in to the north of The Hague. No. 451 went down first, with many of their bombs landing on buildings on either side of the launching ramp. Then came 453, which managed to place four sticks around the ramp and on buildings to its south. They reported causing a large explosion and hits on one of the hangars, a large cloud of black smoke could be seen from 30 miles away. The twelve Spitfires then strafed the airfield before recovering to Ursel and returning to base. Nos 602 and 603 had sections at Ursel for rearming and refuelling after attacks on the railway targets. No. 602's Flight Lieutenant Pullman with Warrant Officers Baerlein, Sollitt and Amies took off at 16.30 with the usual bomb load and flew straight to Ypenburg, which they found easily because of a large fire started by the attack just carried out by the Australians. They dropped their bombs accurately, starting another fire. Ten minutes later 603 arrived, four Spitfires flown by Flight Lieutenant Jack Batchelor, Warrant Officer Godfrey, Warrant Officer Thomson and Flight Sergeant Paddy O'Reilly, and another three flown by Flight Lieutenant Bob Sergeant and Flying Officers Nick Machon and Thomson. They stoked up the fires. Sergeant's group returned to Ursel, landing at 17.40, where he recalled that the ground crews were refuelling 602's Spitfires. He reported to the Intelligence Officer, who asked if it would be possible to make another attack on the way to England. Sergeant thought it would be but he wanted to check first with his 'lads' as it would be getting dark by the time they reached Coltishall and some of them might not be qualified for night landings. But they were happy to carry out the extra job and Sergeant went back to the flights and had the airmen come off the 602 aeroplanes to rearm and refuel the 603 ones first![4]

In the meantime, two sections of four Spitfire IXs of 124 Squadron arrived, twenty minutes apart, to carry out yet more attacks, although three were unable to drop their bombs because of 'mechanical trouble'. They landed back at Coltishall at 17.35 and 18.00.

The three 603 Spitfires were off again at 17.55, fifteen minutes after landing, fast and low back to Ypenburg. They streaked across the airfield as low as they could. Some huts were hit and Sergeant saw Nick Machon's aircraft bursting through debris from them which had been blown skywards. They rounded some hangars and in front he saw what looked

453 Squadron flight commanders, Messrs Clemesha and Leith. The two
on the Spitfire (an XVI) are LAC L.E. McKenzie and LAC D.O.
Herdman.
(Russell Leith.)

like a parade (although why the Germans would be parading just after
being attacked is unclear). Instinctively he jabbed down on the gun button
and hosed the assembled troops. Years before at RAF Sealand he had been
strafed by a German bomber as he and several others made their way across
the open airfield in the evening after flying was finished. Banking round
after dropping its bombs, the rear gunner took a 'squirt' at the airmen and
gave them a real fright. Sergeant saw this as his revenge for that incident.

Nick Machon had an interesting background. Born in Guernsey, to join
the RAF he first had to escape the German invaders of the island,
managing to get away the day before they arrived. His parents still lived
there and to avoid reprisals on relatives in occupied countries, pilots like
Nick flew under assumed names in case they were brought down. The
young Machon had been addicted to the Saint, Simon Templar, and with
his middle name Nicholle, he decided to call himself Nicholas Templar!
Training to fly in the United States, it had been contracted to 'Nick', the
name by which he was still known. It seemed to have slipped his mind
though that his Spitfire was called 'Guernsey's Reply', which might have
been noticed by the enemy and questions asked!

It is probably too much of a simplification to say that these operations were becoming 'milk runs' but few of the pilots were being lost. So it is interesting that in the week following 602's attack on the BIM building, two went down in the sea within hours of each other.

Earlier, at 09.45, Wing Commander Don Andrews led three of 453's Spitfires flown by Flying Officer Norman 'Swamp' Marsh, Rusty Leith and Flight Sergeant J. 'Jim' McAuliffe across to the Netherlands and bombed a railway line near Gouda before landing at Ursel to refuel and rearm. They reported seeing a V2 launch from the grounds of the Hotel Promenade at 09.50 – one is reported landing at Mayland in Essex, not far from Burnham-on-Crouch, at 09.53. Taking off from Ursel, the four made for Noordwijk, where they bombed a railway line, although a strong wind made the bombs scatter. As they turned away, Blue 2, Norman Marsh in FU●S (SM188), reported that he was losing oil pressure, possibly caused by a flak hit. Warrant Officer Eric Mee, flying with 603 on another operation at the time heard Marsh say very coolly and laconically that he was 'going over the side'.

> I decided to make use of the remaining dynamic energy to climb out to sea before baling out with the hope that I would be rescued by the Air Sea Rescue chaps. I baled out from about 3–4000 feet while the aircraft was in a stable glide. The parachute deployed normally and after landing in the sea was able to deploy the dinghy. I had some difficulty boarding it after inflation; the low temperature of the North Sea soon prompted me to follow the correct boarding procedure which I had learned on an Air Sea Rescue course some time earlier in my training.

He was about 6 miles off The Hague in heavy seas and waved to his comrades above to let them know he was alive. They circled overhead calling a Mayday until they had to return to Ursel to refuel. A second section from 453 including Pilot Officer Brian Inglis was airborne and after bombing railway lines near Leiden, made a search for 'Swamp' in his dinghy and found him. They directed a pair of ASR Spitfires to the position. At 11.00 several of 602's Spitfires

'Swamp' Marsh.
(The late Norman Marsh.)

were at Ursel and two, Flying Officers Roberts and Campbell were scrambled to search for a downed pilot – who may have been Flying Officer Marsh. It is possible, but unclear, that they may have been the two ASR Spitfires which took over the patrol from 453. They reported seeing a Walrus but were not able to contact it because of the different radio frequencies in use, so they tried to show the ASR crew where the dinghy was by diving towards it. The Walrus landed on the sea near to the downed airman but shore batteries opened up and it started to taxi away from the dinghy, heading west. Apparently it damaged its rudder on landing. Marsh said later that he did not see the Walrus and it may very well have been searching for another airman, but the location suggests otherwise.

During the afternoon, the same section of four from 453 Squadron attempted to find the dinghy again but failed. As darkness fell, the Aussie pilot settled down for a cold and miserable night as he continued to drift closer to the coast. The same section (Red Section) from 453 was off from Matlaske at 06.15 the next morning to try to find 'Swamp' but their first sighting, at 07.00, was an empty dinghy which they sank. They reported it as being circular which meant that it was not the one they were searching for. Fifteen minutes later, they found their friend still alive. Flying Officer Stansfield climbed to 10,000 feet to radio back the news, then they all continued to orbit the dinghy until relieved by Blue Section, who continued the watch. At 09.30, three of 451 Squadron's aircraft (Flying Officers Ball, Minahan and Hill) took off to relieve the 453 section and at 10.15 sighted two dinghies, one containing Flying Officer Marsh. (It seems that there were at least three dinghies in the area over the period, so the one patrolled by 602 the previous day may not have been the Australian's.)

Soon after their arrival, a Catalina appeared and landed by the empty dinghy but no sooner had it touched down, then shore batteries opened up on it and it had to take off again. Two of the 451 Spitfires bombed and strafed the guns and were joined by Blue Section of another squadron, codenamed 'Heirloom' This was probably 603, which had a section led by Flight Lieutenant Johnnie Welch in the air from Ludham on their second armed recce of the day. Coming across the shelling, they enthusiastically attacked the guns, bombing three German batteries two miles south of IJmuiden with their two 250-pound and single 500-pound bombs, although according to Eric Mee some of the guns were too well dug in and hidden for them to find.

The Catalina returned and was about to try to land again, when more guns opened up on it, this time hitting it so it turned for home. No. 603's Snowy Wheatley saw it going and started after it to try to persuade it to return before realizing that it had no option but to go. The four 603 Spitfires made for Ursel, where they landed at 11.35. In the late afternoon,

'Cupid' Love.
(Courtesy Imperial War Museum.
Negative no. CH14813.)

two of 453's Spitfires yet again made a search for their friend and reported seeing a German Red Cross boat about ¾ mile off IJmuiden with Marsh on board. They said that he waved to them so he seemed to be in one piece. Marsh's own account is slightly different:

Apparently, following the departure of the Catalina, the German authorities were advised on an international frequency that the rescue attempt was abandoned. During the heavy swell I occasionally saw the German launch flying a Red Cross flag but assumed that the flag was flown to avoid attack from Allied aircraft. Later on in the evening, I drifted on to the shore keeping my fingers crossed and hoping that I did not land amongst some 'nasties'. By this time the German troops were awaiting for me and took me to their barracks where I was able to dry out while waiting for a Luftwaffe officer to collect me.[5]

The Australian was safe at last. From the Netherlands, his captors took him to an interrogation centre on the outskirts of Hamburg, where he remained for a week before ending the war in a POW camp on the Baltic. Whilst in captivity he met up with Bill Bennett, who had been shot down during the raid on the flats at Marlot on Christmas Eve. Not long afterwards, Soviet troops liberated the camp and Marsh returned to 453 on 19 May 1945. His log book has the following succinct summary: 'Engine packed up after bombing. Cause unknown. Bailed out over North Sea. Great difficulty with ASR. Search abandoned 11.00 hrs. 21-3-45. Drifted ashore evening of 21-3-45 worse for wear and taken prisoner.'

Coincidentally, one of 602's pilots also found himself in a dinghy in the open North Sea on the 22nd, the day after 'Swamp' Marsh drifted ashore. Flight Sergeant T.L. Love, given the nickname 'Cupid' by his comrades – a name that some say he did not like – was, in the words of a fellow pilot, 'a great little character with a marvellous singing voice, witty and generally good company'. Small in stature and with a disarmingly boyish face that belied a sometimes aggressive character, Love already had a claim to fame as the only man to try to shoot down a ballistic missile in flight. 'Bax' Baxter recalled that incident: 'We went and attacked a V2 target and dropped our bombs and then being very keen we came back to strafe it and as we came back they had obviously started the countdown and the missile came up in front of us.'[6] Love said, 'I remember the V2 coming out of the woods certainly and I can remember exactly what was said to bring everybodys' attention to it. Just as I was pulling out I heard a voice saying "Keerist' would you look at that!" I was still firing.'[7]

Raymond Baxter laughed about the incident later, glad that Love did not hit the missile: 'He'd have blown us all up!'[8] Born in Larkhall in Lanarkshire, Love earned a living as a salesman in Glasgow before joining the RAF in 1941. He completed flying training in Rhodesia and flew operationally in the Mediterranean before being posted to 602 on 5 February 1945.

On 22 March he took off from Ludham in SM361, with five more of 602's Spitfires at 10.55 on an armed recce with the usual bomb load of two 250 and one 500-pound bombs. The section was led by the CO, Squadron Leader Sutherland and the other pilots were Flight Lieutenant Pertwee, Flying Officer Rudkin, Warrant Officer Max Baerlein and Flight Sergeant Zuber. The target of their low-level attack was a railway junction south-east of Voorburg. After dropping their bombs, the section recovered to Ursel, landing at 12.20. A quick turnround found them back at the same target an hour later for a similar attack. On the way back to Ludham, about 60 miles from the English coast, Love's aeroplane

602's Shufti Zuber and Stan Sollitt standing beside Zuber's car at Coltishall.
(Geoff and Richard Zuber.)

developed mechanical problems and he had to bale out. With the other pilots watching and with some difficulty because of the sea swell like Marsh, Love managed to climb into his dinghy. The orbiting Spitfires relayed his position to ASR. Back at Ludham, Michael Francis (by now a Pilot Officer) and Warrant Officer Ellison, who were on readiness, were 'scrambled' to cover the ditched pilot. They took off at 14.20 and vectored to the spot.

> An ASR Thunderbolt had just found him but it returned to base when we arrived and I kept vigil over 'Cupid' alone about 300 feet; W/O Ellison also having returned. Very soon a Catalina landed and taxied up to the dinghy. I continued to circle and watched them take him out of the dinghy and directly on board the aeroplane. I found it a thrilling experience and couldn't believe that it all could have happened in the same day. He told us how he almost gave up attempting to get into the dinghy because he was so exhausted.

But Love was safe; the only loss was his ripcord handle. There was a tradition in the RAF that an airman who had baled out would be charged for the ripcord handle if he failed to bring it back and it was a matter of pride to do this. It seems that the Catalina was American and they did not know this, so when Love scrambled aboard with the ripcord, one of the crew tossed it back into the sea, much to Love's chagrin!

Whilst the drama of 'Cupid' Love's rescue unfolded in the North Sea, the Kurhaus garage at Scheveningen on the coast was the target for a wing 'show', a Ramrod by 453 and 603 Squadrons in fine weather. The British believed that the rocket troops used the building to house transport and in particular *meillerwagen*. Both squadrons were to supply twelve aircraft and after their first attacks, to recover to Ursel for fuel and more bombs and then return for a second go. First thing, 603's CO, Squadron Leader Rigler, Flight Lieutenant Jack Batchelor and their Intelligence Officer, Pilot Officer G Allott, travelled the short distance to Coltishall to clarify the target building because their own photographs of the area were six months old. Full bomb loads being carried, Squadron Leader Rigler led 603 off at 12.55 from Ludham for a straightforward attack. Crossing the coast of the Netherlands at 13.28, they went down in three sections of four, east to west from 9,000 feet to 2,000. By and large their bombs hit the target building and apart from light flak, the whole thing was uneventful. No. 453, led by Wing Commander Andrews followed ten minutes later, bombing south-west to north-east from 9,500 to 4,500 feet with some bombs overshooting. But they reported a lot of black smoke from the target building that could be seen for some distance as they too headed for Ursel. No. 453 departed Ursel at 15.55, with 603 almost half an hour behind them. The Australians' second attack repeated the first almost identically and they reported that 'no spectacular results' were observed. No. 603, however, reported that one bomb hit the nearby railway sheds and caused a violent explosion and that a column of thick black smoke rose to 2,000 feet. They returned to Ludham, landing back at 17.35. Flying Officer Peters' log book notes, 'Bombed garage. Heavy flak. 4 bursts. Landed Ursal [sic].'

From time to time, the squadrons had a day off operations and whilst sometimes they knew this in advance, often they started the day expecting to fly operational sorties only to have no demands made on them. On the 23rd, 453 had the day off and on the 24th, 603 did not carry out any operational sorties. Although they woke up to fine weather, they found themselves at readiness all morning from an early start. They were ordered to maintain a cockpit readiness from 04.00, which meant twenty-four Spitfires sitting at the end of the runway, engines ready to start, pilots freezing in their cockpits until 05.30. Then 603 changed to standby readiness and 602 to fifteen minutes with the readiness states being swapped each hour until 10.00 when the squadrons went on to thirty minutes. The squadrons had been told to have maximum numbers available, but they did not know why until later when it became clear that they were being held as a reserve in case General Montgomery's Rhine crossing assault brought the *Luftwaffe* up in force. In the event it did not, but it meant a cold and miserable start for the airmen involved at Ludham.

In the afternoon, they did some practice flying. By now, 603 had none of its original Auxiliary pilots, and had a distinctly cosmopolitan feel about it, with some Aussies of its own and even two pilots from the Indian Air Force, one of whom died tragically during the practice flying. At 14.40, Flying Officer McConnochie took off with Flight Sergeant Webb, Flying Officer Machon (the Guernseyman) and Pilot Officer Nelson McGinn. Machon flew No. 3 (in SM396) and McGinn No. 4 (in TB396). They flew out to sea and at 16.10, whilst carrying out a 180° crossover turn, McGinn and Machon collided. By this time in the war, the RAF fighters used the same standard combat formation as that introduced by the *Luftwaffe* after the Spanish Civil War, the 'finger four', which called for the four aircraft to fly in a wide formation that can be represented by the positions of the four finger tips of one hand, with No. 1 out in front – the middle finger. A section of two flew so that each pilot looked towards the other, allowing each a good view of his comrade and the sky beyond and behind him to spot any approaching enemy aircraft. If a formation in the finger four spread had to turn, it involved a rather complicated ballet called a crossover turn, requiring the aeroplanes to pass over and under each other so that at the end of the turn, they were in the same relative positions as at the start. As No. 4, McGinn would have to pass underneath Machon and his Spitfire struck Machon's from below. Machon landed on the marshes at Hickling Church, a few miles from Palling, but McGinn died.

It seems that he managed to bale out but because of the low altitude his parachute did not have time to open. The body of Pilot Officer Nelson Arthur Horace McGinn RIAF was recovered from the sea by a Walrus and his funeral took place on 29 March in the Cambridge City Cemetery. Nick Machon suffered strained ribs and got a nasty fright but he survived to be one of 12 squadron aircraft which flew over the funeral service in McGinn's honour.

This particular week had its full share of incidents and losses. Nelson McGinn was 603's second loss in seven days, although the other pilot, the Australian Johnny Green, died in action. It happened on the 17th, the first day that the operations of the 12 Group Spitfires turned towards the railway and communications infrastructure of the V2s and away from The Hague. There were twelve aircraft in the group, led by Jack Batchelor. They were off at 14.10 making for the general area of Utrecht. Having started flying operationally in 1941, Batchelor was a hardened warrior – well used to combat and its stresses. At this stage in the war he focused on each operation, moving from the current to the next in a grimly professional way, any fears well controlled as he moved on. After attacking the railway junction at Maartensdijk at 14.45, they turned for Ursel.

Ten minutes later, passing over Bleskensgraaf, Batchelor (White 1) was thinking through the detail of the next operation this one being more or less completed. There was a call over the R/T from 'Johnny' saying that he had seen a 3-ton truck going into the village. Batchelor thought that the call had come from the other flight commander, Johnny Welch, and asked him to go down to investigate, but Welch, leading 'Blue' Section, decided that it was not worth it because the truck was already in the village, so he did nothing. Batchelor noticed that Welch had not gone to investigate and assumed that he had thought better of it. In fact, the call had come from Johnny Green (White 2) who promptly dived down to have a look at the truck. Nobody realized that he had gone until, as the formation swung away, someone glimpsed the Spitfire going down surrounded by bursts of light flak coming up from the village. Then they all heard a cry of 'I've been hit!' but because most of the pilots had not seen him go, they did not realize who it was from until much later. Nobody saw the Spitfire crash, nor any sign of an explosion, and it was hoped that he had managed to survive the crash. The uncertainty continued for many weeks. But he had been killed, hit by a flak battery on the Heinenoord Bridge.

Johnny Green was engaged to a WAAF in the MT Section. He was buried in the nearby village of Barendrecht. He shared a locker with Eric Mee, who always flew with a little gold monkey on a chain given to him by his wife in the pocket of his lifejacket. Going to the locker the following day, he discovered that Green had taken the wrong lifejacket – and the little gold monkey. It was many years before Mee found out what had happened to Green.

Jack Batchelor worried about the incident, telling himself that if he had insisted on the use of proper R/T procedure then the confusion would not have arisen and Green might have survived. If he had not been thinking about the next operation, might the loss have been avoided? But in truth it was an unfortunate accident of war and Jack Batchelor had no cause to take any blame on himself. Warrant Officer Jack Dawson Green, Royal Australian Air Force was twenty-one when he was killed. His Spitfire was recovered by the Royal Dutch Air Force in 1972.

The remaining eleven aircraft flew back to Ursel where they rearmed and refuelled. At 16.45 they were airborne yet again and bombed railway targets near The Hague before returning to Ludham at 17.30.

The attacks against the infrastructure continued. Increasingly, 602 pilots were reporting that there was no flak and that they could see no sign of the Germans attempting to repair the damage to the railway system, which they thought was 'considerable'. For the pilots the daily routine did not change much other than the targets they sought. Tuesday 27 March illustrates a pretty typical day with five squadrons attacking the infra-structure and one – 602 – not flying operationally. Poor weather first thing prevented operations but from the late morning it cleared sufficiently to allow operations, and by the late afternoon the visibility over the Netherlands was being reported as 15 miles, although with a haze.

Take-off	Squadron	Airfield	Pilots and aircraft	Comment
08.45	603	Ludham	F/O McConnochie XT●T F/O Richmond XT XT●Q W/O Wheatley XT●O W/O Laffan XT●S	Weather/armed recce. Found 9/10ths cloud 5,000 to 15,000 feet. Bombs brought back to base. Landed 10.10.
11.35	453	Matlaske	F/O N.R. Adams FU●G P/O A.T. Bartels FU●F	Weather recce. Landed 12.55.
13.00	453	Matlaske	F/O J.C. Grady FU●P F/O F.N. McLoughlin FU●N P/O R.G. Peters FU●J F/O J.K. McCully	Bombed railway junction at Breukelen. Landed 14.35.
13.15	603	Ludham	F/Lt McAndrew XT●H W/O Maslem XT●G P/O Haupt XT●L W/O Godfrey XT●E	Bombed road bridge over railway south of Amsterdam. Landed 15.00

Take-off	Squadron	Airfield	Pilots and aircraft	Comment
13.30	451	Matlaske	F/O Minahan SM516 P/O Kelly SM417 P/O Stubbs SM391 P/O Roe SM199	Attacked Amsterdam – Hilversum railway line, but all near misses. Landed 15.05.
13.30	124	Coltishall	F/Lt J. Fowler TA813 F/Lt L. Oakshott PV151 W/O J. McCall PV344 W/O A. Williams PV303	Railway junction Woerden/Utrecht. No results seen. Landed 15.00.
13.40	303	Coltishall	F/Lt M. Szalestowski ML339 F/Sgt J. Kmiecik MA422 P/O Z. Krzeptowski MA476 F/Sgt K. Sztuka BS401	Uneventful patrol over Utrecht/ Amsterdam/ Haarlem. Landed 15.50.
13.50	603	Ludham	F/O McConnochie XT●T F/O Richmond XT●N W/O Beckwith XT●R F/Sgt Webb XT●S	Attacked road and rail bridge east of Woerden. Landed 15.35.
14.10	453	Matlaske	S/L E. Esau P/O C.G. Robertson FU●F F/O E.G. Mack W/O D.C. John FU●C	Bombed railway line near Amsterdam and attacked road transport near IJmuiden. Landed 16.15. Mack aborted, landed 14.40.
14.35	603	Ludham	F/Lt Staniforth XT●B F/O Thomson XT●F F/O Cookson XT●O	Bombed railway junction near Utrecht. Landed back 16.15.
14.35	451	Matlaske	S/L Robertson TB592 P/O Sheppard SM480 F/Lt Milner TB744 P/O Vintner SM479	Attacked bridge near Utrecht. No direct hits but bombs all landed near target. Landed 16.10.
14.35	124	Coltishall	F/Lt A. Charlesworth RR252 F/Lt M. Lloyd PL249 W/O J. James PV299 F/O J. Blackett TA796	Bombed railway junction at Breukelen. Landed 16.35.

Take-off	Squadron	Airfield	Pilots and aircraft	Comment
15.00	303	Coltishall	F/Lt J. Franckiewicz BS247 F/O Sikorski MA683 W/O Z. Bartkowiak MH777 W/O W. Skrzydlo BS328	Uneventful patrol over Rotterdam/ Utrecht/ Amsterdam. Landed 17.05.
15.30	453	Matlaske	W/C Andrews P/O C.A.M. Taylor FU●E P/O R.A.J. York FU●M W/O HA Stewart	Bombed bridge near Woerden. Landed 17.30.
15.45	451	Matlaske	F/Lt Sutton SM507 P/O Barrington SM511 F/Lt MacKenzie SM427 F/O Cooper TB913	Bombed railway line Utrecht/ Breukelen. Line cut in two places. Landed 17.30.
15.50	603	Ludham	F/Lt R Sergeant W/O Maslem XT●H P/O Haupt XT●L W/O Godfrey XT●G W/O Thomson XT●A W/O Laffan XT●Q	Bombed rail bridge and road south of Amsterdam. Landed 17.25.
16.00	124	Coltishall	S/L G. Scott PV312 W/O C. Paterson RR209 F/O R. Johnson TA804 F/S F. Oakley TA813	Attacked railway south of Amsterdam. No results seen. Landed 18.05.
16.15	603	Ludham	F/Lt Kirkman XT●T F/O Richmond XT●R W/O E. Mee XT●S	Attacked railway bridge over canal south-east of Amsterdam and road transport near Haarlem. Landed 18.10.
16.30	453	Matlaske	F/O S.L. Cumming FU●N P/O A.T. Bartels FU●D P/O W.R. Mack FU●J W/O J.K. McCully FU●Q	Bombed junction near Woerden. Landed 18.05. Bartels aborted. Landed 16.50.
17.00	451	Matlaske	F/Lt Kemp SM199 F/Sgt Hopper SM417 P/O Ball SM516 P/O Kelly SM391	Bombed junction near Woerden and a midget submarine 2 miles off Zandvoort. Landed 18.40.

Take-off	Squadron	Airfield	Pilots and aircraft	Comment
17.05	124	Coltishall	F/Lt B. Brooks TA800 W/O G. Beadle PV303 F/O H. Fallon PV296 F/Sgt F. Oakley TA813	Attacked railway line Woerden/ Breukelen. Two direct hits which cut tracks. Landed 18.40.
17.05	603	Ludham	Fl/Lt Staniforth XT●B F/O Thomson XT●F W/O Wheatley XT●Q	Bombed railway junction near Utrecht. Landed 19.45
17.15	303	Coltishall	F/Lt M. Szalestowski MA422 P/O Z. Nowinski MA420 F/Lt E. Bartys BS401 F/Sgt K. Sztuka MH694	Uneventful patrol The Hague/ Rotterdam/ Utrecht/ Amsterdam. Landed 19.15.
17.35	451	Matlaske	S/L Robertson TB592 P/O Sheppard SM394 F/Lt Milner TB744 P/O Vintner SM479	Bombed bridge near Woerden. Landed 19.10.
17.50	124	Coltishall	F/Lt K. Lawrence PV344 F/L L. Oakshott RR252 W/O E. Parker PL249 F/Lt P. Phillips TA796	Attacked Woerden/ Amsterdam railway line and midget submarine off Katwijk. Landed 19.20.
18.05	603	Ludham	F/Lt McAndrew XT●L W/O Maslem XT●H W/O Thomson XT●A F/Lt Sergeant XT●E W/O Godfrey XT●G F/Sgt Webb XT●Q	Bombed road/rail bridge near Woerden. Landed back 19.45.

Compared with the similar table produced for 28 October 1944, the pace had certainly hotted up, even with no operations in the morning. With all attacks aimed at the communications infrastructure and not the launch sites, it is noteworthy that five V2s landed in the south of England in the early hours of the 27th before operations started, and only one whilst the Spitfires roamed the Netherlands. It landed at 88 Kynaston Road, Orpington, at 16.54 ,and although those involved in the campaign against the V2s could not realize it, it was the last V2 to be fired at London. At the same time, a final rocket was launched against Antwerp.

The pilots and ground crews of 602 and 603 Squadrons who had endured the early morning freezing cockpit readiness a few days before, apparently for nothing could also not have appreciated that the event they were standing by to cover if needed – the Rhine crossing – would bring a swift end to their current work. As the armies of the western Allies drove into Germany the western Netherlands remained under the control of the Germans, but at the end of an increasingly long supply chain and increasingly at risk of being cut off. The German command, *OKW*, ordered *Gruppenführer* Kammler to withdraw and after this last parting shot, he did so. His troops in The Hague still had a considerable number of rockets left to fire – some sources say about sixty – and everything not able to be moved by road was transported by rail to Kasteel Duivenvoorde, where it was blown up in the early afternoon of the 29th. Other equipment was thrown into a small waterway, the Leidsche Rijn and, protected by poor weather, the rocket troops started to move out from Leiden to Utrecht and thence to Germany.

The V2 that landed at Kynaston Road killed 34-year-old Mrs Ivy Millichamp who lived at number 38 with her husband Eric. Mrs Millichamp was the eighth child in a family of twelve and she married Eric, an engineer, in 1938. She was in the kitchen of their bungalow and the explosion killed her outright. Mr Millichamp pulled her out of the wreckage of their home, but she was already dead and has the sad distinction of being the last civilian in Britain to be killed in the war. She is buried in All Saints churchyard.

For the Spitfires of 12 Group, the campaign continued, although the poor weather which protected the withdrawal of the V2 troops restricted operations almost to nil until the 30th, Good Friday, when they resumed once again with the same intensity as in the past. By now, intelligence had appreciated that the attack on the BIM building carried out by 602 Squadron on the 18th had not destroyed it and another attack was ordered, this time by 603 and using dive-bombing techniques rather than skip bombing, possibly because of the perceived greater accuracy of dive bombing and the nearness of the church across Wassenaarseweg. Over Norfolk the day brought squally showers of hail with thunder interspersed with good visibility. The report included in 603's ORB for that raid is as good an account as any.

F/Lt Batchelor took off 12 Spits XVIs at 09.30 to bomb the Bataafsche Petrol Building. Each aircraft was armed with 1x500lb. bomb and 2x250lb. bombs rused [sic] .025 secs: nose and 11 secs: tail. The aircraft crossed in at the Hague at 8,000ft and flew straight to the target, bombing from East to West in dives from 8,000ft to 1,000ft. The results of the bombing were excellent, one salvo falling on the middle of the building, and three salvoes falling on the N.E. Wing. A very large bright orange flash was seen from the salvo

A view from within the BIM building probably following the attack by
603 Squadron on Good Friday 1945.
(Reproduced by kind permission of Shell International B.V., The Hague.)

*which fell on the middle of the building. Another salvo fell on the road
outside target while other bombs scored near misses. The aircraft then flew
straight to Ursel, being rebombed and refueled in 20 minutes – an excellent
piece of work. They took off again at once and crossed in at the Hook at
9,000ft and flew to the Hague, where they turned to starboard, flying direct
to the target and bombing it again from East to West in dives from 8,000ft
to 1,000ft. Bombing results were again good. Two salvoes fell on the centre
of the building, and three others against its side on the road in front. They
crossed out the Hague at 9,000ft and setting course for base landed at 12.30.
Moderate, heavy, accurate flak (for height) was experienced over the target
during the first attack. No flak during the second attack. The Weather was
good during the operation, being clear over the target.*

The twelve pilots who flew were: Flight Lieutenant Batchelor (XT●A)
as leader, Warrant Officer Maslem (XT●F), Pilot Officer Cookson (XT●R),
Flying Officer Machon (still suffering sore ribs) (XT●G), Flight Lieutenant
Welch (XT●Q), Warrant Officer Mee (XT●H), Flight Lieutenant Kirkman
(XT●N), Flying Officer McConnochie (XT●Y), Flight Lieutenant
McAndrew (XT●B), Pilot Officer Haupt (XT●L), Flight Lieutenant
Sergeant (XT●E) and Warrant Officer Thomson (XT●C). As luck would
have it, when the air-raid warnings sounded for 603's attack, the young

Dutch boy was in the building again. This time, he did not hesitate and ran hell for leather to the high boundary fence which he scaled as if he had wings. After the raid, he realized that not far from where they scrambled over, the fence actually lay flat on the ground. PRU photos showed that six to eight bombs were direct hits and that all the bombs landed within 35 yards but the conclusion remained that the building was effectively undamaged – unlike the 602 assessment that the interior was totally destroyed. Fighter Command concluded on 1 April: 'After attacks by a total of thirty Fighter Command aircraft on 18th and 30th March, 1945, thirty craters are seen within a circle radius 250 yards from the centre point of the building. The target has received at least six direct hits and eight near misses.'[9]

Eric Mee noted in his log book: 'Bombed block of flats in Hague area. Wizard bombing. Many direct hits.' And he added '(Gestapo Head-quarters?)'. Reinforced concrete is difficult to destroy at the best of times and with the bombing amounting to random and relatively small explosions it would need a lot of luck to damage the building fatally. A demolition would need to be designed so that the key elements in the structure would be removed in an appropriate order. Whilst the type of bombing carried out might have caught one of these key structural elements, the chances were always that only parts of the building would

Damage to the BIM building, particularly the roof, probably after 603 Squadron's attack. The elevation is pock-marked from attacks.
(Reproduced by kind permission of Shell International B.V., The Hague.)

be made uninhabitable. It would need a major bombing raid by heavier aircraft to destroy the building, and in the wake of the bombing of Bezuidenhout, this was never going to happen. It is interesting that the two attacks employed different methods: 603's dive bombing was the norm with greater accuracy and less chance of stray bombs causing civilian casualties, while 602's skip-bombing technique – hardly used during the V2 campaign – ran the risk that poorly aimed bombs would overshoot the building completely and cause civilian deaths. There was also the chance that the church would be damaged which, if nothing else, would be a propaganda gift for the Germans. Of course on 18 March, the controversy about the bombing of Bezuidenhout was only getting under way and the risk of more civilian casualties was perhaps not as high on 12

Matlaske. Pilots of 451 Squadron. Back row, l to r. Flying Officer Cliff Stubbs, Flying Officer Jack Vintner, Pilot Officer Dave Cooper. Middle Row: Flight Lieutenant Dave Fisher, Flying Officer Cec Ball, Flying Officer B. Fuller, Flying Officer Jim Minahan, Flying Officer Joe Barrington, Flying Officer Arthur Roe, Flight Sergeant J. McDonald, Flight Lieutenant Bob Milner, Flying Officer Ralph Hill, Flight Sergeant Sid Handsaker, Flying Officer Bob Field, Flying Officer Bruce Robertson. Front row. Flight Lieutenant Reg Sutton ('A' Flight Commander), Squadron Leader C.W. Robertson (Commanding Officer), Flight Lieutenant Doug Davidson ('B' Flight Commander).
(*Australian War Memorial Negative no. SUK14376.*)

Group's agenda as it became only a few days later. Whatever the arguments about different bombing techniques, both attacks damaged the building, but with the V2 troops already well on their way out of the Netherlands by the 30th 603's raid had little effect on the outcome. Of course it easy to say this with hindsight. At the time, 12 Group's Spitfires were still fighting the rockets and for them the campaign continued, but it did start to wind down. No. 303 flew their last operation against the rockets on the 30th – an attack by three Spitfires on a railway carried out in the late afternoon from Ursel. These three, F/O M Maksymowicz, F/O J Krok and W/O A Rutecki landed at Coltishall at 18.05.

Tragedies continued. Later that day, four of 124 Squadron's Spitfire IXs took off from Coltishall at 14.40 but shortly afterwards ran into a thunderstorm and heavy rain, which made the engines of three of the aeroplanes cut. They jettisoned their bombs into the sea but Flight Sergeant C.M. Lett did not get back and was drowned. He was the second 124 Squadron pilot to be lost in the space of a few days. On 25 March, Flight Lieutenant C. Maltby, on an attack by four Spitfires on the railway junction at Breukelen, continued his dive down to about 200 feet and was caught in the explosion of one of the bombs. His colleagues reported seeing the crashed aeroplane, but no sign of the pilot. Unfortunately he was killed. No. 451 also suffered losses during March. On the morning of the 9th, four were tasked to attack a bridge south of Alphen. They reported no flak but Warrant Officer Blake (in NI●X, SM465) baled out. The others saw his parachute open and assumed, correctly, that he survived. Their next loss was Flight Lieutenant N.J. Bray. He was leading a section of four Spitfires which took off at 15.25 to cross the North Sea but shortly after take-off he reported 'oil trouble' and turned back to attempt an emergency landing. His aeroplane, SM346, came down in a field 3 miles to the west of Swannington and Bray was killed.

The weather on April Fool's Day prevented any significant operations, but 2 April saw another full day against the railway and communications targets. Meanwhile, 303 Squadron prepared for a move to Andrews Field. They would be leaving their Spitfires behind to be handed over to an incoming unit. And suddenly, with hardly any warning, it all finished; more with a whimper than a bang. No. 602 and 603 stood down on the 3rd and for them it was all over.

The 603 Squadron ORB described the end of the campaign as an easter egg – a gift – and rejoiced that they were released for the day. Clearly the pilots relished their brief holiday away from the stresses of operations. They ate a leisurely breakfast and the mess bar opened mid-morning. Guinness seems to have been popular! Than at lunchtime, some made for the club at Sutton Staithe and afterwards about a dozen went sailing on the Broads at Potter Higham in two dinghies and what was described as a half-decker. Some were new to sailing and presumably the combination of their inexperience, the alcohol and a gusty wind made the sailing erratic, to put it mildly! No. 602 spent the day in a similar fashion – probably in the company of their colleagues from the Edinburgh Squadron. Eventually, all returned safely and the day ended with more socializing at Sutton Staithe. All in all it was a fine day! Nos 124, 451 and 453 attempted some operations on the 3rd, but these were disrupted because of heavy cloud cover and over the next few days only a few desultory recces were carried out. Effectively, the campaign was over. On the 3rd, Flying Officer Peters of 453 noted in his log-book, 'Bombed railway. The end of V2 war. VII <u>KAPUT</u>.'

Notes

1. *20th Century Architecture* by Jonathan Glancy.
2. 'Spitfire Special Delivery' *Spitfire* Volume 5 No. 2 Autumn 2004.
3. 'Spitfire Special Delivery' *Spitfire* Volume 5 No. 2 Autumn 2004, p7.
4. Although this demonstrates the friendly rivalry between the two auxiliary squadrons, it may be apocryphal. Their ORBs suggest that no 602 aircraft were still at Ursel when Sergeant's section arrived back.
5. Captured Allied airmen were the responsibility of the *Luftwaffe*.
6. From the BBC Radio Scotland programme *Beware the Crossed Lion* broadcast in 1980.
7. From the the same broadcast.
8. The date of the incident is unclear. It is sometimes given as 14 February, but this is not confirmed by the 602 Squadron ORB.
9. Intelligence Report dated 1 April 1945 from Fighter Command HQ summarizing post-attack reconnaissance photographs.

CHAPTER NINE

Endings . . . and Beginnings

The authorities wasted no time dispersing the squadrons into new roles. No. 303 went on the 3rd, then at tea time on the 4th, 602 and 603 started a move to Coltishall, which they completed the next day. They were now in 11 Group, with a new role on the 6th, escorting heavy bombers mainly to northern Germany and the west coast of the Netherlands. On the 5th, the two Australian squadrons left Matlaske for RAF Lympne and 11 Group, where they too were involved in escort duties to heavy bombers – often operating from forward bases on the Continent on many of the same raids as their erstwhile comrades. They were the last occupants of Matlaske, which finally closed in October 1945. No. 124 Squadron moved into 11 Group and RAF Hawkinge on the 7th, where it too helped escort the heavies on many of the same raids as the others.

Although their various departures were short and sharp, there was time for some congratulations. No. 603's 'A' Flight Commander, Jack Batchelor, received a DFC for leading the attack on the BIM building on 30 March. On 6 June he received a signal from Air Marshal James Robb at HQ Fighter Command:

> *Dear Batchelor,*
>
> *I am delighted to see that you have been awarded the DFC. Your skill and courage and fine leadership have been an inspiration to your Squadron, and your leading of the attack on the Bataafsch [sic] Petrol Company's building in the Hague was a magnificent piece of work.*
>
> *All good wishes,*
> *Yours sincerely,*
> *James Robb*

And the C-in-C, Air Marshal Hill, wrote a letter to the units congratulating them on their work:

*With the intermission of the V-2 attacks on this country, and before the rede-
ployment of the six Spitfire squadrons from Coltishall, I should like to take
the opportunity of congratulating all ranks of these Squadrons on the
outstandingly good work which they put in while the attacks were in
progress.*

*The Fighter/Bomber attacks carried out in the Hague Area undoubtedly
did much to prevent the enemy stepping up the weight of his attack, and
thereby achieved a lightening of the burden which the Londoner was called
upon to bear. As fuller information becomes available, it may well transpire
that the attacks had a more powerful dislocating effect than is generally
believed.*

*I fully realise that the targets which the Squadrons were called upon to
attack day after day, were heavily defended by flak, and I am most pleased
at the manner in which the attacks were pressed home in spite of this. The
balance between aggressiveness and caution was nicely struck. This implies
both professional skill and good discipline.*

*I consider that the accuracy attained in bombing was a great feather in
the cap of the aircrews, and that the high number of sorties was an achieve-
ment on the part of the ground crews.*

In a broadcast on 13 May, the Prime Minister mentioned the role that
the RAF had played in reducing the effectiveness of the V-weapons. This
is undoubtedly true, but just how effective was the dive-bombing
campaign? Even with hindsight, it is difficult, if not impossible, to make
a precise assessment, not least because the Spitfires were not working in
strict isolation. The 2nd TAF also operated against the V2s – sometimes
against the same targets, often against others located in the eastern part of
the Netherlands, like the communications network to stop the rockets
being transported to the launching sites, and launching sites themselves
from which the rockets were being fired at targets on continental Europe
like Antwerp. Although 12 Group concentrated on the launching sites in
the western part of the Netherlands, the ability of the Germans to fire the
missiles also depended on their supply routes, which must have been
disrupted by all the Allied air activity. It is interesting that when the rocket
troops finally pulled out of the Netherlands at the end of March 1945, one
source notes that they had sixty rockets waiting to be fired – almost a
week's supply if a generous firing rate of ten a day is assumed. If this
figure is right then clearly the attacks on the supply routes were not shut-
ting them down.

By this time, at the end of March, Fighter Command seemed to be
working on the assumption that the main firing sites in The Hague – the

Haagsche Bosch and the racecourse at Duindigt – had been so comprehensively destroyed that they could no longer be used, hence the decision
to stop attacking the launch sites and turn attention to the supply chain.
But in the final few days of the rocket campaign, a significant number of
V2s landed in England: no fewer than sixteen on the 22nd, eight on the
23rd, one on the 24th and three on the 25th, nine on the 26th and six on
the 27th. This amounts to an average of just over seven a day compared
with an average of over nine during the first week of March. The firing
troops still had rockets to fire and sites from which to fire them. If this was
true, then a very firm conclusion has to be that the attacks by both the 12
Group Spitfires and the aircraft of 2nd TAF *did not* bring the V2 campaign
to an end – the reason they stopped was the advance of the Allied armies
into north and western Germany that made the western Netherlands more
and more isolated and in danger of being cut off as well as extending the
supply lines. They did not come to an end because of the air attacks alone.

The table below gives details of the numbers of V2s landing in England
during the onslaught:

Month	Number of V2s landing	Daily average (incl. 'nil' days)	Daily average (excl. 'nil' days)
September 1944	36	1	2
October 1944	95	3	3
November 1944	154	5	5.5
December 1944	134	4.5	5
January 1945	222	7	8
February 1945	229	8	9
March 1945	226	8	8

'Nil' days are days on which no rockets landed in England.

Because of the progress of the Allied armies through Europe in the
autumn of 1944, the Germans were forced to deploy the rockets before
they were fully ready and so instead of a sudden massive onslaught of a
new and terrifying weapon which might have created panic in Britain,
their campaign started off in a rather piecemeal fashion, and only gradually increased. If the population of London could be told nothing for two
months other than that the explosions were faulty gas mains, then the
rockets can hardly have had a major effect on the population in any
context – physical damage, injury or morale. The Germans can hardly
have gained much comfort from them. In the scheme of things the achieve-
ments could only be limited. It is striking that both the numbers and the
daily average figures increase as time goes on and despite the attentions
of the RAF resources deployed against them, but they never approach a
critical level.

The chart of the number of V2s arriving in England on each of the days of March 1945 shows that the total for the month was 226, slightly less than the 229 in February, but of course March has only twenty-seven operational days against twenty-eight in February. However, the number of days on which rockets arrived are much the same – twenty-five in February and twenty-seven in March. If the Germans had been able to fire the same number on 28 March as they had on the 27th, then the monthly total would have been the highest of any month! As it is, the daily average for March is almost the highest, and this when the RAF stopped attacking the launch sites in The Hague to concentrate on the communications and logistics infrastructure, although with the furore about the bombing of Bezuidenhout in full cry, the fear of causing more casualties might have been an additional factor in the decision not to return to The Hague. Again, it is striking that the greatest number of V2s to land in England on any one day was sixteen, and other than three occasions in March, it only happened once before, on 20 January. March was nearly the best month for the V2s, and yet it was the month during which the RAF's effort was at its maximum and the German troops were being increasingly pressured by the Allied armies moving towards and into Germany to the east of them. Although the attack by the mediums of 2nd TAF on 3 March is remembered for the mistake in bombing Bezuidenhout, part of the force did hit the other correct aiming point in the Haagsche Bosch and must have caused significant damage there. From the 17th, when 12 Group started to concentrate on the supply lines, and following the attack on the

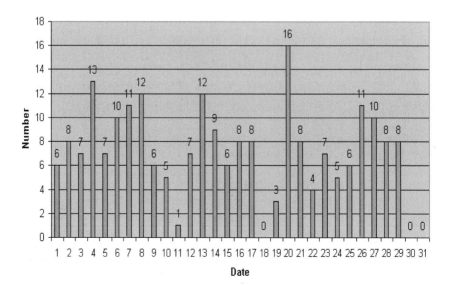

Daily numbers of V2s arriving in England during January 1945

BIM building by 602 on the 18th, there is no apparent effect on the rocket numbers. And of course, when 603 attacked the BIM building again on the 30th, the rockets were away and the campaign over, although 12 Group was not to know it.

It is noticeable, however, that there is little consistency in the daily numbers. The equivalent chart for January shows a similar pattern of varying rates of firing, although without the same peaks and troughs as in March. The 12 Group ORB shows that on most days in January, operations were either not mounted, or were mounted but aborted because of bad weather. On only eight days did the weather allow meaningful operations against the launch sites in The Hague: the 1st, 4th, 5th, 14th, 17th, 19th, 22nd and 23rd. An inspection of the chart for January does not show any clear correlation between the days that 12 Group was flying and the numbers of rockets arriving in Britain – there is no inference that the Spitfire attacks were instrumental in reducing the number of launches.

The maximum daily number reaching Britain during the month was sixteen, on the 20th, a day of no operations. But the next largest number, thirteen, was on the 4th, a day when operations did take place. And on the 11th, when one rocket arrived, and the 18th when there were none, 12 Group was not flying, so the low numbers fired can hardly be attributed to the dive-bombing activities of the Spitfires. Moreover, the charts show the numbers of rockets arriving over Britain, not the numbers being launched, which would include those aimed at targets on continental Europe such as Antwerp. The conclusions drawn from January are mirrored in those for the other months of the campaign.

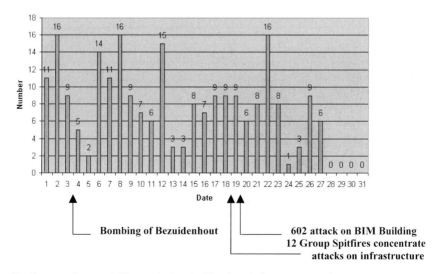

Daily numbers of V2s arriving in England during March 1945

On the face of it, the dive bombing was not achieving much and one, perhaps simplistic, question sometimes asked is 'If the dive bombing was not achieving anything, why did the British continue to do it?' However, this assumes that the only measure of success was the number of rockets arriving, whilst in reality there are other factors to be taken into the equation, albeit that some of them might be difficult to measure with any degree of accuracy.

The attacks clearly forced the Germans to shift operations from 'round the clock' to the hours of darkness, when the British fighters did not operate. Listings of the times of V2s arriving in England in September, October, November and December 1944 demonstrate this. For example on 4 October the first landed at 08.15 and the last at 17.36. On the 9th, the first was timed at 05.52 and the last at 18.30. By 31 October, however launches were moving into the night – the first timed at 02.26 and the last at 23.40. On 29 November, with few daylight hours, explosions are timed at 03.13, 10.55, 15.14, 19.50, 20.20, 21.11, 23.38 and 23.55, and on 31 December, at 00.35, 02.09, 02.55, 03.40,19.12, 19.46, 20.41 and 23.40. The authorities considered that casualties were likely to be fewer at night than in the day, when people would be going about their business, although night-time V2s which exploded on places where people congregated (e.g. the Prince of Wales pub on Boxing Day) still caused large numbers of casualties and much distress.

Other, more nebulous factors also come into play. For the Dutch people, under grinding occupation, there was the boost to morale in seeing the Spitfires flying over them day after day. It is striking that those who suffered often say how much they were heartened by the bravery of the pilots – and this sixty years on, when the events are distant memories. And Freddy van Dyck's encounter with the elderly Dutchman who witnessed the Marlot attack is another case in point. Moreover, the ability of Kammler's rocket troops to operate efficiently must have been affected by the knowledge that on days of good weather, there was the possibility – albeit perhaps slight – that their launch sites might be attacked in the middle of the firing preparations with terrible consequences. Carrying out such work whilst hearing the sound of the Spitfires' Merlins criss-crossing overhead all the time must have been nerve-wracking, and on days of heavy cloud cover when Spitfires could not find them they must have felt some relief. With up to a dozen and more rockets falling on London on a daily basis, the Government could also not acknowledge that nothing could be done to stop them. Even if there had been clear evidence that the activities of the RAF were achieving absolutely nothing (which there is not), the Government would have to be seen to be taking some action.

The way that the Germans conducted the offensive affected the ability of the Allied aircraft to counter it. By early 1944, even if the expected Allied invasion of Europe in the west had failed completely, German hopes of a victory were slim. Those developing the V2 continually promised more than they could deliver and in the end, the strategic situation in the summer and autumn of 1944 found the German High Command looking for something which might turn the tide – or at least suggest to the German people that it might. The 'revenge weapons' fitted the bill even although the V2 was not really ready for operations. The *Luftwaffe* had not been modernized sufficiently to match the British and American air forces. Although some of the fighter aircraft had been improved and new ones introduced to service (e.g the Focke Wulf 190 and the Me262) the bomber fleet still flew the same twin-engined tactical types – e.g. Ju88s, HE111s etc. – that it had flown in the late 1930s, albeit with improvements in electronic and radar equipment. They lacked a strategic heavy bomber. Over the same period, the British had progressed from biplane fighters (like the Hawker Hart and Gloster Gladiator) and light bombers (like the Handley Page Hampden and Fairey Battle) to jet aircraft and sophisticated other types like the Typhoon and the four-engined strategic 'heavies', the best known of which was the Avro Lancaster. Consequently, in trying to conduct their V2 campaign, the Germans had no air cover of any sort. The Allies had complete air supremacy over the west of the Netherlands and this created a very real disadvantage for the V2 troops, who were trying to operate under a roving umbrella of 12 Group's Spitfires. If the *Luftwaffe* had been able to provide worthwhile protection, then the story might have been different, but perhaps not significantly so. The Spitfires could not have fought a defender without getting rid of the long-range tanks and bombs and so it might have been that they were forced to operate with escorts – perhaps not unlike the Circuses and Ramrods that started in 1941 across the Channel to targets in France, and with a similar effect on the V2 launches. The cost to the RAF, however, would have been the commitment of greater resources to achieve this. And if the scale of the attacks on London had increased significantly, no doubt it would have been countered by drawing in the resources of Bomber Command and the medium bombers of 2nd TAF but with the increased risk of major civilian casualties to deal with. And the consequences of the bombing of Bezuidenhout on 3 March demonstrate just how important it was that these be avoided, although if the V2s were perceived as actually being a potential war winner, a greater level of Dutch civilian deaths and injuries would undoubtedly have been considered more acceptable.

Although the RAF could operate over the western Netherlands without interference from the *Luftwaffe*, they did sustain casualties. Thirteen pilots died, although not all on operations. The dangerous nature of their work resulted in some being killed in training and some died because of mechanical problems with their aircraft. The German flak could be ferocious at times, and a hit whilst the Spitfire was diving could easily spell disaster for the pilot. This rather forgotten campaign was no easy number and the operations were anything but benign.

It has to be stressed that the six 12 Group Spitfire squadrons were not the only counter to the V2s. As well as the aircraft of 2nd TAF, it is worth noting that British counter-intelligence operations also appeared to have some success in reducing the effectiveness of the V2s by using double agents supplying false information about where the rockets were landing and the damage they were causing. At the end of October 1944, accurate information passed by a double agent codenamed 'Treasure' was repeated verbatim in a report of the German High Command and this resulted in consideration being given to the use of a tactic which had resulted in some success in the battle against the V1s. By feeding the enemy false information that the missiles were overshooting their intended targets, the firing troops would set them for a shorter range which would, in fact, make them come down in the less heavily populated areas to the east of London. Rockets falling in London between 26 October and 4 November mainly fell in the east, and in particular the dock areas, and this was a cause of concern. Studies suggested that the aiming point of the missiles was in Wapping and intelligence concluded that the maximum range was 200 miles – relatively few fell to the west of London Bridge. Over the months, the mean point of impact of the V2s crept gradually eastwards, and the only apparent reason for this is the false information being fed to the Germans by the double agents. Whilst this did not reduce the numbers, an analysis undertaken by the Ministry of Home Security after it was all over, concluded that the gradual movement

---

RAF WINKLE OUT V2

Daily Sketch, 28 Dec. 1944.

'SAFE' SITES

TWO V2 depots in occupied Holland, placed by the enemy between densely populated civilian areas for security from air attack, were "winkled out" by the R.A.F. yesterday.

One lay in a 300-yard-wide open space between two housing estates and the other within 200 yards of a large hospital, both on the outskirts of towns.

In pin-point attacks R.A.F., Polish and Australian Spitfire squadrons put bombs accurately on these narrow targets.

Near the first target a railway supply line was also bombed. "We didn't put a single bomb outside the target area, despite the distraction of the flak," said one of the pilots.

Pilot-Officer F. W. Doidge, of Brixham, Devon, led another attack on

a V target, which was protected by a good deal of light flak.

A fourth target—a V2 storage and launching site, in a woodland area—was ploughed up by bombs.

None of our aircraft is missing.

Day Raid On Cologne

Lancasters of R.A.F. Bomber Command, escorted by Mustangs and Spitfires, in the afternoon pounded a railway marshalling at Cologne.

More than 1,200 Flying Fortresses and Liberators, escorted by about 700 Thunderbolts and Mustangs of the U.S. Eighth Air Force, attacked ten railway targets between Saarbrucken and Cologne.

It was the sixth consecutive day of Eighth Air Force attacks on com-

munications in support of the ground forces resisting the German counter-offensive.

No enemy aircraft was met. Flak was intense at a few of the targets.

Railway yards and bridges in the region of Neunkirchen, Kaiserlautern, Coblenz and Bonn were attacked. Four bombers are missing. All the fighters are safe.

A huge fleet of R.A.F. bombers which went out in the afternoon took nearly an hour to go over the East Coast.

Article in the *Daily Sketch* at the end of December 1944 reporting the activities of the six squadrons.

(Reproduced by kind permission Daily Sketch/Associated Newspapers.)

east of the mean point of impact saved 1,300 additional deaths, 10,000 additional injuries and 23,000 instances of damage to dwellings.

But the fact is that the V2 in the form that it was employed was never going to be a war winner although it created concern and disruption and tied down Allied resources – not least the six 12 Group Spitfire squadrons. Perhaps if it had been armed with atomic warheads it might have won the war, but in 1944 the Germans were far from developing a viable atomic bomb in any form, never mind one that was small enough to fit into a V2. The Germans employed the V2s without a clear military objective in mind. They saw it either as a straightforward 'terror weapon' that they hoped might so break down the civilian morale in London that peace might be requested, or as a long-range weapon to act in place of the strategic bomber element which the *Luftwaffe* so lacked. But the V2 alone would never crack civilian morale nor could it act in the strategic way that the Allied bombers could because there weren't enough of them, they were not accurate enough and they would never cause enough damage.

Despite this, as the rocket campaign gained momentum and the numbers exploding on London increased the Government had to be seen to be doing something. The hard fact was that the V2s could only be stopped before being fired, and it was very difficult to do this, but the authorities could never have admitted that they could not stop them. It would have been an admission that Britain's capital city was completely at the mercy of a ruthless enemy who, it was being said, was on the brink of defeat. Quite the contrary, with incidents like the New Cross explosion in mind from November 1944 onwards the anti-V2 activities of the Spitfire squadrons featured regularly in the media, with headlines such as this from the *Daily Sketch* on 28 December 1944:

'RAF WINKLE OUT V2 'SAFE' SITES' [1]

> *Two V2 depots in occupied Holland, placed by*
> *the enemy between densely populated civilian*
> *areas for security from air attack were*
> *'winkled out' by the RAF yesterday.*

And there were other similar paragraphs strewn around the papers on many days.

Several pilots gave radio interviews and the ORBs record on several occasions that on returning from raids, public relations staff from Fighter Command asked about results, presumably to brief the press. In these final few months of the war, the British public and the citizens of London needed to be reassured that something was being done to counter the V2s, and the dive-bombing Spitfires could illustrate this.

If there is doubt about what the Spitfires achieved, might they have been used in another way that would have made a bigger contribution to the ending of the war? Most likely they would have been deployed in the 2nd TAF and used to assist the ground troops in their advance, but would this have resulted in a significant shortening of the war? Probably not. Or they might have been sent directly on to the bomber escort duties which they undertook in April 1945. Again, would this have resulted in a significant shortening of the war? Probably not. One is drawn to the conclusion that the six squadrons were unlikely to be employed in a more useful way, and were better employed against the V2s. It may be difficult to demonstrate the precise effects of the dive-bombing campaign but it would be naive to conclude that it had no effect at all. Such a conclusion is incorrect, and demeans the sacrifice of those who died during the campaign and the efforts of the many involved in it. The airmen threw themselves into the campaign with energy and enthusiasm, despite the risks, and some of them at least recognized that their efforts were producing mixed results. They did their best within the limitations of the equipment they were given and there can be little doubt that they saved many lives in the south-east corner of England and much damage to property.

All six of the squadrons disbanded sooner or later. No. 303 successfully converted to Mustangs at Andrews Field and continued to fly them until it disbanded on 11 December 1946 at Hethel. The OC at that time was Witold Łokuciewski, returning to his old squadron from captivity after being shot down by a Bf109 during an operation in March 1942. For the members of the unit, the disbandment represented a stunning betrayal of them and all that they had fought for since 1939, which was an independent Poland. Being allied with the British allowed them to fight the Germans and the goal of a British victory a stepping stone towards the ultimate victory of their own and a triumphant return to Poland. The men in the Polish units of all the fighting arms expected to take part in the liberation of Poland by fighting to free their homeland for themselves, but it was not to be. Since 1939, Poles had been assured that Britain would stand with them against the common enemy, Germany, and that their country would be restored to them. In the latter half of 1944, although Churchill still promised the fighting Poles that they would get their country back, it was becoming clear that it would not be the free country they desired. Roosevelt, Stalin and Churchill were already planning the post-war carve-up of Europe, and Poland would be one of the losers. The die was cast at the conference which took place at Yalta at the beginning of February 1945, when the three leaders met for the last time. One of the points of agreement was that Poland would fall into the Soviet sphere of influence. When Germany surrendered in May 1945, the Poles found themselves losers on the winning side. In Britain's defence, it is clear that Churchill himself seems to have been well aware of what was happening and expressed his misgivings – but was powerless to affect the final outcome decided by the more powerful Soviets and Americans. And there were plenty of Members of Parliament and ordinary Britons who were concerned and ashamed at the treatment given to their long-suffering ally.

By the start of 1946, Churchill had been defeated in a general election and Britain had a Labour government. In March, Poles still in the services were told that they were no longer required and that they could either return to Poland (under Soviet control) or stay. If they decided to stay, there would be no guarantees or safeguards for them; they would be on their own. Yet another insult came with the Victory Parade in London on 8 June 1946. Communist Poland was invited to send a contingent of troops to take part, but the thousands of Poles still wearing the uniform of their Free Forces were ignored. Eventually the RAF pressed for some of the airmen to be allowed to march, and a grudging permission was given, but the offer was refused by the Poles who wanted their army and navy colleagues to be given the opportunity to march also. In the event, Communist Poland did not send a contingent and no Poles took part in the parade, many of those who had fought with Britain and its allies since 1939 watched bitterly from the pavements.

Poles who could not find it in themselves to return stayed in the West and integrated with their hosts. In Britain, the families of Poles who fought there during the Second World War have made homes and livings in all parts of the country from Stornoway to Cornwall. Some did return, including Witold Łokuciewski, 303's last CO, who went back in 1954. He loved to fly and joined the new Communist air force, becoming a colonel. In 1969 he returned to London as a military attaché in the Polish embassy. Looking up his old friends who had not returned, he found many of them were bitter that he had gone over to the hated Soviets and ostracized him. This he found painful to an extreme. He died in 1990. Jan Falkowski moved to Canada, where he continued his love of aviation, being active in the air cadet movement. With the break-up of the Soviet Union and the Warsaw Pact, in 1992 the standard of the Polish air force, safeguarded in London for all the years, was returned to the new, free, air force by some of the old pilots who had fought with the RAF during the Second World War. In their view, Poland was free at last.

No. 602 Squadron did not last long and disbanded at Coltishall on 15 May 1945, but like other squadrons of the Auxiliary Air Force, it re-formed back at its home town a year later with a new complement of pilots but many of the ground crew who had been with it during the war. Based at Abbotsinch initially flying Spitfire F.21s and F.22s, it moved to Renfrew in 1949 and then back to Abbotsinch in 1954, by now flying Vampires. In 1957, all flying units of the Auxiliaries were disbanded, 602 amongst them. For a unit that had such a strong connection with its city this came as a real blow, but the 602 Squadron Association remained strong and kept the memory of the unit alive until it finally re-formed forty-nine years later on 1 August 2006 in an intelligence role. A flight of 603 Squadron split off to become the new 602, but, ironically shared 603's traditional Town Headquarters in Edinburgh. Presumably the long-term aim is to move back to the west of Scotland.

After the Japanese surrendered, Max Baerlein found himself posted to a Transport Command Staging Post in Iraq, where he remained for nine months before being offered the choice of either waiting for a normal demobilization or being released immediately if he would return to his pre-war work on a farm for the period he would have had to wait until normal release. He accepted the early demob but found his new employer unwilling to pay much of a salary – ostensibly because Baerlein had lost his agricultural skills whilst in the RAF. As soon as he could, he moved to work for Decca and then with Plysu Products, which manufactured plastics. Having been not long married and with a daughter, Baerlein was horrified to be made redundant suddenly when the company went through a bad patch, but got another job whilst at the same time becoming interested in radio. A friend with the same interest was a director of a small electronics company and offered Baerlein a job in their laboratory. He stayed there for thirteen years, becoming their Overseas Sales Manager. He then accepted a job in France selling imported electronic products, and after working some years in the import business he joined Motorola Communications (France) becoming an account executive dealing with various ministries. He stayed with them until at the age of sixty-five he retired. He and his wife have enjoyed a long and happy retirement in France with yearly breaks at their other home on the Isle of Wight.

Of all the pilots, 'Bax' Baxter is probably the one who became the best known, as a journalist and broadcaster. His urbane, unhurried BBC accent endeared him to several generations of technically minded people who watched him present *Tomorrow's World* – a BBC television programme about current technical developments and how they might affect day-to-day life – and using his great flying knowledge to describe televised air displays. But that was not all; he was also a distinguished writer and speaker on, amongst other topics, motoring. After leaving 602 Squadron, Baxter was posted to Cairo (with 'Cupid' Love and Max Baerlein) and whilst there entered the world of broadcasting with the Forces Broadcasting Unit. Within a few years he joined the BBC, where most of his work was with the Outside Broadcasting Department. He was involved in a number of other organizations, including some charitable ones, and he was a member of the Committee of Management of the Royal National Lifeboat Institution, an Honorary Freeman of the City of London and an Honorary Admiral of the Association of Dunkirk Little Ships – to name only a few. Born in 1922, he died in 2006.

Michael Francis returned to his other love, art. He applied for a place at the Slade School of Art, part of London University, was accepted and graduated three years later. Then came a postgraduate year. He wrote:

After this I soloed into the world as a portrait painter, being steeped in tradition. Painting a full-length portrait of Richard Todd in the role of Rob Roy for the Royal Command Performance, for which it had been selected. Then it quickly came home to me that I was clinging to the 18th century and in 1946, Modern Art was already fifty years old! I wanted to be in the avant garde, *not the jaded past! So I slowly adopted the abstract mode of painting as my career. In portraiture, I subsequently painted the Queen Mother and Princess Anne.*

He became part of the art 'scene' in Chelsea, and he and his wife have lived there all their lives. In the 1990s, he became involved in a project to restore the control tower at RAF Ludham, then in ruins, and met up with some of the other pilots he had flown with, including Raymond Baxter and Bob Sergeant. This took him back into the cockpit of a Spitfire and the memories this brought back prompted him to write the poem which appears as a postscript to this book. Roderic Hill would have recognized a kindred spirit!

'Cupid' Love, the man reputed to be the first to take a shot at a ballistic

Bob Sergeant, Raymond Baxter and Michael Francis return to Ludham in 1998.
(The late Bob Sergeant.)

602's Stan Gomme and 'Cupid' Love, presumably in Egypt after the end of the campaign against the V2s. *(Max Baerlein.)*

missile was married in 1945. No. 602 having been disbanded, the pilots expected to be posted to the Far East to fight Japan and getting married seemed to be a good idea. According to one fellow pilot, Mr and Mrs Love's first wedding night was spent 'switching off numerous alarm clocks set at different times and hidden in their room by their friends'! Instead of going to the Far East, though, Love found himself with Baerlein and in Cairo, ferrying P51 Mustangs to Nagpur in India. Once delivered, the pilots had to 'hitch' their way back to Cairo to await the next Mustang for the next run. On his last run, Max managed to get a ride in a Sunderland from Bahrein – the end being a memorable landing on the River Nile. In spare moments, he recalled they played Monopoly! Love ultimately returned to Glasgow, where he eventually died. Max Baerlein understood that by then he had gone blind – a tragedy for an old pilot whose eyes must have been so important to him.

No. 603 Squadron, which started off the campaign as 229, found itself in Scotland on VE Day, back at Drem in East Lothian, the same territory that it had covered in the dark days of 1939 when, together with 602, it had shot down the first German aircraft over UK air space. On 11 May they escorted three Ju52s carrying high-ranking German officers into Drem, bringing with them the surrender of German forces in Norway. Then on 15 August, back at Turnhouse, it disbanded. However, like 602, it re-formed again as an auxiliary squadron the following year and flew Spitfire F22s and Vampires until once again it disbanded in 1957 with all the other flying squadrons of the Auxiliary Air Force. However, the story did not end there. In a direct line of succession, No. 2 (City of Edinburgh) Maritime Headquarters Unit (known as '2Mahoo') formed, using as its HQ the same Town Headquarters in Edinburgh that 603 had used. This continued until 1 October 1999, when 2MHU re-formed back to 603 but as a role support squadron and not a flying unit.

In 2003, its young men and women found themselves in Iraq taking part in Operation TELIC, the British part of the invasion of Iraq, and there was a curious coincidence. In Qatar, some of the 603 men found themselves operating on an airfield with the Australian 75 Squadron flying F18s. Recognizing the link between 603 and the Aussies during the Second World War, the Australians designated one of their aeroplanes as the 'Edinburgh aircraft' and it went into battle bearing the three-towered castle of 603's badge and its motto '*Gin ye Daur*'. In future, there will always be a designated 'Edinburgh aircraft' on the unit. In 2006 of the six 12 Group squadrons that fought the V2s in 1944–45 602 and 603 are the only ones that still exist – both non-flying units.

In August 1945, with 603 back at RAF Turnhouse, its Edinburgh home base, Bob Sergeant got a phone call to say that he should have been demobbed a couple of weeks before. Within a few hours, he was on his way south. He initially returned to his home town and the family undertaking business, but he found it difficult to settle down. As a committed Christian, he had been a lay preacher in the Methodist Church before the war and found that everyone wanted things to return to the way they had been then. But for him things had changed, he was now married with a family and he had killed people, and it could never be the same. A few years later, with the RAF now desperately short of Spitfire instructors, a chance encounter with one of his old chums still in the air force led to him rejoin as an instructor at RAF Chivenor. He stayed in the Air Force until 1969, when he retired. He then joined the Construction Industry Training Board at Bircham Newton as a lecturer but took early retirement from it in 1976 to live in Norfolk for many years, taking an active and enthusiastic

interest in the RAF and a number of books written about it. He developed a respiratory illness which he attributed to many years of breathing pure oxygen. Sadly, in September 2001, whilst travelling to Cyprus on holiday, Bob Sergeant took ill on the aeroplane and died shortly after arriving there.

Freddy van Dyck left 603 on 17th January 1945 and following demob joined Sabena as a first officer flying DC-3 Dakotas. After two years, he

Freddy van Dyck in the left-hand seat of a Boeing 747 at Chicago Airport in 1981.
(*Freddy van Dyck.*)

'Paddy' O'Reilly returns to Coltishall, then home to Jaguar strike squadrons. *(Tom O'Reilly.)*

became a captain and flew with the same company until he retired in 1982, by which time he had notched up 27,847 flying hours on all manner of aircraft including Convair 240s, DC-4s, DC-6s, DC-7s, Boeing 707s, DC-10s and Boeing 747s. He now spends his time between his two homes, one in his native Belgium and the other in the south of France.

Paddy O'Reilly left the air force. He remembered his father suggesting that staying in might be a good career move, or perhaps becoming an airline pilot. But like many young men, Tom thought that he knew better and wanted to try his hand at 'civvy street'. He spent some time working in sales and marketing – vacuum cleaners and building trade supplies – and tried his hand at running his own businesses. Latterly, he became a senior manager in the Rank Organization, involved in the newly popular 'bingo' entertainment market, and made a good life for himself, his wife Beryl and his family back in the Wirral. At the start of the twenty-first century, he still held down a part-time job as a branch secretary of the Royal British Legion and kept himself fit playing golf.

Eric Mee died in 2007.

No. 124 Squadron moved to Molesworth where an operational conversion unit for Meteors had been established. Having converted to Meteor F. Mk. 3s, the squadron moved to RAF Bentwaters as part of the defensive screen for London. It stayed there until 1 April 1946 when it disbanded by re-badging as 56 Squadron.

No. 451 Squadron moved to Germany in September 1945, first to Fassberg, then to Wunstorf, where it disbanded in January 1946.

VE Day found 453 Squadron at Hawkinge. It moved subsequently to Lasham and at the end of July, lost its charismatic CO, Ernie Esau. Command was taken over by Squadron Leader D.M. Davidson. It traded in its Spitfire XVIs for XIVs before moving to Germany and Fassberg. By

October it was at Wunstorf, where it remained until it disbanded with 451 on 21 January 1946, at this time commanded by Squadron Leader T.E. Hilton. Neither of the Australian squadrons ever re-formed.

The ebullient Squadron Leader Ernie Esau married an English girl who, his old flying chums heard, was from a wealthy family. They understood that Ernie was going to manage an Australian arm of his father-in-law's business after being demobbed but later word was that he had bought a business in a barren part of north-west Victoria in a place called Nyah West, where he died. One of his pilots, Russ Baxter recalled that Esau was an orphan and commented later that considering a difficult start in life the CO had achieved great things.

Rusty Leith led 453 Squadron on its last wartime operation on 25 April 1945, escorting Halifaxes and Lancasters on a raid against the Frisian island of Wangerooge. With the war in Europe over, he expected to be posted to a squadron fighting the Japanese, but with the dropping of the atomic bombs on Hiroshima and Nagasaki he returned instead to Australia to take up the threads of his interrupted life. He sailed to Sydney

Russell Leith back in the cockpit of the restored TB863, a Spitfire which he flew operationally in 1945.
(From 'Duty Done' by kind permission of Russell Leith.)

on the P&O liner *Maloja* to find Meg there to meet him. Then he went to his father's house, where he found that Colin, who had by now remarried, had visibly aged and seemed to be in some pain, but still working for the Colonial Sugar Refining company. He rejoined the company and married Meg on 12 December 1945. In October 1947 his father died and not much later, Russell came down with tuberculosis, which resulted in him spending sixteen months in a sanatorium. However, the company stuck by him during this spell and he took full of advantage of his free time to complete his accountancy studies, returning to work on a restricted basis, gradually regaining his strength. Over the years, he undertook a series of roles culminating in an appointment in 1970 as Regional Manager for Western Australia. The Leiths moved to Perth and Russell followed a successful career but in 1979, the company was offering early retirement packages to employees who had been with them for more than 30 years. Russell was one and he decided that this opportunity should not be missed.

A man with a strong sense of public duty, he threw himself into voluntary work with charities and has made a success of it. His many posts include being Chairman of the Anglican Diocesan Trustees and the Western Australian Potato Board as well as serving on the Consultative Committee on Prison Industries, the Western Australia Art Gallery, the National Safety Council of Australia – of which he was the Chairman in 1990 – and also work with Alzheimer sufferers. For his services he was made a Member of the Order of Australia in 1994. But sadly, much of this has been done without the support of his wife Meg, who died of cancer in August 1982. Russell and Meg had two children, David and Margaret, who in turn both have children of their own. They form a close family group and Russell values their closeness and support. Many years after he crashed in France, his family discovered that the crash site of his Spitfire had been found and they arranged for the cockpit hood of his aeroplane to be airfreighted to him for a surprise and emotional reunion.

In amongst all his other activities, Russell has become heavily involved in efforts to mark the contribution made by Australian servicemen to the defeat of the Third *Reich*. He has returned to Europe on several occasions to meet the people who sheltered him when he was downed, and to be present at events like the sixtieth anniversary commemorations of the Arnhem fighting, which he witnessed from above. He maintains links with the RAAF and with some other ex-airmen has been 'adopted' by the local RAAF base at Pearce, where he is invited to the graduation ceremonies and dinners for the new generation of the RAAF's airmen who have the opportunity to meet and talk with those who created some of the traditions that live on in the present day. Always the gentleman, but with a keen mind for politics and current affairs as well as people, Colin Russell Leith is a remarkable man who has had a remarkable life.

453 Squadron reunion 1984. From l to r. 'Norm' Stewart, Sir Brian Inglis, 'Cam' Taylor, Digby Johns and Jim McAuliffe.

The temperament that sustained men through the trials of operational flying also seems to have helped them in civilian life. Many of the pilots who flew the dive-bombing raids against the V2s made their subsequent careers in flying, but many returned to civilian life to take up careers that had been interrupted by the war. Brian Inglis was one who had a distinguished and by any standards remarkable life in commerce and industry. Before joining the RAAF in 1942, he had matriculated which meant that on his return to Australia after the war ended he could take up a place at Trinity College, Melbourne University, in 1946 to read mining and metallurgy, which he had always intended to make his career. He graduated three years later with a BSc in Metallurgy to join Ford Canada as a graduate trainee. A year later he received a postgraduate degree in Business Administration from the University of Michigan. Rising through the ranks of the Ford Motor Company, in 1967 he was appointed Director of Manufacturing of the Australian arm and in 1970, by now in his mid-forties, Managing Director of the Ford Motor Company of Australia. Further promotion followed and after an appointment as Vice President in 1983, Inglis became Chairman of Ford Asia Pacific Inc. in 1983. With his business and commercial acumen in demand, he formed associations with other companies and organizations over the years including Amcor, Newcrest Mining, Aerospace Technologies of Australia and Optus Communications.

In addition to all of this, he played a full part in the national business life of his country. In 1977 he was the Chairman of the Australian Manufacturing Council and later, in the 1980s, took an appointment as the Chairman of the Defence Industry Committee. To mark all of his distinguished service he received a number of awards and honours including becoming a Knight Bachelor for distinguished service to industry in 1977, being awarded the James N. Kirby Award by the Institution of Production Engineers in 1979, Honorary Life Membership of the Society of Automotive Engineers (Australasia). In 1988 he became a Companion of the Order of Australia (AC). Finally, in 1992, Sir Brian Inglis became an Honorary Doctor of Laws of Monash University.

In 2005 along with five other Australian veterans of the Second World War from all branches of the service, he received the French *Legion d'Honor* from the French Minister for Veterans' Affairs at a ceremony held at the Australian War Memorial. These awards marked the contribution made by Australian forces to the liberation of France from German occupation. By any standards Sir Brian is a remarkable man with a hugely successful life. He was married and has three daughters and lives out his retirement in Victoria.

'Swamp' Marsh remained a pilot all of his life. He flew with Australian National Airways, Air Ceylon, Union of Burma Airways and Cathay Pacific, flying a wide range of civil aircraft, including DC-3s, DC-4s, de Havilland Doves, Miles Marathons, Lockheed Electras, Convair 880s and Boeing 707s. By the time he retired from Cathay Pacific in 1973, he had reached the board. After retiring, he accepted a position with the Australian Department of Aviation monitoring and flying the Hawker Siddeley 125, the F28, the Boeing 707, the Lockheed Electra and the

European Airbus A300B4. His work included the certification of the Airbus A300 Flight Simulator for the Department of Civil Aviation. One of the many high spots was when he flew as an observer in August 1975 on the Concorde proving flight between Melbourne and Singapore. By the time he finally left flying in 1985, he had amassed 21,860 flying hours. He married an Australian National Airways flight attendant and they had three sons and a daughter, and

Captain Norman Marsh.
(*The late Norman Marsh.*)

The restored 453 Squadron's TB863 FU●P soars over Mount Aspiring in New Zealand. At the time of writing it was based in Australia.
(© *Philip Makanna/GHOSTS (www.ghosts.com) and published with his kind permission.*)

now several grandchildren. Two of the Marsh sons became pilots, one with Qantas and the other with Cathay Pacific. At the turn of the twenty-first century he lived quietly at Eaglemont, and he died peacefully in October 2006.

Few of the Spitfires the squadrons flew survived. Based back at Turnhouse not long after the European war ended, one day the 603 pilots learned that their aeroplanes would soon be taken away, and within hours they stood watching sadly as their beloved Spitfires disappeared into the southern sky and the unmistakable sound of their Merlins dwindled and faded. One, though, which did survive and continued to fly at the beginning of the twenty-first century was TB863, an LF XVIE flown by 453 Squadron. It will be recalled that on 18 March, following the attack on the BIM building, 453's Ernest Tonkin in FU●P SM233 was brought down and became a POW. A replacement Spitfire, TB863, flew in to the squadron a few days later and became the new FU●P. Its first operation took place on the morning of 24 March, piloted by the 'A' Flight Commander F/L Clemesha. This was an armed recce against rail targets. Operationally, the pilot who flew it most often was Rusty Leith. After the war, it managed to survive the scrap merchant's torch but it languished and deteriorated in various places around Britain. It appeared briefly in *Reach for the Sky* and provided spares for other aircraft appearing in *The Battle of Britain*. Eventually the Alpine Fighter Collection bought it for restoration and moved it to New Zealand, where it has been a regular performer in air shows at the hands of Sir Tim Wallis back in the markings of 453 Squadron – FU●P – although with black and white D-Day invasion stripes, which strictly speaking it wouldn't have worn! In 2006 it moved to Australia.

Although the airfields at Ludham, Swannington and Matlaske closed within months of the end of the European war, RAF Coltishall survived. During the Cold War it hosted the RAF's Jaguar light strike aircraft squadrons and continued in this role through to the end of the twentieth century. It fell victim to the Labour government's defence spending review in 2004 and has now closed.

The retreat of the rocket troops meant the end of the campaign for the six 12 Group Spitfire squadrons, but it did not mean the end of the grinding occupation endured by the civilians in the west of the Netherlands although their suffering was perhaps lightened a little with the ending of the noise of the rockets being launched, the risk of a rogue misfire and the constant patrolling of the Spitfires with the attendant risk of civilian injuries – no doubt more in people's minds because of the bombing of Bezuidenhout. But they still had to endure the privations imposed on them; little food, little warmth and little sign of liberation. And although ultimate liberation was not in doubt, the 3½ million Dutch civilians could not but wonder whether the Germans would make the Allies fight for this part of the Netherlands or would eventually surrender. By mid-April the bread ration had reduced to about 500 grams a week – half a loaf for each person – and the people despaired.

The Canadian armies stopped near the Dutch border in anticipation of a battle or a surrender but in fact negotiations were taking place with the Germans near Amersfoort. Eventually they agreed that the Allies could drop food parcels provided that no offensive action was taken from the air. Both British and American aircraft took part – Lancasters of Bomber Command and B-17s of the USAAF. The British operation received the code name Operation Manna and the American Operation Chow-Hound. Eventually the drop started on Sunday, 29 April, with some of the old familiar places being now designated as drop zones – Duindigt racecourse, the airfield at Ypenburg, Valkenburg and Rotterdam. The Lancasters came in low – 1,000 feet, and then because of low cloud had to descend even lower. Just short of the objectives they were hedge-hopping at 300 feet, 200 feet, surrounded by other aircraft with civilians on rooftops waving at them and the gunners waving back. There were heavy bombers everywhere, but dropping food not bombs, and the people scurried to the dropping areas to get what they could. Their relief needs little description. After all their privations it can be readily imagined and felt. The food drops continued for over a week until 8 May, three days after the war came

The BIM building in 2003 – no sign of wartime damage!
(Author.)

to an end and the people of the western Netherlands were truly free again.

The Hague still bears scars of the V2 campaign. The damage to Bezuidenhout was too great for it to be repaired on a building-by-building basis and what was left of it was demolished. A new Bezuidenhout rose from the ashes. The tragedy of the 3 March 1945 bombing has never been forgotten by the citizens of The Hague. Commemoration ceremonies have been held each year, with special ones in 1995 for the fiftieth Anniversary and in 2005 for the sixtieth. Generally, the Dutch bear the British and the RAF no ill feeling about it. They accept it as an unfortunate accident in a terrible war, but it has left an indelible scar on the collective memory of the citizens of The Hague, and it is only natural that there must be some who do bear their erstwhile allies some ill feeling over it. However, if there are they do not make these feelings obvious.

The BIM building was repaired and in 2003 was the office at the Hague of a large international firm of accountants and business consultants. It looked as it looked in 1944, with no visible external sign of the attacks of 1945. At Ockenburg, explosions of faulty V2s and splinters from the RAF's bombs blew holes in the walls of the church and left gouge marks in the dark red brickwork. All of these have been repaired, but the difference in colour and texture between the original and the new brickwork can be clearly seen by an observant visitor. Not far from here, in one of the wooded areas is the crater of a V2 that exploded prematurely. Overgrown

Betty van't Hoff – 1944 *ausweis*.
(Jan and Betty van't Hoff.)

with bushes and undergrowth, it is not obvious to the casual visitor, and even those who know what it is can have difficulty finding it, but it is there, a hidden memorial to what happened in the dark days of 1944 and 1945.

After liberation, Jan van't Hoff went to Britain to help him recover from the ordeal. He stayed in a small Welsh mining village near Ebbw Vale, where he enjoyed a decent diet and as a bonus improved his English tremendously. He became a radio operator in the merchant navy and shortly after the war met the nurse who would become his wife, Betty. Although only fifteen, she had shown tremendous courage during the occupation by carrying leaflets for the Resistance, although like many such people she is quite modest and unassuming about her contribution and the risks she ran. She still has her identity card – the *ausweis* – used at the time as a keepsake.

Jan served in the merchant navy until 1951, when he transferred to the new navy for a two-year stint, then he moved to the marine radio station at Scheveningen, from where he eventually retired. He and Betty had two sons and they live in IJmuiden. Sadly Jan died in 2007. Like many Dutch civilians, Jan had strong memories of the war and occupation and was very appreciative of the risks the pilots of 'their' Spitfires took to help them and to liberate them. Jan and Paddy O'Reilly of 229/603 Squadron met

Jan and Betty van't Hoff in 2003.
(Author.)

much later and have become firm friends. The Dutch civilians who endured all of this are remarkable people, who bear no rancour for the civilian casualties that they suffered, from both the bombing of the Spitfires and the horrors of 3 March. They are grateful that the Allies did not leave them and there is a long-standing friendship and affection for those who fought and lost their lives for them.

Dr Hans Kammler, the commander of the rocket troops, disappeared into the confusion of post-surrender Europe and never resurfaced. Various rumours about his fate circulate, including one that he did research work in the US but there is nothing definite.

Wernher von Braun, trapped at Peenemünde between the armies of the Allies to the west and the Soviets to the east made a conscious decision to surrender to the Americans rather than be captured by the Soviets. Gathering together important documents and equipment, he and many of his technicians headed west and successfully managed to meet an American unit. From there they were taken to America, where they continued their research, which culminated in the giant Saturn rockets used to put American astronauts on the moon in the late 1960s and 1970s. The lineage of these rockets can be traced back directly to the V2s which killed so many in 1944 and 1945. Von Braun became a celebrated engineer and technician, his history of collaboration with the Third *Reich* and the SS conveniently swept under the carpet and out of sight. Many of the engineers who did not flee to the west with von Braun fell into Soviet hands. They used them differently, sucking the knowledge out of them then using it to develop their own arsenal of rockets for the Cold War. One of these, the SCUD, is little more than a V2 in another guise and it was still in use by countries like Iraq at the end of the twentieth century.

And what of Air Marshal Hill? After the war ended, he became the Air Member for Training on the Air Council, then the Air Member for Technical Services. In 1947 his promotion to Air Chief Marshal was promulgated and King George VI appointed him as his Principal Air Aide-de-Camp. But his post-war career in the RAF was not long, and he retired in 1948. He went back to academia and between 1948 and 1954, he held the position of Rector of the Imperial College of Science and Technology, and between 1953 and 1954 Vice-Chancellor of the University of London. But the new path ended abruptly when he died on 6 October 1954. Earlier that year, on 26 February he had suffered a stroke at his office in the Senate House and he never fully recovered from the effects of it. Air Chief Marshal Sir Roderic Hill KCB, MC, AFC, MA, LLD, was a remarkable man, but like the squadrons of 12 Group under his command in 1945, he has never really been given his due place in history. From the mud of the Loos battlefields in 1915, via the deserts and heat of the Middle East, through the corridors of power of the young Royal Air Force to the skies of southern England echoing to the throaty rattle of the V1s, Roderic Hill devoted his life to his country. Overcoming his own self-doubts, he was courageous both physically in the air and intellectually in high command. He flew all types of aeroplanes, from the flimsy biplanes of the Somme in 1916 to the Spitfires and Tempests of the European campaign and then some of the early jets.

He was a man of his time.

Notes
1. Reproduced by kind permission of Associated Newspapers.

Postscript

I n 1990, forty-five years after dive bombing the V2s, Michael Francis, formerly of 602 Squadron, once again climbed into the cockpit of a Spitfire and felt moved to write the following:

The fearful details by
Faded memory suppressed:

The twist-grip
On the decayed throttle
Controlled the gauge of diamonds,
On the gyroscopic gunsight,
Through which we aimed to kill.

The dashboard in the cockpit
–A gothic arch–
Displayed the instruments
Like stained glass windows
Above an altar.

An insidious liaison:
A son of God to kill;
An art with which to arm him.

We re-entered the womb each time.
Our umbilical cord:
The microphone jack,
Oxygen tube,
Dinghy clasp
Parachute and safety harness.

We relied upon the fierce iron heart
And agility of our surrogate mothers
Not to be prematurely ejected into
Eternity.

The careless assuredness of youth
Defied the qualms of fear.

The scar tissue over
The wounded mind
Remains invisible.

APPENDIX I

Roll of Honour

Pilots of the six Spitfire squadrons who gave their lives in the campaign against the V2s

Date	Name	Squadron	Comments
15 September 1944	F/Sgt J. Manley, RAFVR	229	Buried in Bergen General Cemetery
1 November 1944	Sgt J. Wierchowicz, *Polskie Sily Powietrzne*	303	Buried in the Military Cemetery in Amsterdam.
11 January 1945	F/O L.S. Trail, RAF	603	Lost at sea. Commemorated on Panel 268 of the Runnymede Memorial
14 February 1945	F/L G.Y.G. Lloyd, RAFVR	602	Buried in Liverpool (Allerton) Cemetery
14 February 1945	W/O J.F. Kelman, RAFVR	124	Buried in Westduin General Cemetery, The Hague
15 February 1945	F/Sgt P.B. Allen, RAFVR	124	Commemorated on Panel 6 of the Manchester Crematorium
25 February 1945	F/L S. Szpakowicz, *Polskie Sily Powietrzne*	303	Lost at sea
27 February 1945	Sgt K. Prusak, *Polskie Sily Powietrzne*	303	Killed in a flying accident
14 March 1945	F/L N.J. Bray, RAAF	451	Buried in Cambridge Regional Cemetery

Date	Name	Squadron	Comments
17 March 1945	W/O J.D. Green, RAAF	603	Buried in Barendrecht General Cemetery.
24 March 1945	P/O N.A.H. McGinn, RIAF	603	Buried in Cambridge City Cemetery.
25 March 1945	F/L C.J. Maltby, RAFVR	124	Buried in Breukelen (Kerkplein) General Cemetery
30 March 1945	F/Sgt C.M. Lett, RAFVR	124	Lost at sea. Commemorated on Panel 271 of the Runnymede Memorial

Opposite page:

Equivalent to an altitude of about 20,000 feet.
'A', 'B' and 'B1' refer to the raid of 3 March 1945.
Reproduced by kind permission of the National Archives UK. AIR 20/795

Target Photograph –
The Hague

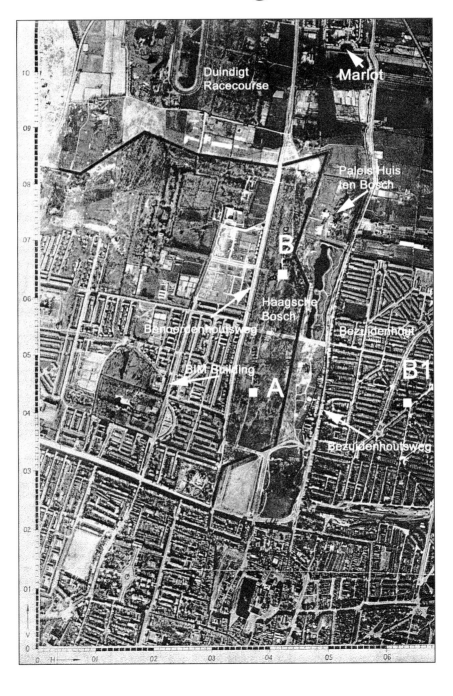

APPENDIX III

Squadron Strengths, 31 December 1944

229 SQUADRON

Pilots
Officer Commanding: Major N.F. Harrison (South Africa), relinquished command to Squadron Leader Patterson.

'A' Flight

Flight Lieutenant McAndrew, Flight Lieutenant R. Sergeant, Flying Officer L. S. Trail, Pilot Officer W. Doidge, Pilot Officer Grant, Flight Sergeant J. Green, Flight Sergeant T. O'Reilly, Flight Sergeant Thomson, Flight Sergeant Wheatley.

'B' Flight

Flight Lieutenant T. Rigler, Flight Lieutenant J. Kirkman, Flight Lieutenant J. Welch, Flying Officer Sanderson, Pilot Officer McConnochie, Pilot Officer F. van Dyck, Warrant Officer Beckwith, Warrant Officer Cookson, Flight Sergeant W. Haupt, Warrant Officer E. Mee.

Others:

Squadron Leader Donovan, Flight Lieutenant Burrett, Flying Officer Richardson, Flying Officer Walker, Warrant Officer Butterworth, Warrant Officer Hayes, Warrant Officer McKenzie.

Aircraft on charge
Squadron code: 9R
Spitfire IXE: Definitive listing not available.

303 (POLISH) SQUADRON POLSKIE SILY POWIETRZNE

Pilots

Officer Commanding: Squadron Leader B. Drobinski.
Flight Lieutenant K. Bartys, Flight Lieutenant J. Franckiewicz, Flight Lieutenant S. Kedzierski, Flight Lieutenant S. Kleczkowski, Flight Lieutenant A. Malarowski, Flight Lieutenant T. Rzyski, Flight Lieutenant S. Socha, Flight Lieutenant S. Szpakowicz, Flight Lieutenant M. Szelestowski, Flying Officer M. Maksymowicz, Pilot Officer Z. Krzeptowski, Pilot Officer E. Martens, Warrant Officer A. Rutecki, Warrant Officer W. Sznapka, Flight Sergeant Z. Bartkowiak, Flight Sergeant M. Michalak, Flight Sergeant W. Skrzydlo, Sergeant A. Benski, Sergeant L. Bisans, Sergeant E. Janicki, Sergeant E. Janiszewski, Sergeant J. Kmiecik, Sergeant S. Magdziak, Sergeant K. Prusak, Sergeant K. Sztuka.

Aircraft on charge

Squadron code: RF
Spitfire VB: AB272, AB282, BL292, BM157, BR140, BS348.
Spitfire IXF (NOTE: Some IXs were upgraded Vs): BS129, BS140, BS281, BS461, BS463, EN182, EN367, EN526, MA416, MA420, MA426, MA528, MA683, MA692, MA694, MA763, MA814, MH692, MH694, MH777, MJ129.

453 SQUADRON RAAF

Pilots

Officer Commanding: Squadron Leader E.A.R. Esau
Flight Lieutenant N.K. Baker, Flight Lieutenant W.R. Bennett, Flying Officer N.R. Adams, Flying Officer W.H. Carter, Flying Officer R.G. Clemesha, Flying Officer J.L. Cummins, Flying Officer C.R. Leith, Flying Officer N.J. Marsh, Pilot Officer B. Fuller, Pilot Officer J.C. Grady, Pilot Officer B.S. Inglis, Pilot Officer G.J. Stansfield, Pilot Officer C.A.M. Taylor, Pilot Officer K.A. Wilson, Warrant Officer J.D. Carmichael, Warrant Officer D.C. Johns, Warrant Officer R. Lyall, Warrant Officer W.W. Mace, Warrant Officer R.G. Peters, Warrant Officer C.S. Robertson, Warrant Officer R.A.J. York, Flight Sergeant J.H. Lynch, Flight Sergeant J.F. McAuliffe, Flight Sergeant J.K. McCully, Flight Sergeant R.J. Pollock.

Aircraft on charge
Squadron code: FU
Spitfire XVI: SM184(D), SM185(M), SM188(S), SM193(Q), SM207(R), SM230(F), SM233(P), SM243(J), SM244(K), SM249(B), SM250(T), SM255(A), SM256(W), SM278 (T), SM281(G), SM282 (Z), SM402(C).

602 (City of Glasgow) Squadron

Pilots
Officer Commanding: Squadron Leader R.A. Sutherland.
Flight Lieutenant J.P. Banton, Flight Lieutenant G.Y.G. Lloyd, Flight Lieutenant H.R. Pertwee, Flight Lieutenant A.O. Pullman, Flight Lieutenant J.D. Stephenson, Flight Lieutenant J.R. Sutherland, Flight Lieutenant J.C.R. Waterhouse, Flight Lieutenant Z. Wroblewski, Flying Officer R.F. Baxter, Flying Officer F.W. Farfan, Flying Officer F.J. Farrell, Flying Officer R.C. Rudkin, Flying Officer R.H.C. Thomerson, Warrant Officer J. Crosland, Warrant Officer H.G. Ellison, Warrant Officer L.T. Menzies, Warrant Officer S. Sollitt, Warrant Officer J. Toone, Flight Sergeant M.V. Francis, Flight Sergeant C.J. Zuber.

Aircraft on charge
Squadron code: LO
Spitfire IXB: MJ253, MJ441, MJ457, MJ522, NH150
Spitfire XVI: SM234, SM235, SM257, SM276, SM287, SM288, SM301, SM307, SM341, SM343, SM350, SM351, SM353, SM361, SM388, SM424.

Squadron Strengths, 31 March 1945

124 (Baroda) Squadron

Pilots
Officer Commanding: Squadron Leader G.C. Scott.

Flight Lieutenant B. Brooks, Flight Lieutenant A. Charlesworth, Flight Lieutenant R. Forth, Flight Lieutenant J. Fowler, Flight Lieutenant F. James, Flight Lieutenant K. Lawrence, Flight Lieutenant C. Maltby, Flight Lieutenant J. Melia, Flight Lieutenant L. Oakshott, Flight Lieutenant P. Phillips. Flying Officer W. Andrews, Flying Officer J. Blackett, Flying Officer H. Fallon, Flying Officer R. Johnson, Flying Officer D. Roy, Flying Officer A. Travis, Pilot Officer W. Andrews, Warrant Officer G. Beadle, Warrant Officer C. Farquharson, Warrant Officer N. Howard, Warrant Officer J. James, Warrant Officer P. Jones, Warrant Officer J. McCall, Warrant Officer E. Parker, Warrant Officer G. Paterson, Warrant Officer A. Williams, Flight Sergeant C. Lett, Flight Sergeant F. Oakley, Sergeant C. Lattimer.

Aircraft on charge
Squadron code: ON

Spitfire IXE: PV151, PV283, PV296, PV299, PV303, PV312, PV318, PV343, PV344, PV354, PK811, PL249, RA804, RK860, RK908, RK911, RR209, RR252, SM515, TA793, TA795, TA796, TA800, TA804, TA811, TA813, TB918.

303 (POLISH) SQUADRON POLSKIE SILY POWIETRZNE

Pilots

Officer Commanding: Squadron Leader B. Drobinski
Flight Lieutenant K. Bartys, Flight Lieutenant J. Frackiewicz, Flight Lieutenant S. Kleczkowski, Flight Lieutenant A. Malarowski, Flight Lieutenant T. Rzyski, Flight Lieutenant S. Socha, Flight Lieutenant M. Szelestowski, Flying Officer J. Krok, Flying Officer M. Maksymowicz, Flying Officer J. Schandler, Flying Officer T. Sikorski, Flying Officer B. Zborowski, Flying Officer S. Zdanowski, Pilot Officer R. Gorecki, Pilot Officer Z. Krzeptowski, Pilot Officer E. Martens, Pilot Officer Z. Nowinski, Warrant Officer Z. Bartkowiak, Warrant Officer A. Rutecki, Warrant Officer W. Skrzydlo, Warrant Officer W. Sznapka, Flight Sergeant A. Bonski, Flight Sergeant J. Janicki, Flight Sergeant J. Kmicik, Flight Sergeant S. Magdziak, Flight Sergeant M. Michalak, Flight Sergeant W. Skrzydlu, Flight Sergeant K. Sztuka, Flying Officer S. Zdamowski, Sergeant J. Kukuc.

Aircraft on charge

Squadron code: RF
Spitfire VB (used for training and communications): AB272, AB273, BL292, BM157.
Spitfire IXF: BR140, BS241, BS242, BS247, BS281, BS328, BS386, BS401, BS542, BS547, BS549, EN129, EN182, ES463, HR140, MA420, MA422, MA475, MA476, MA683, MA694, MH666, MH674, MH693, MH694, MH777, MH787, MJ129, ML339.
Spitfire XVI: SM339.

451 SQUADRON RAAF

(NOTE: The two RAAF squadrons were commanded by Wing Commander D. Andrews as wing leader.)

Pilots

Officer Commanding: Squadron Leader Robertson.
Flight Lieutenant Bray, Flight Lieutenant Kemp, Flight Lieutenant MacKenzie, Flight Lieutenant Milner, Flight Lieutenant Pym, Flight Lieutenant Robert, Flight Lieutenant Sutton, Flying Officer Cooper, Flying Officer Earle, Flying Officer Minahan, Pilot Officer Ball, Pilot Officer Barrington, Pilot Officer Field, Pilot Officer Hill, Pilot Officer Kelly, Pilot Officer Newberry, Pilot Officer Roe, Pilot Officer Sheppard, Pilot Officer Trinoa, Pilot Officer Vintner, Warrant Officer Barrington, Warrant Officer Blake, Warrant Officer Field, Warrant

Officer Stubbs, Warrant Officer Ware, Flight Sergeant Hopper, Flight Sergeant Richards.

Aircraft on charge
Squadron code: NI
Spitfire XVI: SM199, SM314, SM346, SM362, SM391, SM394, SM417, SM418, SM427, SM465, SM471, SM475, SM477, SM479, SM480, SM507, SM511, SM516, SM567, SM665, TB592, TB593, TB520, TB744, TB913.

453 Squadron RAAF

Pilots
Officer Commanding: Squadron Leader E.A.R. Esau.
Flight Lieutenant R.G. Clemesha, Flight Lieutenant J.L. Cummins, Flight Lieutenant C.R. Leith, Flight Lieutenant F.N. McLoughlin, Flying Officer N.R. Adams, Flying Officer E.A. Emmerson, Flying Officer J.C. Grady, Flying Officer G.J. Stansfield, Flying Officer E.A. Wilson, Pilot Officer A.T. Bartels, Pilot Officer B.S. Inglis, Pilot Officer D.C. Johns, Pilot Officer R. Lyall, Pilot Officer J.N. Lynch, Pilot Officer W.W. Mace, Pilot Officer R.G. Peters, Pilot Officer C.S. Robertson, Pilot Officer C.A.M. Taylor, Pilot Officer R.A.J. York, Warrant Officer J.K. McCully, Warrant Officer N.A. Stewart, Flight Sergeant J.F. McAuliffe.

Aircraft on charge
Squadron code: FU
Spitfire XVI: SM184(D), SM185(M), SM193(G), SM230(F), SM243(J), SM250(T), SM256(W), SM278(X), SM281(E), SM348(G), SM402(C), SM484(N), TB619(A), TB743(K), TB863(P), TD152(S).

602 (City of Glasgow) Squadron

Pilots
Officer Commanding: Squadron Leader R.A. Sutherland.
Flight Lieutenant J.P. Banton, Flight Lieutenant H.R.P. Pertwee, Flight Lieutenant A.O. Pullman, Flight Lieutenant G.D. Stephenson, Flight Lieutenant J.R. Sutherland, Flight Lieutenant R.H.C. Tomerson, Flight Lieutenant Z. Wroblewski Polskie Sily Powietrzne, Flying Officer R.F. Baxter, Flying Officer W.M. Campbell, Flying Officer J.F. Farrell RCAF, Flying Officer D. Hunnam, Flying Officer W.J.H. Roberts, Flying Officer R.C. Rudkin, Pilot Officer M.V. Francis, Pilot Officer H.H. HcHardy RNZAF, Pilot Officer J. Toone, Warrant

Officer J.N. Amies, Warrant Officer R.M. Baerlein, Warrant Officer J. Crosland, Warrant Officer H.G. Ellison RNZAF, Warrant Officer L.P. Menzies RNZAF, Flight Sergeant S. Gomm, Flight Sergeant T.L. Love, Flight Sergeant C.J. Zuber RAAF.

Aircraft on charge
Squadron code: LO
Spitfire XVI: SM234, SM235, SM254, SM261, SM276, SM287, SM288, SM301, SM341, SM342, SM343, SM350, SM351, SM353, SM361, SM388, SM400, SM424, TB382, TB595, TB911, TD127.

603 (CITY OF EDINBURGH) SQUADRON

Pilots
Officer Commanding: Squadron Leader T. Rigler
'A' Flight: Flight Lieutenant J. Batchelor.
Flight Lieutenant McAndrew, Flight Lieutenant R. Sergeant, Pilot Officer W. Haupt, Flying Officer Thomson, Warrant Officer Thomson, Flying Officer Burrows, Warrant Officer Maslen, Warrant Officer Godfrey, Warrant Officer Evans, Flight Sergeant T. O'Reilly.
'B' Flight: Flight Lieutenant J. Welch, Flight Lieutenant J. Kirkman, Flying Officer McConnochie, Flying Officer N. Machon, Flying Officer Richmond, Pilot Officer Cookson, Pilot Officer N.A.H. McGinn RIAF, Warrant Officer Wheatley, Warrant Officer Beckwith, Warrant Officer E. Mee, Warrant Officer Laffan, Flight Sergeant Webb.

Aircraft on charge
Squadron code: XT
Spitfire XVI: Definitive listing not available.
Miles Magister: 9276
Taylorcraft Auster I: LB299

Map

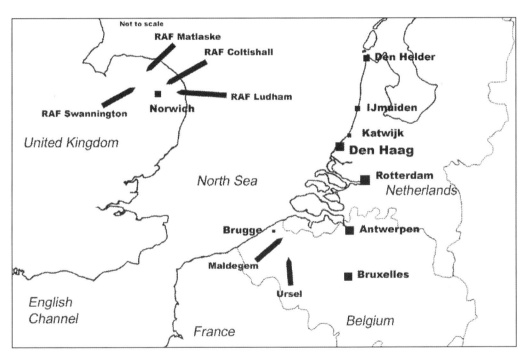

Theatre of Operations

Bibliography

BOOKS AND PUBLICATIONS

Babington Smith, Constance, *Evidence in Camera*, Chatto and Windus 1958

Bennett, John, *Defeat to Victory! No. 453 Squadron RAAF*, RAAF Museum 1994

Bowman, Martin W., *The Reich Intruders*, Patrick Stephens Ltd 1997

Bowyer, Michael J.F., *Action Stations 1. Military Airfields of East Anglia*, Patrick Stephens Ltd 1990

Cameron, Dugald, *Glasgow's Own*, Squadron Prints 1987

Clostermann, Pierre, *The Big Show*, Chatto & Windus 1951

Collier, Basil, *The Battle of the V-Weapons 1944–45*, Hodder & Stoughton 1964

Cooksley, Peter G., *Flying Bomb*, Robert Hale Ltd 1979

Cull, Brian, Bruce Lander and Heinrich Weiss, *Twelve Days in May*, Grub Street 1995

Dibbs, John, and Holmes Tony, *Spitfire Flying Legend*, Osprey Publishing 1996

Foot, M.R.D., *SOE in the Low Countries*, St Ermin's Press 2001

Foster, Alan J., *Airfield Focus 46: Ludham*, GMS Enterprises 2001

Franks, Norman L.R. *Royal Air Force Fighter Command Losses of the Second World War*, Volume 1, Midland Publishing Ltd 1997

Glancy, Jonathan, *20th Century Architecture*, Carlton Books 2002

Goulding, James, *Camouflage & Markings, RAF Northern Europe 1936–45, Supermarine Spitfire*, Ducimus Books Ltd undated.

Hall, Tom, *Typhoon Warfare: Reminiscences of a Rocket Firing Typhoon Pilot – WW2*, published by the author, 2000.

Henshall, Philip, *Hitler's Rocket Sites*, Robert Hale 1985

Hill, Prudence, *To Know the Sky*, William Kimber 1962

Hill, Air Chief Marshal Sir Roderic, Supplement to the *London Gazette, Tuesday, 19 October 1948, Air Operations by Air Defence of Great Britain and Fighter Command in Connection With the German Flying Bomb and Rocket Offensives, 1944–1945*.

Howard, Michael, *British Intelligence in the Second World War*, Volume 5 Strategic Deception, HMSO 1990

Hunt, Leslie, *Twenty One Squadrons*, Crecy Books 1992

Leith, Russell, and Cyril Ayris, *Duty Done*, Cyril Ayris Freelance 2001

Longmate, Norman, *Hitler's Rockets: The Story of the V-2s*, Hutchinson & Co 1985

Mason, Francis K., *Battle Over Britain*, McWhirter Twins 1969

Mack, Joanna, and Steve Humphries, *London at War*, Sidgwick & Jackson 1985

Mee, Eric, Memoirs, unpublished.

Middlebrook, Martin, and Chris Everitt, *The Bomber Command War Diaries*, Viking 1985

Morgan, Eric B. and Edward Shacklady, *Spitfire: The History*, Key Books 1987

Mountfield, David, *The Partisans*, Hamlyn Publishing Group 1979

Neufeld, Michael J., *The Rocket and the Reich*, Harvard University Press 1995

Ogley, Bob, *Doodlebugs and Rockets*, Froglets Publications 1992

Olson, Lynne, and Stanley Cloud, *For Your Freedom and Ours*, William Heinemann 2003

Overy, R.J., *The Origins of the Second World War*, Addison Wesley Longman 1998

Richards, J.M., *An Introduction to Modern Architecture*, Penguin Books 1967

Robertson, Bruce, *Spitfire – The Story of a Famous Fighter*, Harleyford Publications 1960

Ross, David, Bruce Blanche and William Simpson, *The Greatest Squadron of Them All – The Definitive History of 603 Squadron* Volumes I and II, Grub Street 2003

Stokesbury, James, L., *A Short History of World War II*, William Morrow and Co. 1981

Verbeek, J.R., *V2 Vergeltung from the Hague and its Environs*, V2 Platform Foundation, English Edition 2005.

Wallace, Graham, *RAF Biggin Hill*, Four Square Books, 1958

Wood, Derek, and Derek Dempster, *The Narrow Margin*, Arrow Books 1969

Woerkum, P.Th.L.M.van, *Re-Engineering the Vengeance Weapons: a Memoir on Jan W.H. Uytenbogaart*, paper given to the 54th International Astronautical Congress, 29 September to 3 October 2003 at Bremen, Germany

PILOTS' LOG BOOKS

453 Squadron: The late Flying Officer Norman Marsh, Pilot Officer Brian Inglis, Flight Lieutenant Russell Leith, Pilot Officer R.G. Peters

602 Squadron: Warrant Officer Max Baerlein, Flying Officer Michael Francis

229/603 Squadron: Flying Officer Nichole Machon, the late Flight Lieutenant Bob Sergeant, the late Warrant Officer Eric Mee, Flying Officer John Moss, Pilot Officer Freddy van Dyck, the late Wing Commander William A. Douglas, Warrant Officer Tom 'Paddy' O'Reilly

OPERATIONS RECORD BOOKS (FORMS 540 AND 541)

12 Group (AIR25/222), 100 Group, RAF Coltishall (AIR28/169), RAF Swannington (AIR28/789), RAF Ludham (AIR28/496), RAF Matlaske (AIR28/511), RAF Llanbedr (AIR28/494), 26 Squadron (AIR27/319), 56 (Punjab) Squadron (AIR27/531), 486 Squadron (AIR27/1934), 3 Squadron, 453 Squadron (AIR27/1893), 124 (Baroda) Squadron (AIR27/920), 247 (China British) Squadron (AIR27/1489), 236 Squadron (AIR27/1449), 254 (TF) Squadron (AIR27/1516), 602 Squadron (AIR27/2078), 603 Squadron (AIR27/2080), 229 Squadron (AIR27/1420), 540 Squadron (PR) (AIR27/2007), 80 Squadron (AIR27/671), 451 Squadron (AIR27/1890), 303 Squadron (AIR27/1666).

OTHER OFFICIAL DOCUMENTS

2nd TAF Daily Logs (AIR37/718), 2nd TAF Operations Instruction 493 dated 9 March 1945 (AIR24/1516), War Cabinet Report 'German Long Range Rocket Development' dated 27 June 1943 (Premier 3/110), Documents concerning the bombing of The Hague on 3 March 1945 (AIR20/794).

INTERNET AND OTHER SOURCES

'Beware the Crossed Lion'. A radio programme broadcast by BBC Scotland in 1980.
V2Platform Foundation: www.v2platform.nl
V2 rocket.com, A4/V2 resource site
Control Towers.co.uk: www.controltowers.co.uk

Index